An Alphabetical Analysis

Part 3

Terms and texts used in the study of

'Dispensational Truth'

M to P

By

CHARLES H. WELCH

Author of

Dispensational Truth
Just and the Justifier
The Prize of the High Calling
The Testimony of the Lord's Prisoner
Parable, Miracle and Sign
The Form of Sound Words
This Prophecy
Life Through His Name

THE BEREAN PUBLISHING TRUST
52a WILSON STREET, LONDON EC2A 2ER
ENGLAND

First printed	1958
Reset and reprinted	2003

ISBN for complete set of 10 volumes: 0 85156 200 0

ISBN for this volume: 0 85156 203 5

CONTENTS

Main articles are printed in full capitals thus: **MYSTERY**. Subsidiary articles are printed in small capitals thus: **MAN**.

Please ignore the article 'the' when using the Index, i.e. 'THE PRIZE' appears simply as 'PRIZE', and so throughout.

A Subject Index to all 10 Parts of this *Alphabetical Analysis* has been included at the end of each Part.

SUBJECT INDEX

A SUBJECT INDEX
(TO ALL 10 PARTS OF THIS ANALYSIS)
WILL BE FOUND AT THE END OF EACH VOLUME

INTRODUCTION

The reader who has used Parts 1 and 2 of this *Alphabetical Analysis*, needs no introduction here as to its theme, or the method adopted, but it may be an opportunity to put on permanent record how this aspect of truth came about.

The insistence of Dr. E. W. Bullinger upon the need 'Rightly to divide the Word of truth' and to 'Try the things that differ' especially with regard to the several callings made known in the Scriptures, prepared our minds to consider Acts 28 as a 'Dispensational Frontier'. Perhaps the present writer's contribution to the opening up of the Scriptures, dispensationally, could be expressed as follows. While other students of the Word saw that the rejection of Israel at Acts 28 was a crisis, few if any looked upon it as of vital importance. They seem to have come up to the closing chapter of the Acts, and then turned back to epistles like 1 Corinthians as the basis of their assembly and their hope, whereas, when we came to Acts 28 and realized that it was a frontier and that another sphere of blessing lay beyond, we simply said:

'LET US CROSS OVER, AND SEE THIS GOOD LAND'.

This we did and were delighted to realize that here was a sphere of blessing unrelated to Israel's New Covenant, or to the promises made unto the 'Fathers'. Here was a purpose that went back to 'before the foundation of the world' for its inception, that went 'far above all' for its seat of blessing and citizenship, but when we brought back our bunch of the 'grapes of Eshcol' the treatment meted out to us by Christian brethren approximated to that which was received by Caleb and Joshua when they too re-crossed the frontier in days gone by.

The following extract from the writings of B. W. Newton and others will show that he and they saw that Acts 28 was a dispensational frontier, but alas, both he and his followers and other leaders turned back to Matthew 24 and to 1 Thessalonians 4 for their hope, in spite of the fact that 'the hope of Israel' was suspended when Israel became 'Lo-ammi' 'Not My People'. We quote from '*Watching and Waiting*' of March – April 1953:

THREE PERIODS IN ISRAEL'S HISTORY

> I observed also, that the history of Israel during the time of their punishment and subjection to the Gentiles is distributed into three distinct divisions: the first extending from Nebuchadnezzar to their dispersion by Romans, the second being *the present period of their dispersion*, the third, the yet future period of their national re-establishment in unbelief; so, the prophetic visions of Daniel are to be divided into three parts, corresponding to these three periods. But I observed this likewise, that when the first of these periods terminated, *historic detail terminated*. As soon as the dispersion of Israel was effected and they ceased to have a recognized national existence in their land, there is a *pause* in the historic detail of Daniel; no person, no place, no date is mentioned during the present period of dispersion. But when the third period of their unbelieving history commences, when they again have returned in unbelief to their own land, then the historic detail of Daniel *re-commences*, and is given even with greater emphasis than before. So entirely is Gentile history made in the Scripture to revolve around Jerusalem as its centre. Whilst Jerusalem nationally exists, the history of the nations that are brought into connection with it is given; but when Jerusalem ceases to exist nationally, the history of the Gentiles in Scripture ceases too.
>
> We are in the *interval*, the period of dispersion, now. It will terminate when Jerusalem is nationally reconstituted. (*Watching and Waiting*. March – April 1953).

Look at the words 'no person, no place, no date is mentioned during the present period of dispersion'. These words cry aloud that Dispensational Truth demands, during the period of Israel's blindness which commenced at Acts 28:23-31, that no Old Testament prophecy is being fulfilled. Matthew 24 also must belong, not to the present calling of the Mystery, but to the 'third period' when the 'historic detail of Daniel recommences'; that a new revelation with a new sphere, constitution and hope must be given by God if any Gentile is to be saved and blessed during the setting aside of the hitherto exclusive channel of blessing — Israel. Accepting B. W. Newton's view and taking it to its logical conclusion, we have the following threefold division of Israel's history.

FIRST DIVISION	SECOND DIVISION	THIRD DIVISION
From Nebuchadnezzar to Dispersion by the Romans, A.D. 70, a few years after Acts 28.	'There is a pause'. Here comes the dispensation of the Mystery, a parenthesis, unconnected with Israel, Prophecy or Covenants. From Acts 28 to the resumption of prophecy.	Unbelieving history commences, historic detail of Daniel recommences. Daniel 9 is intimately linked with Matthew 24 (Matt. 24:25) and so, completely disassociated from the Second Division.

To the making known of the unique calling of this 'Second Division' wherein Israel is 'dispersed', the writer of this Analysis has devoted the bulk of his life and energies, yet those who advocate the teaching of B. W. Newton as set out in the above quotation, can, at the selfsame time see nothing incongruous in seeing in Matthew 24 with its incisive reference to Daniel 9, characteristics of the hope of the church today. Is it too much to believe that a few, after pondering these things may be led, Berean-like, to 'search and see'?

The May issue for 1952, *Questions and Answers*, edited by Dr. Harold P. Morgan, Riverton, New Jersey, U.S.A. opens with the following headline:

'WHAT WERE THE TEACHINGS OF EARLY PLYMOUTH BRETHREN REGARDING THE CHURCH, THE BODY OF CHRIST?'

Quotations are made in answer to this question from two teachers among the early Brethren, namely C. H. Macintosh, and Richard Holden.

> 'The thought of a church composed of Jew and Gentile "seated together in the heavenlies" LAY FAR BEYOND (*our emphasis*) the range of prophetic testimony .... We may range through the inspired pages of the law and the prophets, from one end to the other and find no solution of "the great Mystery" of the Church ... .

Peter received the keys of the kingdom, and he used these keys, first to open the kingdom to the Jew, and then to the Gentile. But Peter never received a commission to unfold the mystery of the church' (*Life and Times of Elijah the Tishbite*).

How strange to find C. H. M. and C. H. W. saying the same things, yet how strange to note the way in which 'The Brethren' have honoured the one, and repudiated the other!

In 1870 Richard Holden wrote a work entitled:

'THE MYSTERY, THE SPECIAL MISSION OF THE APOSTLE PAUL. THE KEY TO THE PRESENT DISPENSATION'.

Here is a brief quotation from this very precious testimony.

'To make all see what is the dispensation, or in other words, to be the divinely-appointed instructor in the character and order of the present time, as Moses was in the dispensation of "law", is that special feature in the commission of Paul in which it was distinct from that of the other apostles .... If then it shall appear, that, far from seeing "what is the dispensation of the Mystery" the mass of Christians *have entirely* missed it, and, as the natural consequence have almost completely misunderstood Christianity, importing into it the things proper to another dispensation, and so confounding Judaism and Christianity in an inexpressible jumble, surely it is a matter for deep humiliation before God, and for earnest, prayerful effort to retrieve with God's help, this important and neglected teaching'.

It seems almost unbelievable that a movement that could produce such a testimony, could nevertheless perpetuate that 'inexpressible jumble' namely of confusing the NEW COVENANT OR TESTAMENT, made *only* 'with the house of Israel and with the house of Judah' (Jer. 31:31), and make it the very centre of that worship and assembly, thereby 'confounding Judaism' with the truth of the Church of the Mystery, the present dispensation and calling, in which *no* covenant new or old finds a place, but a choice and a promise made 'before the foundation of the world'.

The prophet Hosea makes it abundantly clear that:

(1). A time would come when Israel would temporarily cease to be God's people, and when the Lord would cease to be their God (Hos. 1:9).

(2). This condition is likened to the segregation of a woman who had been unfaithful, the woman abiding many days belonging to no other man, the Lord saying 'so will I also be for thee' (Hos. 3:3).

(3). This is interpreted of Israel's condition from the time this rejection is entered until the Second Coming of the Lord.

> 'For the children of Israel shall abide many days
> (a) Without a king, and without a prince, and
> (b) Without a sacrifice, and without an image, and
> (c) Without an ephod, and without teraphim:
>
> Afterward shall the children of Israel return, and seek the LORD their God, and David their king; and shall fear the LORD and His goodness in the latter days' (Hos. 3:4,5).

It is during the parenthesis that intervenes between Acts 28:28 and their return to the Lord, that the present unique dispensation of the Mystery finds its true place, and to help the reader perceive 'what is the hope' of this calling, this series of Analytical studies has been prepared. May the Berean spirit prevail, while every reader searches the Scriptures to see:

> 'Whether these things be so' (Acts 17:11).

TO THE READER

A distinction has been made in the type used to indicate subsidiary headings from those which are of first importance.

Titles of main articles are printed in Helvetica bold type **capitals**, and are placed *in the centre of the page*, thus:

MANIFESTATION

Titles of subsidiary articles are printed in Helvetica bold type **small capitals**, and are placed at the *left-hand margin* of the paragraph, thus:

Mediator

Cross References

Cross references to articles in Parts 1 and 2, and 4 to 10 of *An Alphabetical Analysis*, are indicated by superscript numbers. For example:

Sons of God[4] refers to the article with that heading in Part 4 of *An Alphabetical Analysis*.

Resurrection[4,7] refers to the articles with that heading in Parts 4 and 7, respectively, of *An Alphabetical Analysis*.

If the reference is to another page in this book, the page number is printed in brackets after the title of the article. For example:

New (p. 105) refers to the article with that heading on page 105 of this book.

Structures

Where the meaning of a term can be illuminated by the structure of the section in which the term occurs, that structure is given, and as the scope of a passage is of first importance in the interpretation of any of its parts, these structures, which are not 'inventions' but 'discoveries' of what is actually present, should be used in every attempt to arrive at a true understanding of a term, phrase or word that is under review. Under the heading INTERPRETATION[2], the uninitiated believer will receive an explanation and an illustration of this unique feature of Holy Scripture. In like manner, other exegetical apparatus such as Figures of Speech, and all such helps, are indicated under the same main heading.

Received Text (Textus Receptus)

This is the Greek New Testament from which the Authorized Version of the Bible was prepared. Comments in this *Analysis* are made with this version in mind.

Where there are textual variances between the Received Text and the Nestle Greek Text (or other critical texts) such variances are noted. The phrase 'in the Received Text' is printed in brackets next to the word or words in question.

MAN. Man created in the image of God, and man fallen, sought and redeemed, comes under the heading rather of doctrinal truth than dispensational truth, for dispensational truth deals with differences, but all mankind are alike in their origin, in their failure and in their need of salvation. Two usages of the word man, however, demand a place in this analysis, namely 'the new man' and 'the perfect man'.

The new man. This term is found only in Paul's epistles, and only in those epistles that are called 'the Prison Epistles' (see article bearing that title p. 160). It therefore belongs peculiarly to the dispensation of the Mystery. In the earlier epistles we have a New Covenant and a new creature, and in the epistles of the circumcision a new commandment and a new heaven and a new earth, but a new man is peculiar to the Mystery. After having observed that, we must make a further observation. Two Greek words are used, *kainos* and *neos*, and they each have their own special connotation.

Kainos means something entirely new, not something recent, but something different from that which had been formerly, something so new as not to have been in use before.

Neos means something young, something recently originated or lately established. Dr. Bullinger has the following note in his Lexicon:

> 'When the two words are used of the same thing, there is always this difference: thus, the *kainos anthropos* "the new man" (Eph. 2:15 and 4:24) is one who differs from the former: the *neos* (Col. 3:10) is one who is 'renewed after the image of Him that created Him'.

The references are as follows:

Kainos

Eph. 2:15	To make in Himself of twain one new man.
Eph. 4:24	That ye put on the new man ... created.

Neos

Col. 3:10 And have put on the new man ... renewed.

While in ordinary usage *kainos* and *neos* often appear interchangeable, their distinctive meanings must be remembered. Ephesians 4 and Colossians 3 are not dealing with dispensational distinctions but with the new man as contrasted with the old. Where the word *kainos* is used, the word 'created' follows, and where *neos* is used the word 'renewed' follows, each passage keeping close to the primary meaning of the words translated 'new', a silent testimony to the accuracy of Scriptural language. The only reference that is specially dispensational in intention is that of Ephesians 2:15. This is a part of the subject introduced into Ephesians 2 under the figure of the 'Middle Wall' and is treated in its place in the article of that name (p, 12). See also article entitled NEW (p. 105).

The perfect man. Where Ephesians 2:15 and 4:24 use the word *anthropos*, 'man', Ephesians 4:13 uses the Greek word *aner*. These two words differ, *anthropos* means not only a man in the sense of a male, but any individual of either sex of the human species. It is a generic name. *Aner* means an adult male person, and never means a woman. *Aner* occurs 213 times in the New Testament and is translated 'fellow' once, 'husband' fifty times, 'man' one hundred and fifty-six times, and 'sir' six times.

Here are the occurrences of *aner* in Ephesians. It occurs seven times as follows:

Eph. 4:13	Unto a perfect *man,* unto the measure ...
Eph. 5:22	Wives submit yourselves unto your own *husbands.*
Eph. 5:23	The *husband* is the head of the wife.
Eph. 5:24	So let the wives be to their own *husbands.*
Eph. 5:25	*Husbands,* love your wives.
Eph. 5:28	So ought *men* to love their wives.
Eph. 5:33	See that she reverence her *husband.*

The apostle has used *anthropos* nine times in Ephesians, yet when he wished to speak of the Church as *the perfect man*, he goes out of his way to use a word that he uses six times afterwards for 'husband'. It is, therefore, evident, if Scriptural language is accurate, that such a Church cannot be 'the Bride', for it would be incongruous to speak of a Church which is the perfect 'Husband' as a 'Bride'. By observing the distinction, a fuller conception of the purpose of the ages is gained. Just as at the beginning man was placed in a garden and provided with a wife, so in the realization of that typical fact, the Church of the Bride, will be associated with (but not confused with) the Church of the Body, the Church which is the perfect Husband. Those who see no other Church than the Bride are looking forward to a Paradise where 'Eve' will have no companion. If it be objected 'Christ is the Bridegroom', we must remember that He also is 'The Head of the Body', and moreover, the Bride is never called the Bride of Christ, but the Lamb. See for further features the article entitled BRIDE and THE BODY[1].

MANIFESTATION

Two Greek words are translated 'manifestation', *phanerosis* (1 Cor. 12:7; 2 Cor. 4:2 and *apokalupsis* (Rom. 8:19). We are not here concerned with the word translated 'manifest' in such a passage as 1 Corinthians 15:27, which should be translated 'it is evident', as in Galatians 3:11; our concern is with the words that are used in relation to the hope that lies before the believer. We are not concerned with 'revelation' as the utterance of an oracle, as Luke 2:26, but only with its use in connection with the hope and the Second Coming of Christ. Both words 'manifest' and 'reveal' suggest something hidden, but the figure underlying the words derived from *phaneroo*, 'to be made manifest', is that of light, whereas the figure underlying the words derived from *apokalupto*, 'to be revealed', is that of a veil. There are two passages of

Scripture that state in plain terms the relationship of 'manifestation' with light.

> 'Every one that doeth evil hateth the light, neither cometh to the light, lest his deeds should be reproved (margin, "discovered" *elegcho*). But he that doeth truth cometh to the light, that his deeds may be made manifest, that they are wrought in God' (John 3:20,21).
>
> 'Have no fellowship with the unfruitful works of darkness, but rather reprove them ... things ... done ... in secret (*krupto*, to hide). But all things that are reproved (margin "discovered", *elegcho*) are made manifest by the light: for whatsoever doth make manifest is light' (Eph. 5:11-13).

Two passages that we have in mind particularly are Colossians 3:4 and Titus 2:13.

> 'When Christ, Who is our life, shall appear, then shall ye also appear with Him in glory'.
>
> 'Looking for that blessed hope, and the glorious appearing of the great God and our Saviour Jesus Christ'.

Here the verb *phaneroo* is translated 'appear' and the A.V. uses 'appear' and 'manifest' interchangeably. It seems that we should come to some conclusion as to the choice of word for the translation of *phaneroo*, for the two English words 'appear' and 'manifest' are not strictly synonymous. We cannot entirely disassociate a sense of movement with the word 'appear', neither can we completely set aside the thought of an 'appearance' in its twofold sense. In the passages where *phaneroo* occurs, there is no sense of movement, but rather of something being made clear and visible by a beam of light. There is attached to the word 'manifest', ideas relating to evidence and proof, as we have already seen by comparing 1 Corinthians 15:27 with Galatians 3:11. The English word 'appear' means primarily 'to become visible', the English word 'manifest' primarily means 'to be palpable', and hence a 'manifesto', a proof, hence, of evidence, a public declaration, but in no sense an 'appearing' or an 'appearance'. The intention of John 3:21 or Ephesians 5:13, is something deeper than mere appearance, but we may never find a word in our language that will entirely rid it of some measure of ambiguity. We must accept this limitation of speech, and avoid drawing erroneous conclusions. The epistle to the Colossians contains another passage where the words 'hid' and 'manifest' are found, and which must be included in those passages that provide us with evidence of the meaning of terms employed.

> 'Even the Mystery which hath been HID from ages and from generations, but now is made MANIFEST to His saints' (Col. 1:26).

The value of this reference is that it links up with a parallel passage in Ephesians:

> 'To make all men see what is the fellowship (dispensation R.V.) of the Mystery, which from the beginning of the world hath been hid in God' (Eph. 3:9).

The words '*to make* all men *see*' are obviously synonymous with '*to make manifest to* His saints'. Now the word thus translated in Ephesians 3:9 is *photizo*, translated in Ephesians 1:18 'enlighten', and in Hebrews 10:32 'illuminated'. It is therefore made abundantly clear, that whether we use the word 'manifest' or 'appear' the underlying thought of illumination must never be absent from our thoughts.

Phaino, the root which supplies *phaneroo* means 'to appear' and is derived from *phos*, 'light'. There are far too many occurrences of the words that are derived from *phaino* to attempt an extended concordance, but we feel it would be right to give at least one example of each.

Phaino and its derivatives

Phaino	'appear' (Matt. 2:7); 'shine' (2 Pet. 1:19).
Phaneros	'openly' (Matt. 6:4); 'outward' (Rom. 2:28); 'manifest' (1 Cor. 3:13).
Phaneroo	'appear' (Mark 16:12); 'manifest' (John 17:6); 'show' (Rom. 1:19).
Phaneros	(adverb) 'openly' (John 7:10); 'evidently' (Acts 10:3).
Phanerosis	'manifestation' (1 Cor. 12:7; 2 Cor. 4:2).
Phantazo	'sight' (Heb. 12:21); *phantasia* 'pomp' (Acts 25:23).
Phantasma	'spirit', ('phantom') (Matt. 14:26; Mark 6:49).
Epiphaino	'to give light' (Luke 1:79); 'appear' (Tit. 2:11).
Epiphaneia	'brightness' (2 Thess. 2:8); 'appearing' (2 Tim. 4:1).
Epiphanes	'notable' (Acts 2:20).
Emphanes	'openly' (Acts 10:40).
Emphanizo	'declare plainly' (Heb. 11:14).
Exaiphnes	'suddenly' (Acts 22:6);
Exapina	'suddenly' (Mark 9:8).
Katepheia	'heaviness' (Jas. 4:9);
Prophasis	'pretence' (Phil. 1:18); 'cloak' (1 Thess. 2:5).
Huperephaneia	'pride' (Mark 7:22);
Huperephanos	'proud' (Luke 1:51), and seven other combinations with 'a' the negative.

Let us return now to Colossians 3. The reference to 'appearing with Christ in glory' is preceded by a statement equally wonderful. 'For ye are dead, and your life is hid with Christ in God' (Col. 3:3). The R.V. more correctly reads 'For ye died'. To say 'ye are dead', to modern ears, is almost the same as saying, 'Ye are at this moment dead and will never be other than dead'. To say 'ye died' points back to an act, and leads the mind to that blessed doctrine of identification 'with Christ' whereby the believer is said to have been 'crucified with Christ', 'died with Christ', 'buried with Him', quickened, raised and seated together with Him, and here at last 'manifested with Him in glory'.

'Your life is hid with Christ in God'. The word 'with' demands that the verb 'hid' shall be true of both 'your life' and 'Christ'. The passage does not say 'your life is hid IN Christ' but assuredly affirms that Christ is hid in God as much as your life is hid in God. Both your life and Christ are at this moment 'hid', the day of the manifestation of both is about to dawn, and then comes the glorious change:

'Hid together with Christ' 'In God'. | 'Appear together with Him' 'In glory'.

The two sets of statements being linked by the words 'When ... then'. Here, in Colossians 3:3,4 the blessed hope of the church of the Mystery is made known. Some believers are to meet the Lord *in the air*, that will be 'in glory', but some are to be made manifest with Him in *that* glory which is associated with the right hand of God. One star differs from another, 'in glory'. We must be acquainted with 'the three spheres' of blessing, and the reader should turn to the article, THREE SPHERES[5], if at all uncertain of the peculiar character of the hope set before us in Colossians 3. Other articles that should be consulted are APPEARING[1]; and HOPE[2].

ME. Self glorification is entirely foreign to the life of faith, and the apostle's words in Galatians 2 give voice to the feeling of every true child of God, 'Not I, but Christ'. Yet the same apostle who could call himself 'less than the least' could say, 'I magnify mine office'. The magnifying of the office, the consciousness of stewardship, the need for faithfulness, the necessity to defend his apostleship, justified the emphasis we find in certain contexts of the pronoun 'me' which would be entirely out of place if used in the ordinary affairs of life. Those references which have a bearing upon the special dispensation entrusted to Paul are the following:

> 'Unto *me*, who am less than the least of all saints, is this grace given, that *I* should preach among the Gentiles the unsearchable riches of Christ; and to make all men see what is the fellowship (dispensation R.V.) of the Mystery' (Eph. 3:8,9).
>
> 'And (pray) for *me*, that utterance may be given unto *me*, that *I* may open my mouth boldly, to make known the mystery of the Gospel, for which *I* am an ambassador in bonds: that therein *I* may speak boldly, as *I* ought to speak (literally "as it becomes me")' (Eph. 6:19,20).
>
> 'Hold fast the form of sound words, which thou hast heard of *me*' (2 Tim. 1:13).

'The things that thou hast heard of *me* among many witnesses, the same commit thou to faithful men' (2 Tim. 2:2).

'Notwithstanding the Lord stood with *me*, and strengthened *me*; that by *me* the preaching might be fully known, and that all the Gentiles might hear' (2 Tim. 4:17).

Unto ME, for ME, as it becomes ME, heard of ME, by ME. The personal pronoun all the time, but all the time the reason for its prominence is the great outstanding fact that Paul, as the prisoner of Christ Jesus, was the appointed channel through whom the truth of the Mystery should be made known.

'All they which are in Asia be turned away from ME'; is balanced by the word 'they shall turn away their ears from the truth' (2 Tim. 1:15; 4:4),

and the sequel is a matter of fact. The first step in apostacy is often the turning away from Paul as the Messenger; it is but a step after that to repudiate his message. Paul would rather subscribe himself as the bond slave of Jesus Christ (Rom. 1:1) than emphasize his office, but for the truth's sake and for the defence of the gospel, he was inspired to devote one and a half chapters of the epistle to the Galatians in defence of his apostleship, so intimately are they linked together.

MEDIATOR. The doctrine of the One Mediator is the central theme of the oldest book in the world, the book of Job, and its glorious presence enriches the types of the law, the visions of the prophets, the praises of the Psalms, as well as the record that announces the birth of Him Who is Emmanuel, and speaks of Him as the Mystery of Godliness, 'God manifest in the flesh'. The only reason for thus introducing so great a doctrine into the pages of an analysis that must keep closely to the dispensational side of truth, is the statement made by the apostle in 1 Timothy 2:5,6:

> 'For there is one God, and one Mediator between God and men, the man Christ Jesus; Who gave Himself a ransom for all, to be testified in due time'.

'To be testified in due time' hardly does justice to the actual intention of the apostle. *To marturion kairois idiois*, should be rendered 'the testimony for its own peculiar seasons', thereby stressing the supreme importance of this basic truth in the present dispensation of grace. We cannot say more without touching upon doctrinal ground, so must content ourselves with the fact that the dispensational importance of this doctrine has at least been acknowledged here.

MEMBER. The Greek word *melos*, which is translated 'member' in the New Testament, is according to *Heyschius*, a grammarian of Alexandria, applied to the parts of the body, from their harmonious adaptation to one another and to the body. For the Greeks call everything congruous and harmonious *melos,* which also signifies musical harmony, songs, etc., whence our word melody. In this latter sense it occurs in Ecclesiasticus 47:9. This relationship of the members of the Body with harmony and melody, appears in a passage in the epistle to the Ephesians:

> 'From Whom the whole body fitly joined together and compacted by that which every joint supplieth' (Eph. 4:16).

The word translated 'fitly joined together' in the Greek is *sunarmologeo* and contains the word *harmonia*, the origin of the English 'harmony'. *Melos* occurs thirty-four times, and is always translated 'member'. Two references only are found in the Gospels (Matt. 5:29,30), all the rest are in the epistles, three being found in James (Jas. 3:5,6; 4:1), the remainder being found in the epistles of Paul. Of this number, three references only are found in the Prison epistles (Eph. 4:25; 5:30; Col. 3:5) the remaining twenty-six occurrences being distributed between 1 Corinthians and Romans, sixteen being found in

1 Corinthians and ten in Romans. The references in Romans 12:4,5 like those in 1 Corinthians 12, use the figure of a body with its many members to illustrate the principle 'diversity in unity' as it relates to the distribution and employment of supernatural gifts. For a fuller treatment of 1 Corinthians 12, see the articles BAPTISM[1] and BODY[1]. *Melos* occurs only in the practical section of Ephesians, and the one reference in Colossians relates to the actual members of the believer's physical body. This means that Ephesians 4:25 is the only reference to the believer in the epistles of the Mystery as a 'member' and although the 'body' is necessarily implied it is not stated.

> 'Put on the new man ... putting away lying, speak every man truth with his neighbour: for we are members one of another' (Eph. 4:24,25).

When we study the implications of the term 'fulness' (see PLEROMA, p. 197), we shall see that the figure of the 'Body' for the church refers only to time and development, but that when the whole company is complete, the figure changes, 'the Church which is His Body' then becomes 'the fulness of Him that filleth all in all' (Eph. 1:22,23).

MEMORIAL. As an adjunct to the article on The Lord's Supper we append the twelve 'memorials' mentioned in the Old Testament which give a good indication of the intention of the Lord when He said 'this do in *remembrance* of Me' (Luke 22:19). The Greek word *mnemosunon* 'memorial', like the Hebrew *zikkaron* 'memorial' and the Greek word for 'remembrance', is a variant of *mnaomai* to remember.

(1) The Passover

> 'This day shall be unto *you for a memorial*' (Exod. 12:14).

(2) The Unleavened Bread

> 'This is done because of that which the LORD did unto me when I came forth out of Egypt. And it shall be for a sign ... and for *a memorial* ...' (Exod. 13:8,9).

(3) The Destruction of Amalek

'Write this *for a memorial* in a book, and rehearse it in the ears of Joshua: for I will utterly put out the remembrance of Amalek from under heaven' (Exod. 17:14).

(4) The Stones on Aaron's Shoulders

'And thou shalt put the two stones upon the shoulders of the ephod for stones of memorial unto the children of Israel: and Aaron shall bear their names before the LORD upon his two shoulders for *a memorial*' (Exod. 28:12).

(5) The Stones on Aaron's Heart

'And Aaron shall bear the names of the children of Israel in the breast-plate of judgment upon his heart, when he goeth in unto the holy place, for a *memorial* before the LORD continually' (Exod. 28:29).

(6) The Atonement money

'And thou shalt take the atonement money of the children of Israel, and shalt appoint it for the service of the tabernacle of the congregation; that it may be *a memorial* unto the children of Israel before the LORD, to make an atonement for your souls' (Exod. 30:16).

(7) The Blowing of Trumpets

'In the seventh month, in the first day of the month, shall ye have a sabbath, *a memorial* of blowing of trumpets, an holy convocation' (Lev. 23:24, see also Num. 10:10).

(8) The Offering of Jealousy

'He shall pour no oil upon it, nor put frankincense thereon; for it is an offering of jealousy, an *offering of memorial*, bringing iniquity to remembrance' (Num. 5:15, see also, verse 18).

(9) The Brasen Censers

'The brasen censers ... and they were made broad plates for a covering of the altar: *to be a memorial* unto the children of Israel ... before the LORD' (Num. 16:39,40).

(10) The Captains' Offering

'And Moses and Eleazar the priest took the gold of the captains of thousands and of hundreds, and brought it into the tabernacle of the congregation, *for a memorial* for the children of Israel before the LORD' (Num. 31:54).

(11) The Twelve Stones

'These stones shall be *for a memorial* unto the children of Israel for ever' (Josh. 4:7).

(12) The Crowns of Silver and Gold

'And the crowns shall be ... *for a memorial* in the temple of the LORD' (Zech. 6:14).

Here we have memorials of redemption, atonement, intercession, acceptance, joy, victory, sin, death, resurrection and glory. The last but one of these memorials is that of the twelve stones raised up at Gilgal by Joshua. The twelfth and last is the pledge of the coming of the great King-Priest, Who shall bear the glory, as He once bore sin, and shall sit as a priest upon a throne, in Whom all the hopes of men are centred.

THE MIDDLE WALL

The epistle to the Hebrews, it will be remembered, uses the figure of the 'rent veil'. The epistle to the Ephesians uses the figure of the 'broken middle wall', the one, the veil, setting aside the law of type and shadow, under which 'the way into the holiest of all was not yet made manifest' (Heb. 9:8), the other, the middle wall, setting aside certain 'ordinances' which caused and perpetuated 'enmity'. Both figures have access in view, the one for the Hebrew, the other for the Church of the One Body; the one setting aside the law of Moses, the other setting aside the decrees of Acts 15. (See article entitled DECREES[1]).

'Having abolished in His flesh the enmity, even the law of commandments contained in ordinances; for to make in Himself of twain one new man, so making peace' (Eph. 2:15).

This verse belongs necessarily to a larger context, which may be visualized, if shorn of all detail, as follows:

A 2:1-3. IN TIME PAST. Children of wrath.
  B 2:4-10. BUT GOD. Entirely new sphere 'made to sit together'.
A 2:11,12. IN TIME PAST. Aliens and strangers.
  B 2:13-19. BUT NOW. Entirely new company 'one new man'.

It will be seen that in the first pair doctrine predominates and salvation by grace is the issue. In the second pair the alienation is not caused by wicked works, but arises out of the fact that there was a dispensational disability in being born a Gentile, quite irrespective of individual merit or demerit. This was cancelled when the time came for the truth of the Mystery to be made known. In both sections the sequel brings the believer into an entirely new or unique position. 'Made us sit together in heavenly places' is a position of grace and glory never before revealed or enjoyed by any believer of any previous calling. 'To make in Himself of twain one new man' we shall see is nothing less than a new creation. The word translated 'to make' in Ephesians 2:15 is the Greek word *ktizo* 'to create'. This word occurs fourteen times in the New Testament and only once, namely in the passage before us, is it translated 'to make'. The word is used of the Creator Himself (Rom. 1:25), the creation of the world (Mark 13:19) and the creation of all things (Col. 1:16). Where the qualifying word 'new' is used of creation, old things (2 Cor. 5:17) and former things (Rev. 21:1) pass away, and come no more into mind (Isa. 65:17).

It has been maintained by some that all Ephesians 2:15 teaches is that, whereas, before Acts 28, the Gentile had a subordinate place in the blessings of Israel, now, the change had come, and the Gentiles have a place of equality. This is not, however, true. It assumes that the change that has been made is in *the status* of the Gentile, leaving the hope, the calling and the sphere of blessing already revealed in Romans, Corinthians, Thessalonians, etc., unchanged. This view by no means fully represents the truth. Such a condition would be but an EVOLUTION, but what we are facing is a CREATION. Let us notice the wording of the passage again, substituting now the correct word 'create' for the word 'make'.

'For to create in Himself of the twain one new man'.

Let us examine the word 'twain', *duo*. This Greek word is translated 'two' over one hundred times in the New Testament. This is but a variation in the wording, for the word 'both' has been used twice already, in Ephesians 2:14,16 and reappears once more in verse 18. Further, the word 'twain' and the word 'both' have the article. It is some specific company that is in view, who can be called '*the* both' and '*the* two'. The two companies have already been named, they are believing Gentiles and believers of Israel, called the uncircumcision and the circumcision, and these 'two' were never so united even during the dispensation that followed Pentecost that they could be likened to 'one body'. The figure which the apostle employs rather emphasizes *the inequality* that obtained, even when Romans was written, for he speaks of the Gentile believer in Romans 11, as a wild olive graft contrary to nature into the true olive tree. This figure continued to represent *the subordinate position* of the saved Gentile up to the end of the Acts.

The new creation of Ephesians 2 did not suddenly turn wild olives into cultivated ones, the truth being rather that all that belonged particularly to Israel was suspended. The olive tree was cut down to the roots, the hope of Israel deferred, and a new dispensation hitherto unrevealed and unsuspected, called the dispensation of the Mystery, was made known. This is something entirely new. Israel *as Israel* has no place in it. A believing Israelite could of course become a member of this newly-created company, but not *as an Israelite*. The Jew must leave behind his promises, his relation to the New Covenant, his descent from Abraham, his circumcision, even as Paul had done. The Gentile must leave behind his alienation, his uncircumcision, his promiseless and hopeless state, and 'the both' must be made one, 'the two' must be created one new man, in which all distinction of every kind ceases to exist, 'so making peace'.

The peace here is not the peace which the saved sinner experiences when justified by faith, nor that peace of God which passeth all understanding; it is a 'peace' that replaces a previously existing 'enmity'. The enmity of Ephesians 2:15 which had been abolished, and which was symbolized by the middle wall of partition, was not a middle wall between the believer and his God, the veil in the temple symbolized that, but a middle wall that separated believers who were Gentiles from believers who were Jews, the enmity being the fruit, not of sin, but of 'the law of commandments contained in ordinances'.

First let us be sure that we appreciate the figure of the middle wall. Josephus says:

> 'When you go through the cloisters, into the second temple, there was a PARTITION made of stone all round, whose height was three cubits; its construction was very elegant. Upon it stood pillars, at equal distances from one another ... some in Greek and some in Roman letters, that no foreigner should go within that sanctuary' (Josephus, *Wars, v. 5.2*).

The apostle likens the middle wall, to the law of commandments contained in 'ordinances'. Here again we must exercise care. It has been common among Christians to refer to Baptism and the Lord's Supper as 'ordinances', the note in the Oxford Dictionary reads, 'applied especially to the sacrament of the Lord's Supper, 1830'. It is extremely unlikely that when the translation of the A.V. used the word 'ordinance' that such an application of the term would have entered their mind. The Greek word translated 'ordinance' is *dogma*, a word having nothing in common with the 'ordinances of baptism and the Lord's Supper' but meaning 'that which appears good or right to one' (Lloyd's *Encyc. Dict.*). Dogma must not be confused with doctrine. Crabb discriminates between dogma and doctrine thus:

> 'The *doctrine* rests upon the authority of the individual by whom it is framed; the *dogma* on the authority of the body by whom it is maintained'.

Dr. Bullinger in his Lexicon says:

> *Dogma*, that which seems true to one, an opinion, especially of philosophic dogmas; a public resolution, decree (occ. Luke 2:1; Acts 16:4; 17:7).

We find this word employed for 'the decrees' of Caesar, and for 'the decrees' delivered to the church, and this reference takes us to Acts 15, where we shall find a decree resting on the authority of a body by whom it was maintained. To quote Crabb again 'that which appears good and right to one', was actually used in Acts 15.

The council that met at Jerusalem was convened to decide what measures could be taken to solve the problems that arose out of the coming into the church of Gentiles whose whole up-bringing, feeding and habits, rendered them obnoxious to their Jewish fellows, and to quote this time from the ordinance itself given in Acts 15, 'it seemed good unto us, being assembled ... to lay upon you no greater burden than these necessary things' (Acts 15:25-28). While there were four items of conduct prescribed for the Gentiles, the added comment 'for Moses of old time hath in every city them that preach him' (Acts 15:21) suggests that the Jewish believer would continue to observe the full ceremonial law. This difference between the two companies of believers set up in effect a middle wall of partition making membership of 'one body' during the Acts impossible. It is this 'decree' which is the ordinance referred to in Ephesians 2:15. This has now been abolished.

This word, 'abolished', translates the Greek *katargeo* which means rather 'to render inoperative', as can be seen in such passages as Romans 7:2 'loosed from the law'; 'done away' (2 Cor. 3:7,11,13,14) and 'to make of none effect' (Gal. 3:17; 5:4). The temporary measures introduced by the Council at Jerusalem were abrogated when the truth for the present dispensation was revealed and this abrogation was seen to have been accomplished, even as access into the true tabernacle had been accomplished by the death of Christ. Instead of this divided company of believers where the Jew was first, where the Gentile was but a wild olive graft contrary to nature, we have the creation of the two, in Himself, of one new man. In this new company neither Jew nor Gentile as such can be discovered; the Church of the One Body is not something carried over from earlier days, remodelled and reconstituted in order to give the Gentile a better place in it. It is a new creation, in which all previous privileges and disadvantages vanish, in which there are blessings hitherto unknown to any son of Adam. To teach that all that Ephesians 2:15 reveals is that the Gentile had been promoted to an equality with the Jew is such an understatement as to be virtually a contradiction of truth. The calling into which these hitherto divided Jews and Gentiles now found themselves is unrelated either to Abraham, the New Covenant, or the New Jerusalem. Neither Jew nor Gentile had hitherto been associated with a calling that went back to *before* the foundation of the world, or went up so high as to be 'far above all' where Christ sits. This calling is unique, and to attempt to see allusions to Old Testament types is to prevent the essential newness or uniqueness of this calling from being perceived.

There is a superficial likeness in the wording of Ephesians 2:15 to the record of the creation of Adam and Eve, and some have been tempted to elaborate that likeness into a definite doctrine. There are one or two essential features that Scripturally characterize the relationship of Adam and Eve that make it impossible that there should be any idea of 'fulfilment' here in Ephesians 2:15. We are distinctly told by inspired comment, that:

> 'Adam was first formed, then Eve' (1 Tim. 2:13).
>
> 'The head of the woman is the man' (1 Cor. 11:3).
>
> 'He is the image and glory of God: but the woman is the glory of the man' (1 Cor. 11:7).

'Neither was the man created for the woman; but the woman for the man' (1 Cor. 11:9).

The same Paul who wrote these inspired comments on Genesis 1 and 2, wrote Ephesians 2, and his comments written AFTER Ephesians (i.e. 1 Tim. 2:13) differ nothing from his comments written before (i.e. 1 Cor. 11). If we import into Ephesians 2:15 the type of Genesis 1 and 2, then the Jew must stand for Adam, and the Gentile must stand in the place of Eve. In this new company the Jew will therefore of necessity be still 'head' even as was Adam, and the explicit teaching of the Mystery thereby nullified. The whole Church of the One Body, the Church that includes within it both Jew and Gentile, is looked upon as a perfect MAN (*aner* 'husband'). The marriage of this perfect 'man' does not take place during this dispensation but *awaits the day of the Lord.* Then another company called 'The Bride' will be ready. Both the Church which is the perfect husband, and the Church that is the perfect wife will *then* fulfil the primeval type, but *that is* not in view in Ephesians 2. In the church of the present calling, the 'Jew' and the 'Gentile' as such do not exist, neither one nor the other is 'head'; this church is 'a joint body' where perfect equality is seen for the first time. Every type will find its anti-type, but like all the ways of God, the realization will be in its own special season. To take an event that is future and attempt to place it on the calendar of God centuries before its legitimate time is what so many have done who were ignorant of the great principle of interpretation 'rightly dividing the word of truth' (2 Tim. 2:15). Under the heading DECREES[1] will be found a fuller exposition of Acts 15.

MILK *v.* MEAT. One of the many arguments in favour of the Pauline authorship of Hebrews, is the employment of certain figures such as the one before us. We set out the seven items that are found in both 1 Corinthians and Hebrews in connection with the figure of Milk *v.* Meat for babes and full grown.

	1 Corinthians 2 and 3		Hebrew 5 and 6	
(1)	Babes	3:1.	Babes	5:13.
(2)	Milk	3:2.	Milk	5:13.
(3)	Meat	3:2.	Meat	5:14.
(4)	Perfect	2:6.	Perfect	5:14.
(5)	Foundation	3:11.	Foundation	6:1,2.
(6)	Fire	3:13.	Fire	6:8.
(7)	Six things erected	3:12.	Six-fold elements	6:1,2.

In the presentation of Dispensational Truth we must remember, that to give advanced truth to those who are spiritually immature may indicate zeal that is not according to knowledge. Toward the close of the Lord's earthly ministry He said:

> 'I have yet many things to say unto you, but ye cannot bear them now' (John 16:12).

There is such a thing as speaking a 'word in season' (Isa. 50:4) and the faithful and wise servant gives meat 'in due season' (Matt. 24:45), knowing that there is 'a time to keep silence, and a time to speak' (Eccles. 3:7).

Although 'The Mystery' was not entrusted to Paul before his imprisonment, he was the steward of many mysteries (1 Cor. 4:1) and as such he desired to be 'faithful'. The R.V. reads 'mystery', in place of the A.V. reading 'testimony' in 1 Corinthians 2:1, where the apostle said:

> 'And I, brethren, when I came to you, came not with excellency of speech or of wisdom, declaring unto you the testimony (mystery) of God'.

Those who adopt the A.V. say that the word mystery is a gloss from verse 7, while those who adopt the R.V. say that the word testimony is a gloss from verse 6.

It is exceedingly difficult to explain what the apostle could mean by 'declaring the testimony of God'. Is it the testimony that God has given? or is it the testimony that has been given for or about God? And why should the apostle especially wish to declare the testimony of God to the Corinthians? The word declare, *kataggello*, is translated 'preach' ten times out of the seventeen occurrences, and to 'preach' the testimony of God does not seem to fit the context. If we look a little further down the chapter where the apostle resumes his subject, he says:

> 'Howbeit we speak wisdom among them that are perfect: yet not the wisdom of this world, nor of the princes of this world, that come to nought: but we speak the wisdom of God in a mystery' (1 Cor. 2:6,7).

This passage seems to be the corresponding fulfilment of the idea commenced in verse 1, and seems to demand the word 'mystery' there instead of the word 'testimony'. Accepting therefore, the R.V. we understand Paul to say, that knowing the high-flown style of eloquence that was so much admired at Corinth, remembering that they had actually said of his speech, that it was 'contemptible' (2 Cor. 10:10), knowing that this high-flown speech was proverbially called *Corinthia verba*, he resolved not to stoop to ingratiate himself into their favour by acting unfaithfully as a steward of the mysteries of God, but, as he goes on to explain in chapter 4, it was a small thing with him that he should be judged of the Corinthian or of man's judgment, for he had already 'judged', *ekrina* 'determined', 'come to a decision' after due deliberation, that in spite of the Corinthian's desire to hear all about 'mysteries', he would know nothing among *them* save Jesus Christ and Him crucified.

This decision cost him something, for he acknowledged that he was with them in weakness, fear and much trembling. However, he would not be misunderstood. He did speak the mystery, he did use words of wisdom, but this was reserved for 'the perfect'. With the opening of chapter 3, he is back to this same theme:

> 'And I, brethren, could not speak unto you AS unto spiritual, but AS unto carnal, even AS unto babes in Christ. I have fed you with milk, and not with meat: for hitherto ye were not able to bear it, neither yet now are ye able' (1 Cor. 3:1,2).

The carnality of the Corinthians kept them in the spiritual category of 'babes' — only the 'perfect' could assimilate any of the mysteries or the strong meat of the Word. This same argument is used in Hebrews 5, as we have already seen, by the parallels set out above. Believers may be unable to receive and assimilate truth for more reasons than one. In the Corinthian Church, their divisions and low moral standard prevented growth; 'are ye not carnal and walk as men?' said the apostle reviewing the condition. The epistle to the Hebrews furnishes another set of reasons why spiritual immaturity may persist. This is introduced in Hebrews 5 upon the introduction into the argument of the Melchisedec priesthood 'of whom we have many things to say, and hard to be uttered' (Heb. 5:11), and we can imagine a number of things that would make such teaching 'hard to be uttered', but the apostle leaves us in no doubt as to what he intended, going to the root immediately saying, 'seeing ye are dull of hearing' (Heb. 5:11). Before we examine this matter more closely, let us get the benefit which can be derived from the structure.

Hebrews 5 and 6

A 5:1-6. Melchisedec. Priest.
  B 5:6-10. The Priest. Perfected.
    C 5:11 to 6:1. Dull (*nothros*) *versus* the Perfect.
  B 6:1-10. The saints. Perfection.
    C 6:11-19. Slothful (*nothros*) *versus* the Overcomers.
A 6:20. Melchisedec. Priest.

It will be seen that the condition, 'dull of hearing', repeated in 6:11-19, and 'slothful', is an integral part of the argument.

The LXX uses the word *nothros* in Proverbs 22:29 to translate 'mean' in the expression 'mean men' and the verse speaks of one diligent in his business. In Proverbs 12:8 it is used for 'perverse'. It would appear from the usage of the word that the A.V. 'dull' is hardly strong enough. The Hebrew word in Proverbs 22:29 is *chashok*

— 'obscure' or 'darkened' and the cognate *choshek* is translated scores of times 'darkness'.

The spiritual ear and eye are of the first importance. Peter in his second epistle uses the word *muopazo* ('cannot see afar off') of those who had become forgetful of the purification of old sins. We trust our readers will immediately remember the strong emphasis upon 'purification for sins' found in Hebrews, especially the fact that in the opening summary this alone is written of the Lord's work on earth, 'when He had made purification for sins' (Heb. 1:3). Peter speaks of 'adding' to the faith, a parallel expression to the words of Hebrews 6, 'things that *accompany* salvation'. These added things have in view the rich furnishing of the entry into the *aionian* kingdom of our Lord and Saviour Jesus Christ (2 Pet. 1:11). So in Hebrews the perfecting is connected with the *aionion* salvation.

This reference to the dullness of hearing is further a gathering up of the words of the great historic type of chapters 3 and 4. 'To-day if ye will HEAR HIS voice'. Some, when they had HEARD, did provoke. 'The word preached did not profit them, because they were not united by faith with them that HEARD'. Dullness of hearing, moreover, is another mode of expressing the truth of chapter 2:1:

> 'Therefore we ought to give *the more earnest heed* to the things which we have heard, lest at any time we drift away' (Heb. 2:1 author's translation).

'Hearing' together with 'seeing' may be reckoned as the chiefest of the senses. How sad to allow any precious sense, even in the physical realm, to be atrophied through lack of use. How doubly sad to have the precious gift of hearing spiritually, and then through not having 'the senses EXERCISED' (Heb. 5:14) to fail, to come short, to drift! Over against this drifting and dullness the apostle places endurance, obedience, suffering, steadfastness unto the end. Surely we, too, need the exhortation of the Lord, 'Take heed *how* you hear'.

The apostle in Hebrews 5:12-14 proceeds to expand what lies in the expression 'dull of hearing'.

(1) It indicates *lack of progress.*
'For when for the time ye ought to be teachers, ye have need that one teach you'.

(2) It indicates *spiritual infancy.*
'Ye have need of milk and not of solid food'.

(3) It indicates *lack of experience.*
'For every one that partaketh of milk is without experience of the word of righteousness'.

(4) It indicates *the opposite of being 'perfect'.*
'But solid food belongeth to them that are perfect'.

(5) It indicates *a culpable neglect.*
'Perfect, even those who by reason of use have their senses exercised'.

(6) It indicates *lack of discernment.*
'Senses exercised to discern both good and evil'.

Let us take some of these points and gather their lessons.

(1) Teachers are placed together with those who can take solid food, have senses exercised and are perfect. No articles could be written for this book or any magazine if we were to understand the word 'perfect' in its ultimate sense. The passage does come to us very solemnly, however, and says that the qualification for teaching is something more than head knowledge and ready speech. In the Sermon on the Mount, breaking the commandments and doing them are associated with teaching men so, and also with losing or gaining a position in the kingdom of heaven. James utters the warning, 'My brethren, be not many "teachers", knowing that we shall receive a greater judgment' (3:1). Instead of progress there was retrogression:

> 'For even when for the time ye ought to be teachers, ye have need that one teach you again certain rudiments of the beginning of the oracles of God' (Heb. 5:12 author's translation).

Ta stoicheia tes arches 'the rudiments of the beginning'.

Stoicheia are the initial steps in knowledge, and also the 'elements' of the natural world. (See Galatians 4:3,9; Colossians 2:8,20; 2 Peter 3:10,12). The verb *stoicheo* comes in Acts 21:24, '*walkest orderly*'; Romans 4:12, '*walk* in the steps of that faith'; Galatians 5:25, '*walk* in the Spirit'; Galatians 6:16 and Philippians 3:16, '*walk* by rule'.

These Hebrew believers had progressed no further than the initial steps of the faith, and indeed needed teaching in these things all over again. An intellectual grasp of the teaching of men on any subject may be sufficient, but a mere intellectual grasp of God's truth is not sufficient. The doctrine and faith of the early church was rightly called 'The Way', for it was *walk* as well as *word, life* as well as *lip.*

> 'Then shall we know, if we *follow on to know* the LORD' (Hos. 6:3).

What these 'first principles' were that they needed to be retaught we shall see better when we come to Hebrews 6.

(2) The spiritual infancy of these saints is indicated by the figurative use of foods for doctrine. 'Ye have need of milk and not of solid food'.

The apostle had occasion to use this same figure when writing to the Corinthian Church, and for similar reasons:

> 'And I, brethren, could not speak unto you AS unto spiritual, but AS unto carnal, even AS unto babes in Christ. I have fed you with milk and not with meat: for hitherto ye were not able to bear it, neither yet now are ye able' (1 Cor. 3:1,2).

The milk, the rudiments of the beginning of the oracles of God, to them had been 'Jesus Christ and Him crucified' (2:2). 'Howbeit', said the apostle, 'we speak wisdom among them that are PERFECT' (2:6). The thought is resumed and developed in chapter 13:8-13.

Milk diet is natural and right for infants, but it has a purpose and a limit. 'As new-born babes, desire the sincere milk of the word, that ye may GROW thereby'. The apostle Peter adds a word to this that links it with Hebrews 6. 'If so be ye have *tasted* that the Lord is gracious' (1 Pet. 2:2,3). Some believe that there is a definite reference to the epistle to the Hebrews in 2 Peter 3:15,16 where Peter speaks of 'our beloved brother Paul' who had written unto the readers of 1 and 2 Peter. In verse 16 there is a word very like the word 'difficult to interpret', *dusermeneutos*, of Hebrews 5:11, where 'some things hard to be uttered', *dusnoetos*, which those that are unlearned and unstable wrest to their own destruction, are spoken of. In contrast Peter urges them to 'grow in grace, and in the knowledge of our Lord and Saviour Jesus Christ' (2 Pet. 3:18).

There is much in Peter's two epistles that bears upon the teaching of the epistle to the Hebrews. Such subjects as the saving of the 'soul', the 'fiery trial', 'suffering and glory', come to mind at once as obvious parallels.

(3) The outstanding feature of the babe that the apostle mentions in Hebrews 5 is that such is 'without experience'. We have drawn attention elsewhere (*The Berean Expositor*, Vol. 33) to the place that 'temptation' occupies in the epistles of the race and the crown, see Hebrews 2:18; 11:17,37; James 1:2,12; 1 Peter 1:6; Revelation 3:10, etc. The Greek word for 'tempt' is *peirazo*. The Greek word for 'unskillful' is *apeiros*, and carries with it the thought 'untested'. Solid food belongs to the perfect. The perfect are placed in opposition to the untested. It is one of the marks of those pressing on to perfection that they endure 'temptation'. The wilderness journey, we have seen, is the great historical type of the early part of Hebrews, and that wilderness journey was a 'day of temptation' in more than one sense.

An important note is struck in the expression 'senses exercised'. In Philippians 1:9 where the apostle prays for the saints who, like the Hebrews, were reaching forward unto perfection (see chapter 3), he writes:

'And this I pray, that your love may abound yet more and more in knowledge and in all *discernment* (or *perception*)'.

The word is *aisthesis*. Luke 9:45 uses the verb *aisthanomai*, 'to perceive'. The word 'senses' in Hebrews 5:14 is *aistheterion*. It will be seen that the senses in their capacity of discernment, of discrimination, of right division, of trying the things that differ, are intended. These senses are 'exercised' in the perfect. The word 'exercise' comes from *gumnazo*, which gives us our word gymnasium, etc. In Hebrews 12:11, where the discipline and correction of the son by the father is subject, the word occurs again:

'But all discipline, indeed as to the time being, does not seem to be joyous, but grievous, nevertheless afterward it gives back the peaceable fruit of righteousness to those who have been EXERCISED thereby' (author's translation).

This exercise of the perception enables the perfect to discriminate between good and evil. It does not necessarily mean moral good and moral evil. *Agathos* is the usual word for 'good', here it is *kalos*. Those concerning whom the apostle entertained doubts had 'tasted the *good* (*kalos*) word of God', but had failed to realize the difference between that which belonged to perfection and that which was 'the word of the beginning'. The two words *kalos* 'good' and *kakos* 'bad' differ only in one letter. The doctrines for which they stand are often confused and said to be 'all one and the same'. We need 'senses exercised' if we are to discriminate and 'go on unto perfection'.

These two outstanding passages which use the figure of Milk *v.* Meat do not exhaust, but illustrate the ways in which truth should be taught, how it can be received and the care that must be exercised in making known Dispensational Truth, lest we choke rather than feed those who for any reason are still 'babes'. The article entitled BABES[1] should be read as a supplement.

MILLENNIAL CONTEXTS

A Positive Approach to a Disputed Theme

When this section of the Alphabetical Analysis was prepared, we had no intention to devote a complete part to Prophetic subjects, but as interest had grown in the subject of the Millennial Kingdom, we felt a few words here would be justified. We have since prepared a complete part devoted to Prophetic truth, but feel that the reader will not think the space and time wasted that is devoted to that great theme here.

The Millennial kingdom has always attracted the attention of students of Prophecy. Its promise of peace, its exemption from external temptation, its recognition of the crown rights of the Redeemer and other associations of peace and safety, so strikingly at variance with the course of this world, act like a beacon light in a dark night, a blessed end to the strife and contention of present-day life.

While, by comparing Scripture with Scripture, light on the Millennium may be gathered from Daniel, Isaiah or the Psalms, strictly speaking one passage, and *one passage only* actually names the thousand-year kingdom, and that is Revelation 20. All the teaching that comparison may bring to light must conform in its every detail to the conditions that are found in this one chapter of the Apocalypse. It is readily granted that the Book of the Revelation is a difficult book to understand. It abounds with symbolism, and like all prophetic utterances, the place and meaning of figures of speech must be allowed for. But when every such allowance is made, one thing stands out as imperative,

REVELATION 20 IS BASIC

Should one interpose — why not start with the lovely foreshadowings of Isaiah 11 — the answer must be, not all students of prophecy agree that this is a Millennial picture. It may be, but it can only be seen to be if and when it is found in accord with the conditions that Revelation 20 demands. Revelation 20 provides the only standard by which all prophetic findings on the Millennium must be measured. The term 'The Millennium' is not found in the Scriptures but is a legitimate term for more reasons than one.

(1) It distinguishes the kingdom of Revelation 20, from the kingdom of God, the kingdom of heaven and other such expressions.

(2) It conveniently expresses the fact that this kingdom is to last for a thousand years, for the Latin *mille* = a thousand, and *annus* = a year.

The first objection we must meet is that this period of time must not be taken *literally*. In answer to this objection we quote the references in Revelation 20 and let them speak for themselves.

> 'An angel ... laid hold on the dragon ... and bound him a thousand years'.
>
> 'That he should deceive the nations no more, till the thousand years should be fulfilled: and after that he must be loosed a little season'.
>
> 'I saw the souls of them that were beheaded for the witness of Jesus ... and they lived and reigned with Christ a thousand years. But the rest of the dead lived not again until the thousand years were finished'.
>
> 'They shall be priests of God and of Christ, and shall reign with Him a thousand years. And when the thousand years are expired, Satan shall be loosed out of his prison, and shall go out to deceive the nations' (Rev. 20:1-8).

This repeated reference to the period of a thousand years cannot be dismissed as mere figurative language, to do so would vitiate the text-books of history, for many an accepted historical date is expressed with less explicit and circumstantial details. The references fall into a perfect pattern as might have been expected.

The Thousand Years

A Satan bound.
  B He will deceive again after he is loosed.
    C Overcomers reign with Christ.
      D The First Resurrection.
    C Priests reign with Christ.
A Satan loosed.
  B He goes out to deceive, after he is loosed.

During the first centuries after Christ, the constant threat of martyrdom turned the believers attention to the promises of the Millennial day, but as persecution waned, and 'other things' entered, the Millennium became spiritualized. This attitude was first noticed in the teachings of Caius at the close of the second century and was greatly furthered by Origen whose spiritualizing is a matter of common knowledge. It was taught later that martyred Christians had risen from the dead, and were spiritually reigning with Christ unseen. Rabbinical tradition held that the seventh thousand years from the creation of man will be a sabbatical thousand, a climax to the heptads of days, weeks, months and years (of which the Jubilee and the prophecy of Daniel 9, are outstanding examples).

During the time of Cromwell, a sect called 'Fifth Monarchy Men' held that a universal kingdom, following the four indicated in the image of Daniel 2, must be set up, and that no single person ought to rule mankind until the Lord's Coming, civil government being provisionally administered by the saints. We must be prepared, it seems, for the continual uprising of many and varied attempts to explain and expound the Millennium, in which of course, the present effort must be included, with the possibility of prejudice and ulterior motive. Prophetic students today are divided mainly into two groups:

(1) Those who believe that Christ must return before the Millennial kingdom can be set up, called Pre-Millennialists.

(2) Those who believe that this kingdom will be the result of the growing activity of the Church, and that Christ will not return until that goal is achieved. These are called Post-Millennialists.

In Volume 6 of *The Berean Expositor,* published in 1916, on pages 65 and 66 we wrote:

> 'As we view these passages of Scripture together (viz. Rev. 5:9,10 and 20:6), it seems that the priestly kingdom is the millennial kingdom, and only those who have overcome, and have had part in the first resurrection constitute its members. We cannot help but feel that Old Testament prophecies concerning future blessings have been too hastily generalized as millennial. We believe that investigation will prove that much that has been considered millennial does not take its place till the thousand years are finished, and that a place in the millennial kingdom is largely a matter of being "accounted worthy". This we will consider in its place. If it is established it will be nothing short of revolutionary in its effect upon the teaching of Scripture relative to the ages to come'.

'In its place' is *now*, and so, forty years after making the initial promise, we have redeemed it. Our findings are published:

(1) In a booklet entitled *Zion, the Millennium, and the Overcomer.*

(2) In several articles in the volumes of *An Alphabetical Analysis* devoted to Prophecy, which are Parts eight and nine of this series.

Turning now to Revelation 20, we observe that it is in *historical* sequence with events that are recorded in chapter 19, and the following conspectus of events is set forth before the reader as an analysis of what *must take place,* and which will lead to the setting up of the Millennial kingdom. Here we are on safe ground. John cannot be accused of writing with preconceived ideas to uphold, he 'received' this book from the Lord.

REVELATION 19 and 20

(1) Babylon Must be Destroyed (Rev. 19:1-4)

By comparing this passage with Jeremiah 25:9-11 it will be seen that it is a reversal of the doom that fell upon Israel at their captivity by Nebuchadnezzar. This condition is referred to again in Jeremiah 33:4-11. The fall of Babylon is given in detail in Jeremiah 50 and 51.

If the destruction of Babylon immediately precedes the Millennium, it follows that it remains and endures throughout any and every 'Pre-Millennial kingdom' since Genesis 10. In like manner, if Israel are to be gathered from the lands of their dispersion at the coming of the Lord, it follows that they cannot have been 'gathered' before as the centre and focus of light and blessing in the earth.

The following items must be included in what we have called 'Millennial Contexts' — if any be excluded, or felt to be an intrusion, that will be a sure sign that our interpretation of the place where the Millennium fits, is wrong. Associated with this final judgment on Babylon should be noted the following features:

(a)	Israel will return and seek the LORD	(Jer. 50:4).
(b)	Israel will be brought back to the LORD	(Jer. 50:19).
(c)	Israel's iniquity will be completely forgiven	(Jer. 50:20).
(d)	Israel is exhorted to leave Babylon	(Jer. 51:6,45).
(e)	As the Alleluias arise in Revelation 19:1-6 so will heaven and earth sing for Babylon	(Jer. 51:48).

The Millennium therefore will be preceded by two noted events, the final destruction of Babylon and the return of Israel. The return of Israel is linked with the New Covenant (Jer. 31:31-37). The history and destiny of the two cities, Babylon and Jerusalem, are intimately related.

(2) The Lord God Omnipotent Reigneth (Rev. 19:6)

The word translated 'omnipotent' is the Greek *pantokrator*, and occurs in Revelation nine times.

Pantokrator in the Apocalypse

> 'I am Alpha and Omega, the beginning and the ending, saith the Lord, which is, and which was, and which is to come, *the Almighty*' (Rev. 1:8).
>
> 'Holy, holy, holy, Lord God *Almighty*, which was, and is, and is to come' (Rev. 4:8).
>
> 'We give Thee thanks, O Lord God *Almighty*, which art, and wast, and art to come; because Thou hast taken to Thee Thy great power, and hast reigned' (Rev. 11:17).
>
> 'Great and marvellous are Thy works, Lord God *Almighty*; just and true are Thy ways, Thou King of saints (or ages)' (Rev. 15:3).
>
> 'Even so, Lord God *Almighty*, true and righteous are *Thy* judgments' (Rev. 16:7).
>
> 'The battle of that great day of God *Almighty*' (Rev. 16:14).
>
> 'Alleluia: for the Lord God *Omnipotent* reigneth' (Rev. 19:6)
>
> 'He treadeth the winepress of the fierceness and wrath of *Almighty* God' (Rev. 19:15).
>
> 'And I saw no temple therein: for the Lord God *Almighty* and the Lamb are the temple of it' (Rev. 21:22).

There is only one true King in the Revelation, namely He Whose name is The Word (Rev. 19:13) and Who is called both King of kings and Lord of lords (verse 16). The time for the assumption of Crown and Sceptre is given in Revelation 11:15 as the days of the sounding of the seventh trumpet when

> 'The kingdoms of this world are become the kingdoms of our Lord, and of His Christ; and He shall reign for ever and ever'.

At this same time, the time of the dead has come that they should be judged, and reward given to the servants of the Lord, and to His saints; the time when they that destroy the earth should be destroyed. Babylon is addressed in Jeremiah 51:25 as the 'destroying mountain, which destroyeth all the earth', which brings this passage into line with the judgment pronounced in Revelation 11:18 when the Lord will 'destroy them which destroy the earth' and as the desolation of Babylon here predicted is to be 'for ever' (Jer. 51:26), this must line up with the destruction of Babylon revealed in Revelation 19:1-6. *Basileo* 'to reign' occurs seven times in the Revelation.

'They reign upon the earth' (Rev. 5:10 R.V.).

'The seventh angel sounded ... He shall reign for ever and ever' (Rev. 11:15).

'Thou hast taken to Thee Thy great power, and hast reigned' (Rev. 11:17).

'The Lord God Omnipotent reigneth' (Rev. 19:6).

'And they lived and reigned with Christ a thousand years' (Rev. 20:4).

'And shall reign with Him a thousand years' (Rev. 20:6).

'They shall reign for ever and ever' (Rev. 22:5).

The association of those who overcome and reign with Christ in the Millennial kingdom, His Own reign and *the ending* of the kingdoms of the earth at the same moment, with *no interval* for any other kingdom good or evil to intervene, is here displayed by the disposition of the word 'reign'.

Reigning in the Revelation

A 5:10. The Throne (6 and 7). They (R.V.) reign upon the earth.
  B 11:15,17. The seventh angel sounds.
    Kingdoms of this world end.
    Power taken and reigning.
    C 19:6. The Lord God Omnipotent reigneth.
      Proclamation at the Second Advent immediately before setting up of Millennial kingdom.
  B 20:4,6. Overcomers live and reign with Christ, as priests for a thousand years.
A 22:5. The servants of the Lamb, reign for ever and ever.
  The Throne (22:1,3).

Two Kingdoms are met with in the Revelation

(1). A kingdom that precedes the Millennium and is followed by it immediately.

(2). A kingdom which is the kingdom of the Lord.

The kingdom that immediately precedes the Millennium and could be called 'The Pre-Millennial kingdom' is called the kingdom of the Beast! and if David's kingdom is in any sense a type of the future kingdom of Christ, that too had a kingdom that preceded it, a kingdom that foreshadowed the kingdom of the Beast, namely the REIGN OF SAUL. Many there are who mistake the rider of the white horse of Revelation 6:2 who is followed by war, famine and death, for the rider of the white horse of Revelation 19:11, Who is followed by the armies of heaven. May the Lord forbid that any of His saints who are so eagerly looking for a Pre-Millennial kingdom to be set up in the absence of Christ, shall be deceived by the apparent 'peace and safety' of that false reign.

The Pre-Millennial Kingdom

'The kingdoms of this world' (Rev. 11:15).

'His kingdom (see the throne of the beast) was full of darkness' (Rev. 16:10).

'The ten horns ... are ten kings, which have received no kingdom as yet; but receive power as kings one hour with the beast' (Rev. 17:12).

'Agree ... give their kingdom unto the beast' (Rev. 17:17).

'And the woman which thou sawest is that great city, which reigneth (lit. having kingship) over the kings of the earth' (Rev. 17:18).

Over against the kingdom of this world, of the Beast, of the scarlet woman (Babylon) is placed

'The kingdom ... of Jesus Christ' (Rev. 1:9),

and upon the casting out of that old Serpent, called the Devil and Satan which deceiveth the whole world, is heard a loud voice saying 'Now is come ... the kingdom of our God' (Rev. 12:9,10).

These passages exhaust the references that contain the Greek word *basileia.* No other kingdoms appear but these two. The Pre-Millennial kingdom *so far as* the Apocalypse is concerned is the kingdom of the Beast. Revelation 12:9,10 is linked with Revelation 20:1,2, for in these two passages we have the title, 'that old serpent, which is the Devil and Satan'; in the first passage he is cast down to the earth, and is said to be he 'which deceiveth the whole world', and in Revelation 20:2,3 he is said to be cast into the bottomless pit, 'that he should deceive the nations no more, till the thousand years should be fulfilled'.

(3) The Marriage of the Lamb (Rev. 19:7)

This is another Millennial context. This is associated in chapter 21 with the holy Jerusalem (Rev. 21:10). This city is called 'New Jerusalem, which cometh down out of heaven from My God' (Rev. 3:12), and is there associated with the overcomer. While the twelve apostles have each a name in one of the twelve foundations of this heavenly city, that does not prevent them in the regeneration from sitting on twelve thrones, judging the twelve tribes of Israel (Matt. 19:28) any more than the fact that Abraham looked for this heavenly city, will prevent him from sitting with those that shall come from the east and west, in the kingdom of God. Neither will the fact that the Saviour is to sit on the throne of His father David, prevent Him from occupying a throne in the New Jerusalem (Rev. 22:3) or from being seated far above all in heavenly places. Even the writer of these lines can sit at a desk, and be at one and the same time Editor, Husband, Principal and Citizen, without inconvenience or involving an impossibility.

The marriage of the Lamb is given a full exposition in chapter 21, for John but introduces the new heaven and the new earth, to leave it immediately, and to step back into the period that precedes that great event. In the same way Isaiah 65:17 takes the reader *up to* the new heavens and new earth, but then steps back and gives all his attention to the creation of the city of Jerusalem with its attendant blessings. If any one is unconvinced that the new creation is not the subject of chapter 21, a reading of verse 27 will surely suffice.

Following the announcement of the marriage of the Lamb comes THE Revelation.

(4) The Second Coming of The Lord

Here in Revelation 19 we have THE Apocalypse, the Second Coming of the Lord. He comes according to this record, *not to a world at peace,* and not after a kingdom of heaven has been functioning for years and waiting for Him, He comes in righteousness to 'make war'. He is followed by the armies of heaven, and is seen 'clothed with a vesture dipped in blood'. The word translated 'vesture' is the same in the LXX as that translated 'apparel' in Isaiah 63:1, and is closely associated with that prophecy. At His coming, the Lord is to 'rule the nations with a rod of iron' — not merely with a rod, but with a rod of iron.

> 'The Syrian Shepherd has two implements of his calling, neither is wanting when he is on full duty ... Hung to his belt ... is a formidable weapon of defence, a stout bludgeon. The guardian of the flock who carries a long shepherd's staff ... its use answers to that of our shepherd's crook, namely to guide the sheep, to rescue them from danger, to rule the stragglers into order, and at times to chastise the wilful ... This conveys the full meaning of the royal Psalmist, the one valiant shepherd-boy, when he writes under inspiration:
> "Thy club and Thy staff they comfort me"'.
> (*Palestine Explored*, by Rev. James Neil, M.A.).

When the Scriptures speak of a 'rod of iron' there is little of the 'gentle shepherd' either in the term itself or in the context where it is found, and any explanation that focuses attention on the 'rod' but omits all reference to the peculiar feature 'of iron' cannot but be held suspect. Let us note the terms which accompany and qualify this use of the rod of iron, both in Revelation 19 and elsewhere. 'Make war'; 'a vesture dipped in blood'; 'armies'; 'sharp sword'; 'smite the nations'; 'tread the winepress of the fierceness and wrath of Almighty God'; 'eat the flesh of kings'. If this rod is a symbol of blessing, surely it must be what is called an intruder here! The fact that the 'rod' is sometimes associated with the Shepherd and his sheep, taken by itself, cannot set aside the twofold fact that here we have war and wrath, and that the rod is not merely a rod, but a 'rod of iron'.

This 'rod of iron' appears in the first place in Psalm 2. This Psalm speaks of Christ as the Anointed, but this has been denied, one of the 'proofs' being that as it speaks of 'the Lord' as well as 'His anointed', and as 'The Lord' of the Old Testament is the Lord Jesus Christ of the New, the 'Anointed' here must be someone else! The same argument would risk the same disastrous results if applied to Psalm 110. In the first place Acts 4:25-27 makes it clear that Peter accepted the Messianic import of Psalm 2, and there is no need to labour the Messianic character of verse 7 of Psalm 2, with its reference in Acts 13:33; Hebrews 1:5 and 5:5. The LXX reads Psalm 2:2 *tou Christou autou* and identical language is found in Revelation 11:15. If the principle of interpretation eliminates Christ from Psalm 2:2, it would eliminate Christ from the prophecy which reads:

> 'The kingdoms of our Lord, and of His Christ' *tou Christou autou* (Rev. 11:15.)

Psalm 2:8,9 where again 'The Lord' and His 'Christ' come together, is quoted in Revelation 2:26,27 as of Christ and it is in a context of rebellion. The Lord's action is revealed to be drastic. 'Thou shalt break them with a rod of iron'.

(5) The Rod of Iron

The Companion Bible has the following note here on Psalm 2:9.

> 'Break them = rule, or govern them. So Sept., Syr., and Vulg.'

That is certainly interesting, but Psalm 2 was written in Hebrew, and written centuries before the Septuagint, the Syriac or the Vulgate were thought of. If Ginsberg's Massoretic text be accepted, and the word translated 'break' in Psalm 2:9 be rendered 'rule' or 'shepherd' as it is in Revelation 2:26,27; 12:5 and 19:15, is it a true inference that this 'shepherding' of the nations is a gentle treatment by a shepherd of his flock? Surely there is a case here for Right Division! A shepherd has a *twofold* obligation: (1) to *look after* his flock and (2) to *defend it* against the attack of robber or wild beast, as David knew only too well. For this the Eastern shepherd was provided with two instruments: (1) the rod for the enemy, (2) the staff for the flock. What sort of shepherding would it be that used a ROD OF IRON to guide or even to correct sheep! This word 'rod' occurs in the A.V. Old Testament thirty-four times, and is associated with 'smiting' (Exod. 21:20; Isa. 10:24), 'beating' (Prov. 23:13), with 'oppression' (Isa. 9:4), 'the fool's back' (Prov. 26:3) and the like. The references to sheep are exceedingly few. Leviticus 27:32 and Ezekiel 20:37 referring to the use of the rod in counting, and Micah 7:14, 'the flock of Thine inheritance', and Psalm 23:4, 'Thy rod and Thy staff they comfort me'.

It will be seen that out of thirty-four references, four only refer to sheep, and even so, we are now dealing with a 'rod of IRON', and so with something different and special.

The context in Revelation 19 and the usage of the term will not allow us to take the verb 'to shepherd' as of *one phase only* of the Shepherd's work. He acts as Shepherd equally when he fends off the robber with his 'club of iron' as when he guides a wandering sheep with his 'staff'. Ask Paul and Silas what *rhabdizo* (from which *rhabdos* 'rod') means in Acts 16:22,23 or ask the Corinthians what they expected by the threat of 1 Corinthians 4:21. It is impossible to read into the rod of iron of Revelation 19:15 anything other than that which is associated with *smiting* the nations with a sharp sword, or treading the winepress of the *fierceness* and *wrath* of Almighty God. These form the 'context' of the rod of iron.

Revelation 2:27 employs a different word reading, 'and He shall rule them with a rod of iron; as the vessels of a potter shall they be broken to shivers' (which is another

New Testament rendering of the passage in Psalm 2). *Suntribo* means 'to bruise' a reed, or a person, and 'to break' as fetters, or an alabaster box. If the reader has any compunction about the translation offered in the A.V. of Revelation 2:27, let him try 'bruising' iron fetters, he will soon discover that facts are like mules, 'stubborn things'. Psalm 2 is closely related to Psalm 1. They cover the same ground and period, but look at the state of affairs from two points of view. In Psalm 1, blessedness is predicated of the man who does not walk in the COUNSEL of the ungodly, in Psalm 2, though a different word is used, the counsel of the ungodly is seen where 'the rulers take COUNSEL together against the Lord'. Two types of mankind are set before us in Psalm 1. The one is likened to a tree planted by rivers of water, the other, the ungodly, are not so, but are like the chaff which the wind driveth away. The references to chaff which is driven away takes us straight over to Daniel 2. 'Then was the iron, the clay, the brass, the silver, and the gold, broken to pieces together, and became like the CHAFF of the summer threshingfloors; and the WIND CARRIED them away' (Dan. 2:35).

Psalm 1 ends with the words, 'the way of the ungodly shall PERISH', and Psalm 2 ends with warning, 'and ye PERISH from the WAY'. We are asked to believe that the words of Psalm 2:7, 'Thou art My Son, this day have I begotten Thee', do not refer to the Lord Jesus Christ, but to David in spite of the fact that Acts 13:33 applies this prophecy to the resurrection of Jesus Christ, coupling it with 'another Psalm' which says 'Thou shalt not suffer Thine Holy One to see corruption' and immediately goes on to deny that *this* can apply to David. How is it that an inspired apostle can say one thing and an uninspired teacher, however godly and however earnest, can say another? We are at liberty to ask, but it is God alone who will give the answer. Moreover, and more wonderful still, how is it that anyone, with an eye to the integrity of the Word can let such exposition go by without protest! We cannot.

Peter goes out of his way to assure us that David spoke of Christ, and knew that God 'would raise up Christ to sit on his throne' (Acts 2:30). A system of teaching that denies that the Lord's Anointed is the Christ (Psa. 2:2), that denies that the begotten Son of Psalm 2:7 is the Christ, that denies that 'the Messiah' of Daniel 9:25,26 is the Christ, is surely suspect, and if the Lord's own people do not make some protest, then truth is dying and its defenders asleep.

For the moment we do not say that Isaiah 11 when 'the lion shall eat straw like an ox' is or is not a prophecy of the Millennium, that can wait, but one verse in that chapter demands attention.

> 'He shall smite the earth with the rod of His mouth, and with the breath of His lips shall He slay the wicked' Isa. 11:4).

First, some codices read *ariz* 'the oppressor' for *erez* 'the earth', and *The Companion Bible* throws the passage into an introversion thus:

g He shall smite the *oppressor.*
  h With the rod of His *mouth.*
  h With the blast of His *lips.*
g Shall he slay the *lawless one.*

Who is this 'oppressor' or 'lawless one'? Is there any other reference that would link Isaiah 11 with Revelation 19?

First we note that 2 Thessalonians 2:2 should read 'the day of the Lord' according to the Revised Text, and this brings the passage into the same period that spans the Apocalypse (Rev. 1:10, 'I became in spirit in the Lord's Day', i.e. the future Day of the Lord). That day will be prefaced by the rise of the Man of Sin and in verse 8 we read:

> 'And then shall that Wicked be revealed, whom the Lord shall consume with the spirit of His mouth, and shall destroy with the brightness of His coming: even him, whose coming is after the working of Satan with all power and signs and lying wonders' (2 Thess. 2:8,9).

In Revelation 19:17 the application of the 'rod of iron' is seen in the 'supper of the great God', and then we read of the Beast and with him the False Prophet that wrought miracles before him, with which he deceived them that had received the mark of the Beast. Mark the words, 'he deceived them that *had received* the mark of the beast' and compare them with 'with all deceivableness of unrighteousness in them that perish; because they *received not* the love of the truth, that they might be saved. And for this cause God shall send them strong delusion, that they should believe a lie: that they all might be damned who *believed not* the truth, but *had pleasure* in unrighteousness' (2 Thess. 2:10-12). The Lord 'in flaming fire' will take vengeance *upon such is* revealed in 2 Thessalonians 1:8.

Another of the items that constitute the 'context of the Millennium' is the reference in Revelation 20:4 to the martyrs of the period who sit upon thrones and live and reign with Christ a thousand years. The references to these 'overcomers' constitute an unbroken chain, linking the record of the book as one.

(6) The Overcomer

***Nikao* 'to overcome'**

> 'To him that overcometh will I give to eat of the tree of life, which is in the midst of the paradise of God' (Rev. 2:7).

Here we have a distinct link with Revelation 22:2.

> 'He that overcometh shall not be hurt of the second death' (Rev. 2:11).

Here is a definite link with the close of Revelation 20.

> 'To him that overcometh will I give to eat of the hidden manna, and will give him a white stone, and in the stone a *new name written, which no man knoweth* saving he that receiveth it' (Rev. 2:17).

This links us with Revelation 19:12, 'He had a *name written, that no man knew,* but He Himself'.

'He that overcometh, and keepeth My works unto the end, to him will I give power over the nations: and he shall rule them with a rod of iron; as the vessels of a potter shall they be broken to shivers: even as I received of My Father' (Rev. 2:26,27).

Those thus addressed were to 'hold fast till I come' (verse 25) and *there is no possible interval* (let alone a kingdom lasting centuries), indicated between the time when this overcomer is enduring, and the time of his reward, namely in the Millennium. This passage obviously links up with Revelation 19:15.

'He that overcometh, the same shall be clothed in white raiment; and I will not blot out his name out of the book of life' (Rev. 3:5).

Again an obvious link with Revelation 20:15.

'Him that overcometh will I make a pillar in the temple of My God, and he shall go no more out: and I will write upon him the name of My God, and the name of the city of My God, which is New Jerusalem, which cometh down out of heaven from My God: and I will write upon him My new name' (Rev. 3:12).

Here the link with the heavenly Jerusalem of Revelation 19:7-9 and 21:2 is apparent.

'To him that overcometh will I grant to sit with Me in My throne, even as I also overcame, and am set down with My Father in His throne' (Rev. 3:21).

This points to the Millennial thrones of Revelation 20:4.

'He that overcometh shall inherit all things (or these things)' (Rev. 21:7),

which takes us to the same Millennial day and city.

We believe there is an unbroken link between chapter and chapter, not necessarily in strict historical sequence, for John retraces his steps, as may be seen comparing Revelation 6:17 and 7:1, but admitting no interval of centuries for any administration of God on the earth, no Pre-Millennial kingdom, except the kingdom of the Beast, as we have already indicated. We ask the question, what warrant is there to introduce a period of some 500 years in Daniel 2:45? The Stone strikes the feet of the image that symbolizes Gentile dominion, and shatters it to pieces, and immediately supplants it and fills the earth, setting up a kingdom that shall never be destroyed. Again we ask, where is there room for a Pre-Millennial kingdom in Daniel 7?

> 'I beheld even till the beast was slain, and his body destroyed, and given to the burning flame' (Dan. 7:11).

This chapter brings before us four beasts, the first like a lion, the second like a bear, the third like a leopard, and the fourth 'dreadful and terrible' with a 'mouth speaking great things' (Dan. 7:1-8). This fourth beast appears at the time of the end in Revelation 13:1,2. It is composed of the three first named in Daniel 7. It is like a 'leopard', it had feet like a 'bear', it had the mouth of a 'lion' and it had a 'mouth speaking great things' (Rev. 13:5) *stoma laloun megala* in both LXX and Greek New Testament. In Daniel 7:13 the Son of Man is seen coming upon the clouds of heaven, identical words being used in Matthew 24:30.

> 'And they shall see the Son of Man coming in the clouds of heaven' *epi ton nephelon tou ouranon.*

The time of this Coming is indissolubly linked with Daniel 9:27 as Matthew 24:15 will show:

> 'When ye therefore shall see the abomination of desolation, spoken of by Daniel the prophet, stand in the holy place ...'

and the reference to tribes of the earth mourning in Matthew 24:30 is a reference back to Zechariah 12:10-14.

(7) Shall We Substitute 'Government' for 'Kingdom'?

There are different forms of government in the world today, ranging from a monarchy down through a republic and the Soviet conception, to the local government of a village council. Such a word cannot and does not represent the Greek word *basileia.* This word, in classical Greek means, according to Liddle and Scott, 'a kingdom, dominion, hereditary monarchy, a diadem, and as a form of address, majesty'. Any appeal to the pagan use of the word but substantiates the claim, that the only form of government that prophecy foreshadows is 'a kingdom, dominion, associated with hereditary monarchy, a diadem and majesty' which terms are foreign to any other form of government, save one, that of a king. God's answer to the anarchy of the last days is to announce:

> 'Yet have I set (or anointed *see margin*) My KING upon My holy hill of Zion' (Psa. 2:6).

Christ, as King, is to sit upon a throne; the word government is not sufficient for this idea. The U.S.A. has a 'government', but the President has neither *crown, throne* nor *sceptre*. The Son of God is to wear a crown, wield a sceptre and have dominion from sea to sea. As King He is the Anointed, of whom David is the type. He is also to 'reign', a term inapplicable to any form of government other than the monarchical. We cannot stand by and hold our peace while the Lord is robbed of His crown rights, or of His place, as He is when it is suggested that Psalm 2 cannot refer to Christ, because it reads 'against the Lord, and against His Anointed' (*tou Christou autou* LXX). As we have seen, the same argument would dethrone the Son of God in Revelation 11:15 where we read 'the kingdom of our Lord, and of His Christ' (tou *Christou autou*), identical language. Again, to suggest that because in many passages of the Old Testament the 'Anointed' refers to Aaron, David, Elijah and others, the Saviour Himself cannot be intended in Psalm 2 or in Daniel 9 is unwarranted. The 'Messiah' was on the lips of the common people, as can be seen in John 1:20,41; 4:29 as well as in use by inspired speakers like Peter (Matt. 16:16) or of educated men like a High Priest (Matt. 26:63). The Church of the One Body can be *in* a kingdom without confusion, as surely as a 'corporation' can be *in* the kingdom of Great Britain without confusion.

The phraseology of the Apocalypse is much like that of the Old Testament and noticeably in the use of the conjunction 'and'. Thus the book of Exodus commences with the word 'now' in the A.V. The Hebrew word is *vav* which is generally translated 'and'. A modern writer would not, as a rule, commence a book with 'and' but Moses does, in order that no break shall be made between the record of Genesis and Exodus. Leviticus opens with the word 'and' — so does Numbers.

So in the book of Revelation there is an interlocking of the narrative by the continuous use of the conjunction 'and' (Rev. 5:1; 6:1; 7:1; 8:1) and so on up to chapter 22. There can be no appreciable break between Revelation 19 and 20, certainly not one of 500 years.

What can we say of the theory that has been advanced of a 'Pre-Millennial kingdom' that shall last about 500 years? *What we have to say may matter little*, but what saith the Scripture is the responsible quest of every believer.

We cannot sit back and see a beloved and respected brother, who has valiantly stood for the principle of Right Division and its consequences for so many years, do harm to his testimony without uttering a word of protest. We implore all who read this article to 'search and see', to re-examine the materials set forth by any and every God-fearing commentator, and to be prepared to lose even their greatest friend, rather than be found wanting in that day.

We would echo the comment of Dr. Bullinger in another context, when he said, 'O that you would make a chart of it'.

In Daniel 2 we have Gentile dominion stretching to the moment of impact of the stone cut out without hands. Can anyone see how it is possible to set out that vision and introduce into verse 44 an interval of 500 years? If there be a Pre-Millennial kingdom of that duration what is the explanation for its complete absence in Daniel 2:44, Daniel 7:1-14 or Revelation 19 and 20?

MIRACLE

The following definition of a miracle we have found written in the margin of a theological work, but are not sure that it is a quotation. If it is, it may be taken from *Theological Institutes*, by Rev. R. Watson.

> 'A miracle is an effect or event contrary to the established constitution or course of things; or a sensible suspension or controlment of a deviation from the known laws of nature, wrought either by the immediate act, or by the concurrence, or by the permission of God, for the proof or evidence of some particular doctrine, or in attestation of some particular person. The force of a miracle is that it is beyond human power and must be a special interposition of God'.

Under the heading BAPTISM[1], some of the teaching of the New Testament concerning supernatural gifts has been discussed, and that article should be considered as a supplement to the one now before us. There are seven words used in the Greek New Testament which are translated miracle, which we will set out before the reader:

DUNAMIS — An act of power. The English dynamo, dynamite and dynamics have power as their dominant note.

SEMEION — A sign. Used chiefly by John.

TERAS — A wonder, a prodigy, something which strikes terror. John 4:48 and Acts 2:22 are the only references to Christ, the remaining fourteen occurrences are used of false Christs, the apostles and Moses.

ERGON — A work. The miracles are spoken of as the *work* of God, good *works*, and *works* which none other man did.

EUDOXIA — Glorious things (Luke 13:17).

PARADOXIA — Strange things (Luke 5:26).

THAUMASIA — Wonderful things (Matt. 21:15).

Many of the miracles of Christ were miracles of healing. Never did He work a miracle of judgment upon a son of man. The withered fig-tree and the destruction of the herd of swine are the nearest approaches to miracles of judgment, but in neither case did they touch a human being. On the contrary, the blind receive their sight, the dumb speak, the deaf hear, lepers are cleansed, and infirmities are cured. Even the dead are brought back to life again, thousands are fed with a few loaves and fishes, and the marriage at Cana is graced by His miraculous provision. The winds and the waves obey the voice of the Lord, the fish of the sea yield themselves to the net, or to pay the tribute at His command; demons and evil spirits are cast out and the possessed set free. On two occasions the Lord passed through a crowd unseen.

The first record of miracles in the Gospels is that of Matthew 4:23,24:

> 'And Jesus went about all Galilee, TEACHING in their synagogues, and PREACHING the gospel of the kingdom, and HEALING all manner of sickness and all manner of disease among the people. And His fame went throughout all Syria: and they brought unto Him all sick people that were taken with divers diseases and torments, and those which were possessed with demons, and those which were lunatic, and those that had the palsy; AND HE HEALED THEM'.

The result of these mighty works was that:

> 'there followed Him great multitudes of people from Galilee, and from Decapolis, and from Jerusalem, and from Judæa, and from beyond Jordan'.

A glance at the map shows that early in the Lord's ministry His mighty works were known through the length and breadth of the land. It is important to observe the setting in which these miracles were wrought. The miracles were not mere exhibitions of power, neither were they performed to strike terror into the observers, for they were all of one character, viz., miracles of healing, and attracted followers from all parts of the country. The miracles formed a supplement, to TEACHING and PREACHING. The last reference to miracles in the Gospel narrative says the same thing, 'and they went forth and PREACHED every where, the Lord WORKING with them, and confirming the WORD with signs following' (Mark 16:20).

Again in Matthew 10 we find the same connection, 'As ye go, PREACH, saying, the kingdom of heaven is at hand. Heal the sick, cleanse the lepers, raise the dead, cast out demons'. Yet again the necessary association of preaching and miracles is implied in Matthew 11. 'He departed thence to TEACH and to PREACH in their cities. Now when John had heard in the prison the WORKS of Christ'. The object (or at least a prominent object) with which the miracles were wrought is given in Matthew 11:20, 'Then began He to upbraid the cities wherein most of His mighty works were done, *because they repented not*'. The close connection between miracles and the testimony is also indicated in Matthew 13:58, 'He did not many mighty works there *because of their unbelief*'. Matthew 9:35 presents a practical repetition of Matthew 4:23, as the reader can observe, and should be read in connection with the commission of Matthew 10.

One of the characteristic accompaniments of the preaching of the gospel of the kingdom was the *presence* of miracles. One of the characteristic features of the preaching of the Mystery is the *absence* of miracles. We might notice the extent of the miraculous healing given in Matthew 4:23,24, 'healing *all manner* of sickness and *all manner* of diseases'; 'all sick people that were taken with *divers* diseases, and torments, and those which were possessed with *demons*, and those which were *lunatic*, and those that had the *palsy*, and He healed them'.

Details are given more fully as the narrative advances, and when we see the complete list of the mighty works that are recorded in the Gospels we shall begin to realize what a confirmation is given to His ministry; and when we add to that the testimony of John 21:25, 'there are also many other things which Jesus DID, the which, if they should be written every one, I suppose that even the world itself could not contain the books that should be written', the confirmation of Messiahship must have been overwhelming. Yet they crucified Him! Yet they repented not. What a testimony then to the nature of the human heart.

The three miracles that are recorded in Matthew 8:1-15 are suggestive of much teaching.

1-4	THE LEPER	Israel	The Lord *touched* him.
5-13	THE CENTURION'S SERVANT	Gentile	Healing at a *distance.* Faith compared with that of Israel.
14,15	PETER'S WIFE'S MOTHER	A Woman	The Lord *touched* her.

The Pharisee in his prayer thanked God that he was not born (1) a Gentile, (2) a Slave, or (3) a Woman (see the Jewish Prayer Book), which position of 'splendid isolation' is gloriously done away 'in Christ' for Galatians 3:28 shows that there is

(1)	Neither Jew nor Greek	The Gentile
(2)	Neither bond nor free	The Slave
(3)	Neither male nor female	The Woman

Here in these three opening miracles the Lord breaks through traditional barriers; He touched a *Leper*! He healed a *Gentile*! He healed a *Woman*! There is a dispensational lesson here which the reader should observe, as well as a moral one. Both the leper and the woman were healed by personal contact; the Gentile, however, was healed at a distance. The peculiarity comes out again in Matthew 15:21-28; in both cases, too, reference is made to the *great* faith of the Gentile. The miracles, like the parables, are distributed with reference to the purpose before the writer. Let us observe the way in which they occur in the Gospel of Matthew.

(1) THE TWELVE MIRACLES THAT PRECEDE REJECTION

Matthew 8 to 12

Twelve separate miracles are recorded by Matthew. Eight separate signs are recorded by John. Evidently, therefore, the writers of these 'Gospels' made a choice of the event to suit the purpose of their respective narratives.

We know that twelve is associated with Israel, and with government. Let us look at these twelve miracles together, and notice anything that will help us to see what their special purpose may be:

(1) THE LEPER CLEANSED (8:2).

(2) CENTURION'S SERVANT (8:5).

(3) PETER'S WIFE'S MOTHER (8:14).

COLLECTIVE MIRACLES (8:16), and Old Testament quotation 8:17: 'That it might be fulfilled which was spoken by Isaiah the prophet, saying, Himself took our infirmities, and bare our sicknesses' (Isa. 53:4).

(4) THE STORM (8:24).

(5) THE DEMONS (8:28).

(6) PALSIED MAN. SINS FORGIVEN (9:2). Brought by others. Old Testament quotation, 'Go ye, and learn what that meaneth, I will have mercy and not sacrifice' (Hos. 6:6).

(7) RULER'S DAUGHTER (9:18).

(8) ISSUE OF BLOOD (9:22).

(9) BLIND MEN (9:27).

(10) DUMB DEMON (9:32). Brought by others.

COLLECTIVE MIRACLES (9:35) and Old Testament quotation (9:36): 'As sheep having no shepherd' (Zech. 10:2).

(11) WITHERED HAND (12:13).

COLLECTIVE MIRACLES (12:15), and Old Testament quotation (12:17-21): 'that it might be fulfilled which was spoken by Isaiah the prophet saying, Behold My Servant, Whom I have chosen; My beloved, in Whom My soul is well pleased: I will put My spirit upon Him, and He shall show judgment to the Gentiles. He shall not strive, nor cry; neither shall any man hear His voice in the streets. A bruised reed shall He not break, and smoking flax shall He not quench, till He send forth judgment unto victory. And in His name shall the Gentiles trust' (Isa. 42:1).

(12) BLIND AND DUMB DEMON (12:22). The peoples' inquiry, 'Is not this the Son of DAVID?' (12:23). The Pharisees' objection, 'He casts out demons by Beelzebub' (12:24).

The miracles of rejection occupy Matthew 13 to 28, and these too fall into a well-defined group.

The Miracles after the rejection

A_1 13:58. Not many because of unbelief.

B_1 SEVEN MIRACLES
- C **a** 14:14. Many healed.
  - **b** 14:15-21. 5,000 fed.
- D 14:22-33. The Sea.
  - E 14:36. Perfectly whole.
- *D* 15:21-28. The Woman of Canaan.
- *C* ***a*** 15:29,30. Many healed.
  - ***b*** 15:31-39. 4,000 fed.

A_2 16:1-4. The demand for a sign refused —
no sign but that of the prophet Jonah.

B_2 SEVEN MIRACLES
- F 17:14-21. Lunatic. Faith removes mountains
  - G 17:27. Tribute.
    Kingdom not yet come.
    (19:2 Multitudes healed).
    - H 20:30. Blind. Son of David.
    - *H* 21:1-11. Colt. Thy King cometh.
  - *G* 21:14,15. Blind and Lame. Son of David
- *F* 21:19,21. Fig tree withered.
  Faith to remove mountains.

A_3 27:42-44. Demand for evidential miracle refused.

B_3 27:52 to 28:8. THE SIGN OF JONAH.

The first set of seven miracles are not so much signs, as miracles of compassion. 'And Jesus ... was moved with compassion' (14:14). The feeding of the 5,000 resembles the feeding of the 4,000 and there again the Lord says, 'I have compassion on the multitude'.

The second series of seven begins to foreshadow the development of events. Immediately after the glory of the Transfiguration, the Lord deals with a difficult case of demon possession, and makes reference to a faith capable of removing mountains. Then follows the miracle of the tribute money and its question:

> 'Of whom do the kings of the earth take custom or tribute? of their own children, or of strangers? Peter saith unto Him, Of strangers. Jesus saith unto him, Then are the children free. Notwithstanding, lest we should offend them, go thou to the sea, and cast an hook, and take up the fish that first cometh up; and when thou hast opened his mouth, thou shalt find a piece of money: that take, and give unto them for Me and thee' (Matt. 17:25-27).

Has the reader observed one great difference between the miracles performed before the twelfth chapter and those after it? In the case of those that are detailed in the first half of Matthew, Christ works them entirely alone. A change comes with this new series.

The disciples are the ones first addressed with regard to the feeding of the 5,000. 'Jesus said unto them, They need not depart; *give ye* them to eat'. While the disciples were utterly unable to comply with the task, they have an ample share in its outworking. Peter evidently began to realize that the working of miracles in conjunction with the Lord was now expected, for he asks the Lord to bid him come to Him upon the water!

The repetition of the feeding of the 5,000 by the feeding of the 4,000 seemed intentional, but the disciples did not at the time appear to grasp the Lord's purpose. The Lord rebukes both lack of memory and lack of faith as to these two miracles (16:5-12). He rebukes the lack of faith again when the disciples confessed their inability to cast out the demon (17:20), and reminds them that prayer and fasting were essentials. Peter shares, however humbly, in the miracle of the tribute money; the disciples take a part in the miracle of the colt, and when the disciples marvelled at the withering of the fig tree, they are again reminded of the faith which removes mountains. There is a reason for this; 'greater works than these *shall ye do*, because I go to My Father', said the Lord, and Mark 16 closes with the following words, 'the Lord working with them, confirming the Word with signs following'. These are, therefore, all indications of the coming dispensation of Pentecost. All was now awaiting that sign of all signs, *the sign of the prophet Jonah.*

The references to the coming of the King, and the Hosannas to the Son of David, again indicate how near the common people were to accepting the Lord as the Messiah. What a dreadful charge lies at the door of their spiritual rulers, who instructed them to choose Barabbas instead of Christ! How soon will this piece of history be repeated on a grander scale? Spiritist activity seems to indicate that the Lord and the False Christ are near.

There are two miracles which we reserve for more detailed consideration owing to their bearing upon the dispensational outlook, namely, that of the woman of Canaan, and that of the withered Fig Tree. We will now deal with these.

(2) TWO MIRACLES OF DISPENSATIONAL IMPORTANCE

Matthew 15:21-28 and 21:19

All the miracles, as well as all the parables, have a definite dispensational character, but the two we select in this article have that character in a very prominent way. The first of the two took place near the close of the Lord's ministry as the Son of David, the second near the close of His ministry as the Son of Abraham. Soon after working the first miracle the Lord began to speak of His approaching death, while soon after the second He was led away to be crucified. A simple outline of the miracle of Matthew 15:21-28 is as follows:

A Have mercy, O Lord, Thou Son of David
    B But He answered her not a word
A Send her away for she crieth after us
    B But He answered I am not sent but to the lost sheep of the house of Israel
A Lord, help me
    B But He answered; take not children's bread and cast to dogs
A True Lord, yet the dogs eat of the crumbs
    B Then Jesus answered, O woman, great is thy faith.

The woman was a woman of Canaan, a Gentile, a Syrophenician (Mark 7:26), and she approached the Lord, calling Him by His title, 'Son of David'. Now as Son of David He came to be King, 'King of the Jews' (Matt. 2:2; 27:37,42). This sovereignty was primarily of an exclusive character. The promise to David regarding his throne will be fulfilled in Christ, and in its primary interpretation it has no place for any nation but Israel. When the kingdom is established and that King is reigning, then world-wide blessing will result. So it was that the Saviour, Who so often was moved with compassion as He contemplated fallen and suffering man, 'answered her not a word'.

His reply to the disciples' request reveals the reason of this strange silence, 'I am not sent but unto the lost sheep of the house of Israel'. These words, to weak faith, would have sounded as the death-knell of hope. The woman, however, penetrated the reply, and learned its lesson. As Son of David He could do nothing for her; she must therefore drop that title and approach Him simply as *Lord*; she had no such rights in Him as Son of David as Israel had. 'Then came she and worshipped Him saying, Lord, help me'. This request draws from the Lord a personal answer, but what will He say? Will He grant her request? 'He answered and said, It is not meet to take the children's bread, and to cast it to *kunarion* (little dogs)'. At first sight this answer seems as forbidding as the former one. Israel were the lost *sheep*, what had He, their Shepherd, to do with *dogs*? Israel were the children of the house; surely it was not right to take the children's bread, and cast it to dogs?

The faith of this woman enabled her to believe that what He spoke to her was absolute truth, and she seized upon the word He had used for *dogs*. As the reader will know, the dog is a term of reproach throughout the East, and is a symbol of all that is depraved, forsaken, and cast out, e.g. 'without are dogs'. The Lord in His reply said '*little dogs*', or, as we say, *puppies*. The rule regarding the dog has an exception in the case of the little puppy; children in the East, like children in the West, like to pet and fondle the little puppies, and for a short time they are allowed inside the house. 'Truth, Lord,' replied the woman, 'yet the puppies eat of the crumbs which fall from their masters' table'. She knew that the exclusiveness of the Lord's ministry to Israel was not for any mean or narrow reason; a saved Israel will be saved not for their own sake, but that all the families of the earth may be blessed in them.

The twofold aspect of this phase of God's dealings is emphasized in Romans 15:8,9, 'Now I say that Jesus Christ was a minister of the circumcision for the truth of God, to confirm the promises made unto the fathers' — this is an exclusive ministry to Israel with reference to promises made in the past — 'and that the Gentiles might glorify God for His mercy' — this follows as the designed sequence. So it was that the woman sought the crumbs. She gave Israel their rightful place; they were *the Masters* (the very same word twice rendered 'Lord'). She was but a little dog; *they* sat at the table and she could only expect the crumbs. As soon as this was recognized, blessing came. How vital to this woman's case was a correct appreciation of dispensational truth! How many today are perplexed because the Lord answers not a word, simply because they are asking amiss! The miracle clearly shows us what was the relationship between Israel and the nations at the time of the Lord's earthly ministry. In Romans 11, the figure changes to that of *wild olive branches grafted into the true olive.* In Ephesians 2 it further changes to the *creation of one new man.* Which shall we believe, the Scriptures rightly divided or those who speak against 'dispensational' truth?

The second miracle has also a dispensational character. Here is a symbol of Israel as a nation, the fig tree. The fig, the vine, and the olive represent Israel in various capacities:

> 'And when He saw one single fig tree by the way, He came to it, and found nothing thereon, but LEAVES ONLY, and said unto it, Let no fruit grow on thee henceforth for ever, and immediately the fig tree was withered' (Matt. 21:19).

In the prophecy of Luke the Lord separates the fig tree from all others — 'Behold the fig tree, and all the trees' (Luke 21:29-31). The sign of the Lord's return is found in the budding of the nation, and all the nations; a day is coming when 'Israel shall blossom and bud, and fill the world with fruit' (Isa. 27:6). At the time, however, when the miracle was performed, the Lord found 'leaves only'.

The crowd had spread their garments in the road, had cut down branches from the trees and scattered them on the road, they had shouted saying, 'Hosanna to the Son of David'; but it was 'leaves only'. The same crowd within a few days were prevailed upon to cry, 'away with Him, crucify Him'. The Lord had foretold this in Matthew 13:5,6:

> 'Some fell upon stony places, where they had not much earth: and forthwith they sprung up, because they had no deepness of earth: and when the sun was up, they were scorched; and because they had no root, they withered away'.

The Hosannas were *leaves only*, fruit depends upon root. The scorching sun indicates persecution:

> 'He that received the seed into stony places, the same is he that heareth the word, and anon with joy receiveth it; yet hath he not root in himself, but dureth for a while: for when tribulation or persecution ariseth because of the word, by and by (immediately) he is offended' (Matt. 13:20,21).

The fig tree and those hearers on stony ground withered. Such was the parable of Israel, they began to cumber the earth; soon the word would go forth, 'cut it down'. Israel will bring forth no fruit until the age (translated 'for ever').

It is deeply suggestive to us all to note the fact that the only miracle of judgment which the Lord performed was upon a tree. Never did He work such upon a human being. The only other occasion where anything resembling a judgment might be found is the case of the swine which were choked. Yet here it was the swine, not the men, who were drowned. Thus these two miracles concerning the Syrophenician woman and the fig tree, taken together, speak of the blessing going out to the Gentiles, and the cutting off, for the time being, of an unfruitful people. In this case there are lessons for all to learn, lessons not rendered the less pointed by seeing them in their true dispensational perspective.

We will conclude this section with a word concerning the presence of the miraculous in the Scriptures. One of the most obvious reasons for a miracle is that it 'confirms' that which purports to be a revelation from God. Anyone can declare that what he has to teach is a message received direct from heaven, and there are always enough gullible souls ready to make a following. Consequently we find that the miracle is referred to as a confirmation in several passages of Scripture:

Mark 16:20	'Confirming the word with signs following'.
1 Cor. 1:6,7	'The testimony of Christ was confirmed in you: so that ye come behind in no gift'.
Heb. 2:2,3,4	'The word spoken ... was confirmed unto us ... God also bearing them witness, both with signs and wonders, and with divers miracles, and gifts of the Holy Ghost, according to His own will'.

When the apostle defended his office against those who would have discredited him, he appealed unto this confirming evidence of miracle:

> 'Truly the signs of an apostle were wrought among you in all patience, in signs, and wonders, and mighty deeds' (2 Cor. 12:12).
>
> 'Through mighty signs and wonders, by the power of the spirit of God; so that from Jerusalem, and round about unto Illyricum, I have fully preached the gospel of Christ' (Rom. 15:19).
>
> 'Then all the multitude kept silence, and gave audience to Barnabas and Paul, declaring what miracles and wonders God had wrought among the Gentiles by them' (Acts 15:12).

The confirmation is most obvious in the cases of Moses. It demanded the greatest courage on the part of Moses to go to Pharaoh and demand the release of Israel, and it was extremely unlikely that Israel would respond without some clear attestation from above:

> 'And Moses answered and said, But, behold, they will not believe me, nor hearken unto my voice: for they will say, The LORD hath not appeared unto thee' (Exod. 4:1).

The answer of the Lord was in the nature of miraculous signs: the serpent, typifying Satan, and leprosy typifying sin. Even the Lord Himself appealed to the miracles He wrought saying:

'The works that I do in My Father's name, they bear witness of Me'.

'If I do not the works of My Father, believe me not. But if I do, though ye believe not Me, believe the works' (John 10:25,37,38).

'Believe Me for the very works' sake' (John 14:11).

Thus it is demonstrated that miracles were given to confirm the revelation to Moses, to the apostles and to Christ Himself. This is so natural, so expected, that the very ones who object to the presence of miracle in the Bible, would be the first to affirm that the Bible could not be a revelation from God if no miracles accompanied its unfolding. Then again, it is objected that miracles are unscientific. The laws of nature cannot thus be set aside. Miracles cannot happen, and no 'proof' can be entertained. We all know this kind of argument. One would imagine that the laws of nature actually exist outside the mind of the scientist who frames them. Many so-called laws of nature have been deposed from their throne, to be taken by others, which in turn will be eclipsed. We see a stone fall to the earth and we speak of 'the law of gravitation'. God, the Creator, Who planned that stones should fall downward, is supposed to be utterly unable to do what is done every minute of waking life. We have only to introduce a PERSON into creation, and water flows upward, light produces sound, masses of metal float on water or fly through the air, in every case breaking or altering the operation of certain 'laws of nature'.

Take a simple illustration. We spend several hours on the edge of a cliff, letting pebble after pebble go, and demonstrating that it is a law of nature, that anything that is let go at the top of the cliff will most certainly fall to the bottom. A little child comes toddling to the edge of the cliff, slips and begins to fall, *but mother love* brushes aside the laws of nature so patiently and so scientifically demonstrated by us, puts out an arm, intercepts the child and saves its life. That is all that a miracle is. The interposition of a *Person*, and if that person be God, what limits shall we put to His power? Instead, therefore, of speaking of miracles as though it were unreasonable to expect them, it is altogether the other way. Grant a God of almighty power, grant a people redeemed by love, and we have granted all that is necessary for the interposition of miracle wherever and whenever it should be so demanded. Finally, if the ordinary chain of cause and effect binds the hand of God as with a fetter, prayer would be just a waste of time. Every answer to prayer, is the interposition of a Father's hand athwart the otherwise remorseless sequence of cause and effect. So from every angle that the matter of miracle is approached it is found to be rational, to be expected if God is God, and if the Scriptures are His revealed will to man. See article entitled CONFIRMATION[1].

MYSTERY

The Greek word *musterion* occurs twenty-seven times in the New Testament and is translated 'mystery' throughout. The word is distributed as follows:

Gospels. Three references. No occurrence in John's Gospel.

Epistles. Eight occurrences in Paul's pre-prison epistles (Rom.; 1 Cor.; 2 Thess.).

Ten occurrences in Paul's prison epistles (Eph.; Col.).

Two occurrences in the Interim epistle (1 Tim.).

Four occurrences in the Revelation.

The word does not occur in Hebrews, nor in any of the circumcision epistles. The LXX contains eight references, all of them in the book of Daniel. In addition there are twelve occurrences in the Apocrypha which indicate, by the way the word is employed, something of the meaning it must have attached to it when it is found in the New Testament.

As this word occupies such an important place in dispensational truth we must waive our rule of not giving a concordance of more than ten occurrences of any word, and set out a complete concordance both in the Old Testament and in the New Testament.

Musterion in the New Testament

Gospels

Matt. 13:11	The mysteries of the kingdom of heaven.
Mark 4:11	The mystery of the kingdom of God.
Luke 8:10	The mysteries of the kingdom of God.

Pre-prison epistles

Rom. 11:25	Not ... be ignorant of this mystery.
Rom. 16:25	The mystery, which was kept secret.
1 Cor. 2:7	The wisdom of God in a mystery.
1 Cor. 4:1	Stewards of the mysteries of God.
1 Cor. 13:2	Though I ... understand all mysteries.
1 Cor. 14:2	In the spirit he speaketh mysteries.
1 Cor. 15:51	Behold, I show you a mystery.
2 Thess. 2:7	The mystery of iniquity doth already work.

Prison epistles

Eph. 1:9	Having made known unto us the mystery of His will.
Eph. 3:3	He made known unto me the mystery.
Eph. 3:4	My knowledge in the mystery of Christ.
Eph. 3:9	The fellowship of the mystery.
Eph. 5:32	This is a great mystery.
Eph. 6:19	To make known the mystery of the gospel.
Col. 1:26	The mystery which hath been hid.
Col. 1:27	This mystery among the Gentiles.
Col. 2:2	The mystery of God.
Col. 4:3	To speak the mystery of Christ.

Interim epistles

1 Tim. 3:9	Holding the mystery of the faith.
1 Tim. 3:16	Great is the mystery of godliness.

Revelation

Rev. 1:20	The mystery of the seven stars.
Rev. 10:7	The mystery of God should be finished.
Rev. 17:5	Mystery, Babylon the great.
Rev. 17:7	The mystery of the woman.

Musterion O.T. (LXX)

Dan. 2:18	Mercies ... concerning this secret.
Dan. 2:19	Then was the secret revealed unto Daniel.
Dan. 2:27	The secret which the king hath demanded.

Dan. 2:28	There is a God in heaven that revealeth secrets.
Dan. 2:29	He that revealeth secrets.
Dan. 2:30	The secret is not revealed to me for any wisdom.
Dan. 2:47	Lord of kings, and a revealer of secrets, seeing thou couldest reveal this secret.
Dan. 4:9	No secret troubleth thee, tell me.

The Greek Christian 'fathers' used the word of any such sign, whether of words or actions. They spoke of the offering of Isaac as a *musterion*, i.e., a sign or a symbol of the secret purpose of God concerning His Son, Jesus Christ. And they used it interchangeably with the words *tupos* type, *sumbolon* symbol, and *parabole* parable.

So far we have been concerned with the material that we are to use. We must now inquire into the essential meaning of the term, and this we shall gather (1) from its etymology and (2) from its usage.

Etymology of *Musterion*

Etymology used alone is an unsafe guide, for language is living, and the folk who use it are not necessarily students; it is therefore wise to balance etymology with usage. This we will do.

Muo does not occur in the New Testament but is the basic word from which *musterion* is derived. It means 'to close', especially the lips or the eyes. *Muzo*, which likewise does not occur in the New Testament means 'to murmur with closed lips, to mutter'. It will be observed that in the English words *mur*mur, *mu*tter, *mu*mble and *mu*te this meaning persists.

Mueo. To initiate into the mysteries, this is not only found in classical Greek but is used by the apostle in Philippians 4:12, 'I am instructed', better, 'I am initiated'. Moffatt translates the passage, 'I have been initiated into the secret', Rotherham renders the word, 'I have been let into the secret'.

Muopazo (myopia in English) 2 Peter 1:9, 'cannot see afar off'.

Kammuo (derived from *kata muo*) to shut, especially the eyes (Matt. 13:15; Acts 28:27).

The etymology, therefore, of the word *musterion* suggests something 'hidden', a secret, something that requires initiation, something not discoverable by ordinary methods. It is an unsafe analogy to argue from the use of the word 'mystery' as employed in the articles of indenture, and referring to the mysteries of a trade, for this word should really be spelled 'mistery' coming as it does from the French *mestier*, or *metier* which in its turn is derived from the Latin *ministerium*. It will not do, therefore, to teach that there is no more 'mystery' about the mysteries of the Bible than there is about trade secrets, for this approach to the subject omits the presence and influence of the pagan mysteries, that will eventually come to a head in 'the mystery of iniquity', even as the mysteries of the Scriptures come to a head in 'the mystery of godliness'.

Is there any one who knows all that there is to know concerning either the mystery of iniquity or the mystery of godliness? Are there not 'depths of Satan' and 'the deep things of God'? Are there not 'unspeakable words, which it is not lawful (or possible) for a man to utter' (2 Cor. 12:4)? And is there not in the same epistle the offering of thanks to God for His 'unspeakable gift' (2 Cor. 9:15)? From very early times there were vast and widespread institutions in the pagan world known as mysteries, celebrated for their profound secrecy, admission to which was only by initiation. The Greek, Egyptian and Persian mysteries can be traced back to a common source, namely Chaldea, and constitute one of the travesties of truth that is so characteristic of Babylonianism. Babylon is represented as bearing a golden cup, and to drink of 'mysterious beverages' says Salverte, was indispensable on the part of all who sought initiation into these mysteries.

'*To musterion*'. This is not the only term borrowed from the ancient mysteries, which Paul employs to describe the teaching of the deeper truths of the Word. The word *teleion* (Col. 1:28 'perfect') seems to be an extension of the same metaphor. Philippians 4:12 we have already noted, and in Ephesians 1:13 *sphragizesthai* ('sealed') is perhaps an image derived from the same source. So too the Ephesians are addressed as *Paulou summustai* 'fellow initiates of Paul' in Ignatius' epistle, and the Christian teacher is thus regarded as a *heirophantes* (see Epict. 3.21,13 seq.), who 'initiates his disciples into the rites' (Bishop Lightfoot).

It becomes very clear that no knowledge of the mysteries was obtainable apart from initiation, and this fact must be borne in mind when we approach the mysteries of Scripture. No mere instruction, or quoting of verses of Scripture, not even the most lucid presentation of Dispensational Truth will ever 'convince' any one apart from the gracious enlightening that God alone can give.

> 'It is given unto you to know the mysteries of the kingdom of heaven, but to them it is not given ... many prophets and righteous men have desired to see those things which ye see, and have not seen them; and to hear those things which ye hear, and have not heard them' (Matt. 13:11,17).
>
> 'Who hath ears to hear, let him hear' (Matt. 13:9).

The recognition of this great fact of initiation would save the believer many hours of fruitless anxiety on the part of others. The truth of the Mystery is not to be made known by the organizing of campaigns, it will never be a subject of popular appeal, our attitude must be a readiness at all times to help and guide wherever we see a desire to know and follow on, being assured that none will come to see the Mystery apart from the Lord's own illuminating; we ourselves can at best be but the earthen vessels that He stoops to use in this most wondrous work.

Usage of *Musterion*

When we come to usage, there are several avenues of approach. (1) The Pagan mysteries and (2) the references in the Apocrypha. These two give an idea what the word mystery stood for in the great outside world; and (3) the usage of the word in the LXX book of Daniel, and (4) its usage in the New Testament, these show how it was used in Holy Scripture. We can say little to profit of the Pagan mysteries. The Greek mysteries which were prevalent in the days of the apostles, were derived from Egypt, which in its turn received them from Chaldea, and so in them we have the mystery of iniquity in germ. A search into the annals of the past would bring to light some of the horrible doctrines and corresponding practices associated with the mysteries, but the attitude of the apostle must be ours:

> 'It is a shame even to speak of those things which are done of them in secret' (Eph. 5:12),

and pass on to positive teaching.

In the Apocrypha the word '*musterion*' rarely rises above the idea of a secret, either of a king or a friend. Twice it refers to secret rites and ceremonies, but nothing more. The fact that the LXX did not use *musterion* until translating the book of Daniel, may be accounted for by many natural explanations, but when all is said, there must still be room left for the exercise of Divine Providence. Some lexicographers say that the Greek *musterion* is derived from the Hebrew *mister*, which is translated 'secret' a number of times, yet the Greek translators never use *musterion* for that or its cognate *sether*. The only word translated *musterion* in the Greek Old Testament is the Chaldee *raz*, which is used constantly throughout Daniel 2, and as this word does not occur anywhere else in the Old Testament we have no means of comparison.

While the Chaldee word *raz* stands alone, we are not left entirely without help, for on one occasion Daniel uses the Chaldee form of the Hebrew word *sether*, a word translated 'secret' and 'secret place' in many passages. This provides us with the link that we felt we needed, teaching us that in the Chaldee *raz* we have the equivalent word. The passage in Daniel 2:22, 'He revealeth the deep and secret things', the LXX render '*bathea kai apokrupha*', reserving apparently the use of the *musterion* for the Gentile term. Its usage is confined to the dream of Nebuchadnezzar and in two ways. Nebuchadnezzar had either actually forgotten the substance of his dream, or as a matter of policy withheld it in order to make sure that the interpretation should be something more than a clever human invention (Dan. 2:8,9,10,11). When Daniel went into the presence of the king, he did not concentrate his attention on the substance of the dream, but its interpretation (Dan. 2:16), but of course, as the substance of the dream had to be known before the interpretation could be given, both dream and interpretation were included in the 'secret' concerning which Daniel and his fellows prayed (Dan. 2:18,19). When Daniel went in before the king, Nebuchadnezzar asked him, 'art thou able to make known unto me the dream which I have seen, and the interpretation thereof?' (Dan. 2:26). One cannot avoid the feeling that there is a Divine overruling in the choice of this word *musterion* here, and for this reason. We discover that when Israel began to make it manifest that they were going to reject the Saviour (Matt. 11 to 12), that the word 'mystery' enters into the New Testament (Matt. 13), and that whereas the apostles had been commanded earlier 'go not into the way of the Gentiles' (Matt. 10:5), a change is indicated by the quotation of Isaiah 42, 'in His name shall the Gentiles trust' (Matt. 12:21). Again at Acts 28, when Israel were set aside, Paul the prisoner commits to writing the epistles which reveal the dispensation of the Mystery (see ACTS 28[1] and PARABLE, p. 122).

At this point it may be useful to reproduce a chart that has been designed to illustrate the idea behind this thought that *musterion* is rightly reserved for the book of Daniel, an idea summed up in the words, 'where HISTORY (that is Israel's) ceases, MYSTERY begins'.

In this Chart, opposite, we seek to demonstrate the principle that where *history* ceases (so far as Israel is concerned) some element of *mystery* comes in. It might be the mysteries of the kingdom of heaven; it might be the mysteries of God's purpose in appointing Nebuchadnezzar; it might be the introduction of the present dispensation of the Mystery, but the sequence is the same. Daniel is the Old Testament Paul. He became the prisoner of the Lord for the Gentiles. In the LXX of the Old Testament the Greek word *musterion* occurs for the first time in the book of Daniel, where it is translated 'secret'.

In the Chart a series of downward steps is indicated by the passages referred to, commencing with the failure of Hezekiah, which introduces the prophecy concerning Babylon. The times of the Gentiles are coincident with the down-treading of Jerusalem, as Luke 21:24 will show. As Israel passed off the scene, the Gentile came into prominence.

The second illustration is taken from the first thirteen chapters of Matthew. The Messiah, Who must be the Son of David and of Abraham, is revealed as having come in the person of Jesus Christ, Emmanuel, God with us. He also is attested by the witness of a divinely equipped forerunner and a voice from heaven. By observing our Lord's words in Matthew 11:20-24, we understand that one of the objects for which the miracles were wrought was the repentance of Israel. Their non-repentance leads to the threefold rejection of Matthew 12:6,41 and 42, where Christ is rejected in His offices of Priest, Prophet and King. Upon this non-repentance and rejection comes mystery in Matthew 13. It is suggestive too, that in Matthew 12:14-21, consequent upon the Council of the Pharisees, we find the reference to the blessing of the Gentiles.

BEREAN MYSTERY CHARTS
No 8.
AN ILLUSTRATION OF THE PRINCIPLE, THAT:-
where HISTORY ceases MYSTERY begins.
ISRAEL'S FAILURE — GENTILE ASCENDANCY
Daniel Prisoner of the Lord for Gentiles.
Hezekiah's failure. Isa. xxxix. 6. 7.
Eliakim appointed by Pharaoh. 2K. xxiii. 34.
Zedekiah app: by Nebuchadnezzar " xxiv. 6-17.
Temple destroyed. 2Ch. xxxvi. 11-21.
Times of Gentiles. Ez. xxi. 25-27. Luke xxi.
ISRAEL REJECT — GENTILE BLESSED Mt xii. 21.
Genealogy. Matt. i. 1-24.
Forerunner. Matt. iii. 1-3.
Miracles, their object. Matt. iv & xi. 20-24.
Threefold rejection. Matt. xii. 6. 41-42.
Mysteries of kingdom. Matt. xiii.
ISRAEL SET ASIDE — MYSTERY REVEALED
Paul Prisoner of the Lord for Gentiles.
Prophecy of Joel. Acts ii.
The miracle and its object. Acts iii. iv.
The wane of Israel. Acts x.
The twofold ministry. Acts xx. & xxvi.
The last signs. Acts xxviii.
ACTS XXVIII. DISPENSATIONAL BOUNDARY
DENOTES ISAIAH VI. 10. A CRISIS
ISA. VI. 10. IN DAYS BEFORE NEBUCHADNEZZAR 2 CHRON. XXXVI.
ISA. VI. 10. IN DAYS OF CHRIST'S REJECTION MATT. XIII. 14. 15.
ISA. VI. 10. IN DAYS OF ISRAEL'S REJECTION ACTS XXVIII. 26. 27.
C.H.W. 34.

The third illustration is the chief purpose of the Chart, to prove that the present dispensation of the Mystery is consequent upon the rejection of Israel in Acts 28. The prophecy of Joel which underlies the teaching of the day of Pentecost is insistent upon repentance (Joel 2:12-14). The restoration of Israel is set forth in the miracle of the lame man (Acts 3), and the vision of the sheet that Peter saw (Acts 10) is an indication that Jewish exclusiveness is going.

The twofold ministry of the apostle Paul now comes to light (see Acts 20:17-24 and 26:16-18), revealing that his second ministry would be accompanied with imprisonment, would be related to a second revelation from the Lord, and would be directed particularly to the Gentiles. The last 'signs and wonders' that fulfil the promise of Mark 16:17,18 are recorded (Acts 28:1-10), the last reference to the 'hope of Israel' is made (Acts 28:20), the last citation of Isaiah 6:10 is made, and Israel become *lo-ammi* (not My people, Hosea 1:9), the 'salvation of God is sent unto the Gentiles', and the dispensation of the Mystery is made known.

The way in which Isaiah 6:10 is cited at great crises in Israel's history is worthy of study.

As we have dealt very fully with Matthew 13 under the heading PARABLE (p. 122), we pass on to those references to the mysteries that have a bearing upon Dispensational Truth and the high calling of the Church. These references we will subdivide as follows:

(1) The mystery of Romans 16:25-27.

(2) The mystery as revealed in Ephesians and Colossians.

(3) The mystery as spoken of in 1 Timothy.

(1) THE MYSTERY THAT HAD BEEN SILENCED (Romans 16:25-27)

We now come to the closing section of the epistle to the Romans, a section that it is of the utmost importance to understand, and about which a great deal of discussion has arisen.

The genuineness of the doxology has been disputed (1) on the ground that its position is unsuitable either at the end of chapter 14:23, where it stands in 190 manuscripts, or at the close of chapter 16; (2) on the ground of its 'un-Pauline' lack of simplicity. The doxology is unusually elaborate for Paul's epistles, but there is of course no rule governing such a matter, and the nature of the subject in the case in point fully accounts for any complexity in its composition. The doxology is found:

(1) After 16:24, in MSS. B, C, D, E, Aleph, Syr., Copt., Alth., Vulg. Lat. Fathers.
(2) After 14:23 by L., most cursive MSS., Chrys., Theod., etc.
(3) Both after 14:23 and 16:23 by A5,17,109 Lat.
(4) Nowhere D, F, G, Marcion.*

When we consider the structure of the epistle as a whole, we shall see two things:

(1) It can stand nowhere else but where it comes in the A.V.
(2) If it were omitted, the epistle would remain for ever imperfect.

To appreciate the latter of these two statements it is essential that we give the structure of the epistle.

---

* For explanation of these symbols see:
Scrivener's *Introduction to the Criticism of the New Testament*,
J.W. Burgon's *The Revision Revised*, and
The Berean Expositor, Vol. 21, page 169.

The Structure of the Epistle to the Romans as a whole

	A	1:1-17.	Gospel. Promise afore. For obedience of faith among all nations.	
	B	1:18 to 3:20.	Jews equally with Gentiles guilty before God.	In the outer portion of Romans we read of sins, law and Sinai, Abraham, Israel, Jew and Gentile.
	C	3:21-31.	The Glory of God. Come short of.	
	D	4:1-25.	His own body now dead.	
	E	5:1-11.	Reconciliation. Doctrinal.	
The Mystery of Romans 16:25-27	**F**	**5:12-21.**	**Condemnation in Adam**	**In the inner portion of Romans, we have sin, law of sin, Adam, and Man, but no references to Abraham, Jew or Gentile.**
	G	**6 and 7.**	**Question: Repudiation.**	
	F	**8.**	**Answer: No condemnation in Christ**	
	E	9 to 11.	Reconciliation. Dispensational.	The outer portion, Rom. 9:1 to 16:24, the same features as Rom. 1:1 to 5:11, but from a dispensational and practical point of view.
	D	12 and 13.	Present your bodies a living sacrifice.	
	C	14:1 to 15:7.	The Glory of God. Received to.	
	B	15:8 to 16:24.	Gentiles equally with Jews acceptable before God.	
	A	16:25-27.	Mystery silenced afore. For obedience of faith unto all nations.	

From this structure it will at once be seen that Romans 16:25-27 is essential to complete the epistle. The reader who is acquainted with the teaching of this epistle will be able to fill in the details of every section, so completing the structural analysis. We must, however, show the relationship of A 1:1-17 and *A* 16:25-27 as that is the subject now before us.

THE OUTER SECTION **A. Romans 1:1-17** The Gospel of God	THE INNER SECTION **A. Romans 16:25-27** My Gospel
Concerning His Son Jesus Christ	The preaching of Jesus Christ
Promised afore	Kept silent in age times, now manifested
Prophets in the Holy Scriptures	Prophetic writings
Unto obedience of faith among all nations	For obedience of faith to all nations
Grace from God our Father	Praise to the *aionion* God, and to the only wise God
To the end ye may be established	To Him Who is able to establish you
The power of God unto salvation	To Him Who is of power
Righteousness revealed ... as it is written.	Revelation of mystery ... scriptures, the prophets.

It is evident that there is an intended contrast between these two passages. From the days of Abraham onward the gospel was no secret:

> 'The Scripture, foreseeing that God would justify the heathen through faith, preached before the gospel unto Abraham' (Gal. 3:8).
>
> 'Your father Abraham rejoiced to see My day: and he saw it, and was glad' (John 8:56).

Here, however, in Romans 16:25-27 is a mystery, and that mystery something that had been silenced. It cannot, therefore, possibly be the same thing as the gospel preached in Romans 1.

It is not stated, however, in Romans 1:1,2, or in any of the passages that link the gospel with the Old Testament Scriptures, that the gospel was fully made known before the coming of Christ. Take for example Romans 1:17:

> 'For therein (i.e. the gospel of Christ, 1:16) is the righteousness of God *revealed* from faith to faith: according as it hath been written (in Hab. 2:4), The just shall live by faith'.

Without the fuller light of the gospel of Christ, it would not be evident from the passage in Habakkuk that the power of the gospel of Christ resided in the provision of a righteousness by faith. This will be evident if we quote the passage:

> 'For the vision is yet for an appointed time, but at the end it shall speak, and not lie: though it tarry, wait for it; because it will surely come, it will not tarry. Behold, his soul which is lifted up is not upright in him: *but the just shall live by his faith*' (Hab. 2:3-4).

But this provision is now 'revealed', and in the hands of an inspired apostle can be confirmed by such passages as Habakkuk 2:4, although the teaching does not lie on the surface. Again, having quoted many passages from the Old Testament Scriptures, the apostle says:

> 'But now (in contrast to the period "then") the righteousness of God, apart from law, has been manifested (perfect tense) being borne witness to (present tense) by the law and the prophets, even the righteousness of God which is by faith of Jesus Christ' (Rom. 3:21,22).

Here the 'manifestation' takes place before the 'witness' can be borne by Old Testament prophets. So in Romans 16:26, we read of something that has been kept in silence, but which was then made manifest.

(2) THE REVELATION OF A MYSTERY

Let us set out this doxology so that we may the better consider it in detail.

Romans 16:24-27

A	16:24,25.	**a**	Grace be with you. Amen.
			b To Him Who is able to establish.
B_1	16:25.	*Kata.*	Gospel proclaimed. According to my gospel.
B_2	16:25,26.	*Kata.*	Mystery manifested. According to revelation of mystery.
B_3	16:26.	*Kata.*	Made known. According to commandment.
A	16:27.	*b*	To God only wise.
		a	Glory unto the ages. Amen.

We observe that the section begins with 'grace' and ends with 'glory', both the statements contained in it being sealed with an 'Amen'. The words 'to be able' are a translation of *dunamai*, which literally means 'to be of power'. This is balanced by the only 'wise' God, the two statements revealing 'the power of God and the wisdom of God' working together. Salvation is not in view in the same sense as it is in Romans 1:16. The apostle here desires that those who are saved shall be *established*. He had desired this at the beginning of the epistle (Rom. 1:11), where, however, the establishing was connected with 'some spiritual gift'. Here in Romans 16 the establishing is associated with what the apostle calls 'my gospel'. This expression 'my gospel' is used three times by Paul, and if we consider the context of each reference we shall be impressed with the magnitude of its sphere.

The first occurrence is in Romans 2:16. The apostle is speaking of the Gentile world, unevangelized and unenlightened by the law; a world left to the voice of conscience and the witness of creation. To argue from Romans 2 that *anyone* who patiently continues in well doing will be saved, whether he believes the gospel or not, is to handle the Word of God deceitfully. Obviously, where no gospel message has ever penetrated it cannot be believed (Rom. 10:14), yet it is wrong to infer that Romans 2 teaches salvation by works. The truth is that salvation for any is neither by works, nor by faith, but by the finished work of Christ. The man who hears the gospel and believes is saved, but that salvation is a secret unknown to anyone, and unconfirmed to himself, apart from those good works that manifest the reality of the faith. The point of this passage is that while the unevangelized heathen cannot believe a message he has never heard, yet if he manifests by his works that he would have believed had he been given the opportunity, God reveals that this will be fully recognized 'in that day'.

'(... For when the Gentiles, which have not the law, do by nature the things contained in the law, these, having not the law, are a law unto themselves: which shew the work of the law written in their hearts, their conscience also bearing witness, and their thoughts the mean while accusing or else excusing one another;) in the day when God shall judge the secrets of men by Jesus Christ according to my gospel' (Rom. 2:14-16).

The second occurrence of 'my gospel' is in Romans 16:25, and the third in 2 Timothy 2:8 :

'Remember that Jesus Christ of the seed of David was raised from the dead according to my gospel'.

These three occurrences have reference (1) to the unevangelized heathen, (2) to the revelation of a mystery hitherto kept in silence, and (3) to the position of the Lord Jesus Christ in the dispensation of the Mystery. Three concentric circles, each narrower than the preceding one, yet each vitally associated with the peculiar ministry of Paul.

It is, then, evident that what Paul calls 'my gospel' is a distinctive message, not to be confused with the good news proclaimed by others. Associated with this gospel is the preaching of Jesus Christ, 'according to the revelation of a secret which hath been silenced in *aionion* times, but is now made manifest, and through prophetic writings'.

The reader will be conscious that there is something missing in the above rendering. He naturally feels that the phrase 'and through prophetic writings' should be followed by 'as well as ... '. In other words, the particle *te* is often followed by *kai*, so that there appears to be an ellipsis here. Elsewhere *te* is passed over in our Version, but to be accurate it should always be translated. Look at the difference the recognition of the particle makes in 1 Corinthians 1:30 :

'But of Him are ye *in* Christ Jesus, Who of God is made unto us wisdom, *as well as* righteousness, and sanctification, and redemption'.

Consequently we read Romans 16:26 as follows:

> 'But now made manifest, both through prophetic writings as well as' (by the apostle's preaching) 'according to the commandment of the *aionion* God'.

Every commentator speaks of the grammatical 'gaps' that appear in this great doxology, as though the apostle's thoughts were too great to find expression.

(3) WHAT WAS THE SECRET?

'According to the revelation of a secret'. It is entirely unnecessary to assume that this is the secret, or mystery, revealed in Ephesians 3. The dispensational section of Romans had a secret, the making known of which illuminated the problem resulting from Israel's failure (Rom. 11:25), and this is the theme of another doxology, namely, that which closes Romans 11 at verses 33-36.

When examining Romans 5:12 to 8:39, we see that it constitutes a unique section of the teaching of the epistle. It goes back to a period before there was a Jew, and before Abraham, to Adam. No one can read Genesis 3 without being conscious that there is much unexplained. Solomon writing in Ecclesiastes 3 says, 'To every thing there is a season, and a time to every purpose under heaven', and in enumerating them he says, 'A time to keep silence, and a time to speak' (Eccles. 3:1,7). The word translated in the A.V., 'kept secret' (Rom. 16:25), is *sigao*, translated elsewhere in the New Testament, 'keep silence' and 'hold one's peace'. Much important truth latent in Genesis 1 to 11 was 'hushed' until the 'time to speak' had arrived, and that was when Paul was inspired to write the epistle to the Romans. The study of Genesis 1 to 11 in the light of Romans 5:12 to 8:39 is therefore of the utmost importance to the believer who would realize the peculiar character of his calling. From Genesis 12 until the end of the Acts, one nation holds the pre-eminent place, and that part of the Old Testament which deals with Israel knows no salvation apart from that chosen race, or from the covenants made with Abraham.

If Israel should fail and fall, the *prophets* had nothing to tell us of how God would cope with the resulting problem. It is, accordingly, the purpose of the central section of Romans to reveal the relationship of man, as such (i.e. as neither Jew nor Gentile), to Adam and to Christ, irrespective both of promises made to 'the fathers', and the failure or success of 'the chosen people'. But this is not the theme of the Old Testament prophecy in general. The period covered by the Scriptures from Genesis 12 to Matthew 1, is as long as that covered by Genesis 1:3 to chapter 11. In that same space of eleven chapters is written all that can be known of the first 2,000 years of this present creation. What is written is pregnant with truth, but it must await its appointed time, and just as the gospel itself revealed teaching hidden in Old Testament Scriptures (as we have already seen in Habakkuk 2:3,4), so these early chapters of Genesis hold much basic teaching, throwing light on the position of the believer who is saved and justified without reference to the law of Moses. Volumes have been written to associate the obedience of Christ with the law of Moses, whereas this law was but transient, it was 'added because of transgressions', it was 'found fault with', and passed away (Heb. 8:7). This secret has been hushed in *aionion* times. We read of some part of God's purpose as being related to a period 'before *aionion* times' (Tit. 1:2; 2 Tim. 1:9), and in 1 Corinthians we read of 'the wisdom of God in a mystery', which has been 'hidden', and which God 'foreordained before the ages' (1 Cor. 2:7). The Mystery of the prison epistles was 'hidden from the ages, and from the generations' (Col. 1:26). These hidden subjects had 'their own seasons' of manifestation, which manifestations were through the medium of 'preaching', and 'according to' a 'commandment' (Tit. 1:3).

The mystery of Romans 16 is not said to be related to a period 'before age times', but silenced in or during age times. This secret is the theme of the central section of

Romans, and its subject is *Adam*, not Abraham, *man*, not Israel or Gentile; the law of *sin*, not the law of *Sinai*.

What are the 'prophetic writings' that Paul refers to? The words translated in the A.V., 'the scriptures of the prophets', are not exactly the same as those used in Romans 1:2. In Romans 1:2 the original reads: *dia ton propheton autou en graphais hagiais*, whereas Romans 16:26 reads: *dia te graphon prophetikon*. The suggestion is made by some that not only a difference of expression is intended here, but a real difference, and that the reference in Romans 1:2 is to Old Testament prophets, whereas that in Romans 16 is to New Testament prophets. It may be so, but the reader should be aware that nothing in the language used constitutes a proof of this. *Prophetikos* is to *prophetes*, what *pneumatikos* is to *pneuma*, simply the adjectival form. As the only other occurrence of the word will show, every one of the Old Testament prophecies are 'prophetic writings' (2 Pet. 1:21). It was when the apostle received commandment to make this early truth known, that the prophetic writings which had for generations held their secret began to speak. The fact that what was made known both in Romans 1 and 16 was 'for the obedience of faith to all nations', establishes the unity of purpose that links the whole of Romans together as an indivisible whole. There is no need to adopt the suggestion of *Lightfoot* that the doxology was added some years after. The ascription of praise is to the only wise God, and wisdom is associated with the unfolding purpose of the ages (Rom. 11:33; 1 Cor. 2:7; Eph. 1:8,9; 3:10). On this high note the epistle ends.

We have already demonstrated that Acts 28 forms a dispensational boundary, having on the one side Abrahamic covenants and promises, and having on the other an entirely new dispensation. The terms of the Abrahamic covenant cannot operate here, for Galatians 3:13,14 makes it clear that the blessings of Abraham to the Gentiles and the redemption of Israel go together, and

Israel went into their *Lo-ammi* condition at Acts 28. If, therefore, the Gentile is to be saved, and not only saved but called to a height of glory that transcends all revelation hitherto given, then God must put into operation some new way of dealing with men; in other words, a new dispensation must begin, and did begin, at Acts 28:28. It is to the demonstration of the fact that this new dispensation is the dispensation of the Mystery, that we now ask the reader's attention.

(4) The Mysteries in Ephesians, Colossians & 1 Timothy

There are four epistles that bear the marks of Paul's imprisonment, and two of them deal very fully with the subject of the Mystery. These epistles are Ephesians and Colossians. Let us note the references to the subject:

'The mystery of His Will'	(Eph. 1:9).
'The mystery'	(Eph. 3:3).
'The mystery of Christ'	(Eph. 3:4).
'The dispensation of the mystery'	(Eph. 3:9 R.V.).
'The great mystery'	(Eph. 5:32).
'The mystery of the gospel'	(Eph. 6:19).
'The mystery'	(Col. 1:26).
'The mystery among the Gentiles'	(Col. 1:27).
'The mystery of God'	(Col. 2:2).
'The mystery of Christ'	(Col. 4:3).

The first epistle to Timothy is not a 'prison' epistle, but it bears marks of having been written after Paul had been liberated, and so describes the newly-formed Church as it was at the beginning. There we have two more references to the Mystery, which we will add for the sake of completeness:

'The mystery of the faith'	(1 Tim. 3:9).
'The mystery of godliness'	(1 Tim. 3:16).

This makes a total of twelve references to the subject after Acts 28, and an examination of these, together with their contexts, should, under God, prove a means of help and blessing in the appreciation of the high and holy calling of the Church of the One Body.

The Mystery in Ephesians

Let us observe the use of the word *mystery* in Ephesians. We find that the six references fall into two sections of three each, the second section supplementing and explaining more fully the first:

A Eph. 1:9,10. The Mystery of His Will ... a dispensation.
  B Eph. 3:3. The Mystery.
    C Eph. 3:4. The Mystery of Christ.
A Eph. 3:9 (R.V.). The dispensation of the Mystery.
  B Eph. 5:32. The great Mystery, Christ and His Church.
    C Eph. 6:19. The Mystery of the gospel.

(5) THE DISPENSATION OF THE MYSTERY

The first mystery mentioned in Ephesians is 'the Mystery of His will' which has in view a 'dispensation of the fulness of the seasons' when Christ is to head up all things, 'both which are in heaven and which are on earth'. We have already seen that the corresponding reference to this is Ephesians 3:9, which we here quote from the R.V.: 'and to make all men see what is the dispensation of the Mystery, which from all ages hath been hid in God Who created all things'. We have quoted the Revised Version because it recognizes the reading 'dispensation' instead of 'fellowship'. The expression 'all ages' is a free rendering — the 'all' is not to be taken as though it existed in the original. Paul uses the word *oikonomia* 'dispensation' five times. It may be as well to see the references together. We give Conybeare and Howson's translation, which, though it is a little free, seems to convey the intention of the apostle:

> 'For although I proclaim the glad tidings, yet this gives me no ground of boasting; for I am compelled to do so by order of my Master. Yea, woe is me if I proclaim it not. For were my service of my own free choice, I might claim wages to reward my labour; but since I serve by compulsion, I am a slave entrusted with a stewardship (dispensation)' (1 Cor. 9:16,17).

To this selfsame 'bond-slave of Jesus Christ' a further dispensation or stewardship was granted upon the failure of Israel at Acts 28:

> 'For this cause I Paul, the prisoner of Jesus Christ for you Gentiles, if ye have heard of the dispensation of the grace of God which is given me to you-ward: how that by revelation He made known unto me the Mystery' (Eph. 3:1-3).

Here we have a series of statements that put the new dispensation in a clear light:

(1) It was given to Paul as 'the prisoner of Jesus Christ'.
(2) It was given to Paul 'for you Gentiles', 'to you-ward'.
(3) It had immediate relation to 'the Mystery'.
(4) Which was received by 'revelation'.

A parallel passage in Colossians 1 makes Ephesians 3 even more clear and emphatic:

> 'His body ... the church: whereof I am made a minister, according to the dispensation of God which is given to me for you, to fulfil (complete) the word of God ... the Mystery which hath been hid from the ages and from generations, but now is made manifest to His saints' (Col. 1:24-26).

Additional items that give further light are the following:

(1) The Church which is His Body is intimately associated with this new dispensation.
(2) This new dispensation *completes* the word of God, and
(3) Finds its expression in a Mystery which had never been made known before it was entrusted to the apostle Paul.

We can now go back to Ephesians 1 and read again the first reference to this dispensation:

> 'Unto a dispensation of the fulness of the seasons, to unite all things under one head, in union with Christ, both which are in heaven and which are on earth' (Eph. 1:10 author's translation).

Where Colossians tells us that this dispensation of the Mystery 'completes' the word of God, Ephesians tells us that this dispensation of the mystery of His will is 'the fulness of the seasons'. There is a contrast in Ephesians 2:12-19:

> 'At *that season* ye were without Christ ... aliens ... strangers ... *now* therefore ye are no more strangers and foreigners, but fellow-citizens with the saints ...' (author's translation).

The 'now' of verse 19 is the *present season* in contrast with 'that season' when the Gentile was an alien. A new creation intervenes between verses 12 and 19. 'The both' have been 'made one'; this deals with the reconciliation of Jew and Gentile. Ephesians 1:10 speaks not of the Jew and the Gentile, but of the things in heaven and on earth being made one under the headship of Christ. This is the reconciliation spoken of in Colossians 1:20. Now all this is absolutely new. Nowhere else in the whole range of the Scriptures can such things be discovered as are made known by the apostle in these epistles to the Ephesians and Colossians. Lest we be misunderstood, it is evident, we trust, that we speak of the 'dispensational' revelations. Such blessed doctrines as redemption and forgiveness of Ephesians 1:7 have already been revealed and explained in earlier Scriptures.

To complete our references, we quote 1 Timothy 1:4 R.V.:

> 'Neither to give heed to fables and endless genealogies, the which minister questionings, rather than a dispensation of God which is in faith'.

This has more to do with the faithful exercise of ministry, whatever it may be, than the revelation of any new truth, and, while including the dispensation of the Mystery so far as Timothy shared it with Paul, does not actually deal with it.

We trust it is clear that the dispensational standing of the Church, the calling of the Gentile, and the revelation of the Mystery after Acts 28, constitute a unique revelation and stewardship.

It is essential that the reader should distinguish 'The Mystery' of Ephesians 3:3, which had been hid in God until it was revealed to Paul, and the Mystery of Christ, which has been the subject of revelation right down the ages.

Ephesians 3 speaks not only of the Mystery as it relates to the new dispensational dealings of God with the Gentiles, but also with the Mystery of Christ. Now this mystery must not be read as meaning simply the fulfilment of prophecy. While many in Israel saw the teaching of their Scriptures as to the coming of the Messiah in glory and dominion, few saw the Mystery of the Messiah which related to His Coming in lowliness, rejection and suffering. Christ said, speaking of the mysteries of the kingdom of heaven, 'many prophets and righteous men have desired to see these things … but have not seen them' (Matt. 13:17), and into the Mystery of Christ 'angels desired to look' (1 Peter 1:12). Mystery necessitates revelation. It is something that cannot be inferred or arrived at by study.

First we will set out the structure of Ephesians 3:1-13 where the two mysteries occur:

Ephesians 3:1-13. The prisoner of Christ Jesus

A 1. Prisoner for you (*huper humon*).

B Dispensation of *grace* of God. Revelation of the Mystery.
- **a** 2. Dispensation given.
- **b** 2. To you-ward.
- ***b*** 2. To me.
- ***a*** 3. Mystery revealed.

C Two Mysteries and two ministries.
- **d** 4. Mystery of Christ.
- **e** 5. Apostles and prophets (*plural*).
- **f** 5,6. The Mystery.
- **g** In Spirit.
- $\mathbf{h}^1$ Joint-heirs.
- $\mathbf{h}^2$ Joint-body.
- $\mathbf{h}^3$ Joint-partakers.
- ***g*** In Christ.
- ***e*** 7. Paul alone (*singular*).
- ***d*** 8. Unsearchable riches of Christ.

B Dispensation of the Mystery. Making known wisdom of God.
- **a** 9. Dispensation hidden since the ages.
- **b** 9. By God Who created through Christ.
- **c** 10. Knowledge through the church.
- **a** 11. Purpose of the ages.
- **b** 11. Which He made in Christ.
- **c** 12. Access through faith of Christ.

A 13. Afflictions for you (*huper humon*).

We draw attention to the ending of this passage which indicates that verses 4-7 are a parenthesis and that verse 3 reads on to verse 8. We have therefore the means of a clearer view of the theme before the apostle, by leaving the parenthesis out for a time, and observing his teaching concerning the wondrous dispensation which he had received.

The Mystery; its special Characteristics (Eph. 3)

(1) A special minister	Paul, as prisoner (1). Me (2,3,8).
(2) A special ministry	For you Gentiles (1). To you-ward (2). Among the Gentiles (8).
(3) A special communication	Made known by revelation (3).
(4) A special theme	Unsearchable (8). Mystery (3,9). Hid (9).
(5) A special period	The dispensation of the grace of God (2). The dispensation of the Mystery (9). Now (10).
(6) A special witness	Unto principalities (10). Manifold wisdom (10).
(7) A special purpose	According to the purpose of the Ages (11).

Such is the theme of verses 1-11, omitting the parenthesis. Coming to verses 4-7 we learn more concerning this Mystery by way of contrast. The Mystery of verses 1-3 and 8-11 is contrasted with the Mystery of Christ. Let us again seek an analysis.

(6) THE MYSTERY OF CHRIST*

(1) Not exclusive to this dispensation. It was made known in other generations (5).

(2) Not exclusive to the apostle Paul. It was revealed unto prophets and apostles (5).

The Mystery

(1) It was exclusive to the apostle Paul. Verses 1,2,3,8 and 9 already considered, and verse 7, 'whereof I was made a minister', the words defining the gospel intended in verse 6.

---

* See under SECRETS OF THE SON[4].

(2) It was peculiar in its composition. It gives a threefold equality to the Gentile believer never before known or enjoyed (6).

Verse 6 in the A.V. reads on from verse 5, being connected by the word 'that'. The R.V. makes the connection closer by adding in italic type the words 'to wit'. Any literal translation, however, is obliged to render *einai* as a statement of fact, and there is no word nor construction which necessitates 'that' or 'to wit'. Instead of connection, contrast is intended. Instead of the threefold fellowship of the Gentiles being the Mystery revealed to the apostles and prophets and before them to the sons of men in other generations, it is entirely associated 'with that gospel' whereof Paul was made a minister, who in that capacity received the commission *to enlighten all* as to the dispensation of the Mystery, which instead of being revealed in other ages, or at the time to many prophets and apostles, had never been revealed at all, but had been hid from the ages in God and revealed only to the one chosen apostle, Paul, when the time for its publication had arrived. Instead, therefore, of linking verse 6 with 5, we should link verse 6 with 7.

We do not arrive at the truth if we stop at the word gospel in verse 6. Scripture speaks of a series of sets of good news or 'gospels' and to ascertain the truth we must know that the gospel under consideration was that which the apostle Paul preached according to the gift of grace of God who had given him the dispensation of this secret to administer. The parenthesis of verses 4-7 stands therefore thus:

THE MYSTERY OF CHRIST	Made known in other ages. Revealed now to apostles and prophets, including Paul.
THE MYSTERY	The threefold fellowship of the Gentiles. Revealed in the special gospel of Paul. Given to him to the exclusion of others.

Isaiah, when he penned the 53rd chapter of his prophecy, entered in some degree into the 'Mystery of Christ' and shared with Paul, Peter and others that blessed truth. David too, when he wrote Psalm 22 perceived the sacred secret of Christ's rejection. But neither Isaiah, David, nor Peter had any knowledge of the terms of the Mystery as revealed in Ephesians 3:6. That was hidden by God in Himself. It constituted a part of the purpose of the ages, but was a part, pertaining to the heavenly section, which had never been made known. It is difficult to decide between the A.V. rendering of Ephesians 3:5, which joins the words *en pneumati* (by the spirit) to the apostles and prophets, thereby declaring the source of their inspiration, and the alternative rendering which makes the words 'in spirit' commence the statement as to the threefold fellowship of the Gentiles.

Matthew 22:43 supplies an instance where *en pneumati* is used of inspiration. 'How then doth David *in spirit* call him Lord?' Romans 8:9 supplies an instance where the words are used not of inspiring apostles and prophets, but as indicating a sphere of blessing. 'You are not in flesh, but *in spirit*'. The general trend of the context and the recognition of the canon that the apostle's style allows of no superfluous words, causes every sentence to be pregnant with meaning. No item can be eliminated without injury to the sense and teaching. The question of inspiration is not in view. Whatever had been made known of the subject under discussion, either to Paul or to the other apostles, had been 'revealed' which carries with it the thought of inspiration.

On the other hand a change of sphere is a feature which the apostle emphasizes in this epistle. Its blessings are 'in the heavenlies' as well as 'in Christ'. Its practical outworkings are 'in the Lord', and the special feature with which Ephesians 3:6 is in direct contrast is given in Ephesians 2:11, *en sarki* 'in flesh'. In verse 12 another sphere is mentioned, 'in the world'.

In the world	is contrasted with	in the heavenlies.
In flesh	is set over against	in spirit.

With the addition of the word 'one' the change is found indicated in 2:18, 'access to the Father in One Spirit', and again in 2:22, 'an habitation of God *in spirit*'. In chapter 3 the apostle pursues the theme of the change of dispensation. The inspiration of Scripture or of apostles is extraneous to the subject. Consequently, as we are free to choose, we feel that 3:6 must commence with the words 'in spirit'. This is the essential condition of blessing in this dispensation. The blessings themselves are 'all spiritual' and can only be received by those who are 'in spirit'.

In the next place we pause to note the class who are spoken of as being thus blessed *in spirit*. It is usual for the words to be added, at least mentally, to make the verse read, 'that the Gentiles *together with the Jews* should be fellow-heirs, etc.', but this idea is unwarranted. If for the moment we concede that the Jew is in view, the teaching then must be accepted as a veritable revelation of an hitherto hidden mystery, for where, since the call of Abraham to the writing of the epistle to the Romans (where the apostle says 'the Jew first', etc.) has the Gentile ever received the threefold *equality* revealed here?

Millennial blessings which fulfil the promises to Israel, necessarily give the blessed Gentile a secondary place; they who were once aliens to the commonwealth of Israel, but who are finally blessed under the covenant of promise, are nevertheless 'tail' and not 'head', and their *national* distinctions remain. Here, in the dispensation of the Mystery, the sphere is 'in spirit' and the equality is concerning the Gentiles. The only place that a Jew can have in the dispensation of the Mystery is to lose his nationality and enter this equal calling as a sinner saved by grace, even as the Gentile does.

The threefold equality of this new sphere must now be noted:

Sunkleronoma *Sussoma* *Summetocha*

In each case the word commences with *su* which means 'with'. The best word in English to fit the three statements is the word 'joint'. We can say 'joint-heirs', a 'joint-body', and 'joint-partakers'.

In Hebrews 11:9 we read of Isaac and Jacob who sojourned with Abraham as 'heirs with him of the same promise'. God does not call Himself merely the God of Abraham, or the God of Abraham and Isaac. His full title in this connection is 'The God of Abraham, Isaac and Jacob'. They were co-heirs. In 1 Peter 3:7 the husband, though recognizing his wife as a 'weaker vessel', is nevertheless enjoined to remember that they were both 'heirs together of the grace of life'. The equality among all believers in the dispensation of the Mystery is expressed in similar terms, namely co-heirs. This inheritance is the subject of Ephesians 1:11 and 18, and of Colossians 1:12. It is a predestinated allotment, it is 'in the light'.

The joint-body (*sussoma*) is as unique as is the word used to express it. The word occurs nowhere else in the New Testament or in the LXX. Words arise in response to needs, and never before in all the varied ways of God with man had there been the necessity for such a term. Kingdom, Firstborn, Church, Bride, Wife, Flock, these and other terms had been necessitated by the unfolding of the purpose of the ages, but not until the revelation of the Mystery was there necessity to use such an expression as 'joint-body'. The equality in the Body is opened up in Ephesians 4:16. There is but One Head and the rest of the Body are members one of another on these equal terms.

The third item is 'joint-partakers', but such an expression does not convey the truth until the statement is completed:

> 'Joint-partakers of the promise in Christ Jesus, through the gospel of which I became minister'.

The better readings omit the words 'of His', and give the title 'Christ Jesus'. ('His promise' in the A.V.).

'The promise in Christ Jesus'.— Paul, when writing to Timothy his last 'prison epistle', calls himself:

> 'An apostle of Jesus Christ by the will of God, according to the promise of life which is in Christ Jesus' (2 Tim. 1:1).

Writing to Titus between the two imprisonments he speaks of the:

> '... hope of *aionion* life, which God, that cannot lie, promised before age times; but hath in due times (or, its own peculiar seasons) manifested His word through a proclamation with which I (*ego*) was entrusted' (Titus 1:2,3).

The Gentiles, here called and blessed, may indeed have been 'strangers from the covenants of promise' while 'in flesh', but 'in spirit' they are 'joint-partakers' of a promise which goes back before the age times, and before the overthrow of the world.

Such is the sphere and character of the unity created by the Lord during this time of Israel's blindness.

We rejoice at the testimony of 'All Scripture' to the joys and blessings which are stored up for all Israel, the nations, the groaning creation, and the Church of God. Nevertheless, we, according to His promise, look for higher things than Abraham hoped or the Prophets dreamed.

> 'There is one glory of the sun, and another glory of the moon, and another glory of the stars: for one star differeth from another star in glory' (1 Cor. 15:41).

THE MYSTERY MANIFESTED

(1) THE MYSTERY AMONG THE GENTILES

The Mystery that was manifested to the saints through the ministry of the apostle Paul had been 'hid from ages and from generations'. This we saw in our last study. The next theme before us is the manifestation of the riches of the glory of this Mystery among the Gentiles:

> 'But now is made manifest to His saints: to whom God would make known what is the riches of the glory of this Mystery among the Gentiles; which is Christ among you, the hope of glory' (Col. 1:26,27).

Being an Israelite by birth, the apostle of the Gentiles would realize better than would the Gentiles themselves the riches of grace that were the source of the preaching of the Mystery among them. Apart from the Epistle to the Romans, it is to the epistles of the Mystery that we turn in order to learn about the riches of grace, and riches of glory, yea, the exceeding riches of His grace; and the apostle connects the manifestation of the Mystery with the making known what is the riches of the glory of this Mystery among the Gentiles.

Left to ourselves, what would be our answer to the question, 'What is the riches of the glory of this Mystery among the Gentiles?' We should be wise if we turned at once to what is written. We could say without fear of contradiction, that 'redemption through His Blood, even the forgiveness of sins' must be included, for that is 'according to the riches of His grace, wherein He hath abounded toward us' (Eph. 1:7,8). We should certainly include the 'inheritance in the saints', though we could not speak in detail of what constitutes 'the riches of the glory' of this inheritance (Eph. 1:18). Looking forward to 'that day' when the inheritance shall be enjoyed, to our amazement we learn that whereas redemption is spoken of as 'the *riches* of His grace', the kindness that He will show to us in the days to come is of such transcendence that the apostle speaks of it as 'the *exceeding riches* of His grace in His kindness toward us in Christ Jesus' (Eph. 2:7).

With all this the apostle would naturally be in hearty agreement. In Colossians 1:27 he focuses attention upon one important aspect of present truth that reveals the ground upon which we may entertain such a hope: 'Which is Christ in (among) you, the hope of glory'. The margin draws attention to the fact that the word 'in' should be translated 'among', as it is in the earlier phrase of the verse, '*among* the Gentiles'. The apostle is not here speaking of the blessed realization of the indwelling Christ, but of the dispensational change that had followed the setting aside of the children of Israel, 'the salvation of God is sent unto the Gentiles, and they will hear it' (Acts 28:28). Up till then salvation had been 'of the Jews' (John 4:22). The gospel had been intimately associated with the promise made to Abraham (Gal. 3:8). What the Gentiles had heard through Peter had been, 'the Word which God sent unto the children of Israel' (Acts 10:36). Even the gospel preached by Paul in Romans was 'to the Jew first' (Rom. 1:16), and the Gentile believer was warned not to vaunt himself against Israel, seeing that he was but a 'wild olive' grafted in among the natural branches (Rom. 11).

But when we commence the epistle to the Colossians we are conscious of a great change. The hope that was laid up for these believers and which was made known in the truth of the gospel, had been preached to 'all the world' (Col. 1:5,6), and 'to every creature which is under heaven' (Col. 1:23), and it is in immediate association with this last quotation that Paul goes on to speak of his special ministry and the manifestation of the Mystery. Consequently we come back to Colossians 1:27, and learn that the very fact that Christ is now 'among the Gentiles' is proved by the preaching of the gospel to them, irrespective of Israel, the once-appointed channel, now set aside. That, of itself, bespeaks a change of dispensation.

'Christ among you', says the apostle is 'the hope of glory'. The hope of *Israel*, which extended right through to the last chapter of the Acts (Acts 28:20), is not in view here, but something distinct. *This* hope is the 'one hope of your calling', 'the hope of His calling', 'the hope that is laid up for you in heaven'; it is a hope of 'glory', and will be consummated when Christ, Who is our life, shall be made manifest, for then, said the apostle, 'Ye shall also be made manifest with Him *in glory*' (Col. 3:4).

The Mystery receives a present manifestation because Christ is among the Gentiles, through the preached Word. *He is* the hope of glory. The Mystery receives its final manifestation when the Church of the One Body is manifested *with* Him in glory. It is good to keep these two passages, Colossians 1:27 and 3:4 together, and to remember that in both the present anticipation and the future realization, it is Christ Himself who is both Manifester and Hope.

(2) THE MYSTERY OF GOD — CHRIST

Our text here has been, and still is, much in dispute. The A.V. reads: 'the acknowledgment of the Mystery of God, and of the Father, and of Christ' (Col. 2:2). The R.V. reads: 'that they may know the Mystery of God, even Christ'. Alford reads: 'The thorough knowledge of the Mystery of God', and rejects all the rest. *The Companion Bible* agrees with the reading of the R.V. Scrivener says: 'We would gladly adopt *tou Theou Christou* (the R.V. reading), so powerfully do internal considerations plead in its favour, were it but a little better supported'. Hilary, who was born A.D. 300, appears to have read the passage as does the R.V.: '*In agnitionem sacramenti Dei Christi*' — 'to the recognition of the Mystery of God, Christ'. For what it is worth, the Numeric New Testament, by its own peculiar method of testing, also gives this reading as the true one.

Accepting then the R.V. as the more accurate, let us proceed in our study, keeping in mind that the special feature of our search is not only to ascertain what the Mystery of God is, but how it is manifested. The Mystery of Colossians 2:2 is not the Mystery of Ephesians 3:3, which speaks of the Church, nor of Ephesians 3:4, which speaks of Christ, but it is the mystery 'of God', the manifestation of which is Christ. Alford draws attention to a most important correction in the translation of Colossians 2:3. The A.V. reads: 'In Whom are hid all the treasures of wisdom and knowledge'. Alford's reading is: 'In which (mystery) are all the secret treasures of wisdom and knowledge'. He says: 'The rendering which I have adopted is that of Meyer, and I am persuaded on consideration that it is not only the only logical but the only grammatical one also'.

There are eleven occurrences of *apokruphos* which is used consistently as an adjective, and never as a verb. For example, in the passage: 'He shall have power over *the treasures* of gold and silver' (Dan. 11:43), the LXX uses the word *apokruphois* for 'treasures', evidently with the idea that treasures would be hidden by reason of their value.

Again, in Daniel 2:22 the same word is used of 'secret things', and it is interesting to observe that in chapter 2:19 the word 'secret' is the word *musterion* or 'mystery'. In Isaiah 45:3, 'the hidden riches of secret places', is, in the LXX, *apokruphous aoratous*, 'secret, unseen'. The context speaks of treasures, using the same word as is so translated in Colossians 2:3. Psalm 27:5 provides a good illustration of the use of the verb and the adjective: 'He shall hide me (*krupto*) in His pavilion; in the secret (*apokruphos*) of His tabernacle'. In 1 Maccabees 1:23 we have a parallel with Colossians 2:3 which cannot be ignored: 'He took the hidden treasures which he found' (*tous thesaurous tous apokruphous*). Therefore instead of reading as in the A.V., we must read: 'In Whom are all the secret treasures of wisdom and knowledge'. These treasures are priceless. They include 'all riches of the full assurance of understanding'. They involve the 'knowledge of the Mystery of God' which is manifested only to those who know Christ in the light of the revelation of the Mystery. Often men talk of God as though it were a simple matter to comprehend Him. They argue about His person as though He were subject to the same laws and limitations as themselves. To such philosophers and expositors God might well say, as He said to the wicked in Psalm 50:21: 'thou thoughtest that I was altogether such an one as thyself'.

Yet God is spirit, and, apart from revelation, what do we *know* of that realm of being? Even angels, who are spirits, take upon themselves the forms of men before man can perceive them. The Saviour declared, in the days of His early ministry concerning the Father, 'Ye have neither heard His voice at any time, nor seen His shape' (John 5:37). God Himself must ever remain a mystery, indeed the greatest of all mysteries, unless He manifests Himself in such a way that His creatures can apprehend and understand. In general, our knowledge of the outside world is derived through the medium of the senses of sight, hearing and touch, supplemented by taste and smell. In that other sphere where the answer to the Mystery of God is Christ, we can understand what may be known of God only by the manifestation of it in His Person. The works of His hands reveal 'His eternal power and Godhead' so that the nations of the earth are without excuse (Rom. 1:19-23). Yet that is but a step, for it is only in the face of Jesus Christ that we see the glory of God. He came to 'declare' the invisible God; He came and said, 'He that hath seen Me hath seen the Father'. He was looked upon, and handled, and the conclusion of those thus privileged is written: the confession of Thomas, 'My Lord and my God' (John 20:28), the record of John, 'This is the true God, and eternal life' (1 John 1:2; 5:20). Whatever glimpses we may have obtained through other aspects of truth, we must all agree that, 'In Him are all the secret treasures of wisdom and knowledge' (Col. 2:3). When one's completeness is found to be in Him, in Whom all the fulness of the Godhead dwells bodily, the folly of turning aside to vain, deceitful philosophy or of being shackled by tradition, or loaded with ceremonial ordinances, is apparent.

The Mystery of God is Christ. That Mystery has been manifested. We thank God that we have seen not only the 'eternal power and Godhead' that is witnessed to by creation, but we have seen in Him and by Him 'The Father, and it sufficeth us'.

One further passage dealing with the manifestation of the Mystery of God must be examined, and that is 1 Timothy 3:16, and we propose to examine this passage under the following headings:

(3) GOD WAS MANIFESTED IN THE FLESH

To write a set of studies on the subject of 'The Mystery Manifested' and to omit 1 Timothy 3:16 would be remiss in the extreme, yet, if the subject is to be dealt with at all, the problem of compressing what is essential to be said into a limited space, is somewhat perplexing. While, as we have said, our problem is partly due to limitations of space, it is also due to the fact that not all our readers will easily follow the subject, and that in dealing with Greek manuscripts we need photographs and the use of Greek type. Acknowledging these limitations we nevertheless make the attempt in the hope that great grace may more than compensate for a little Greek.

We propose, therefore, an examination of 1 Timothy 3:16 under the following headings:

The evidence of the structure of the epistle as a whole.
The meaning of the actual passage itself.
The evidence of the A.V. gives the correct reading.

There are two passages in the R.V. in which the hand of the Modernist is evident. They are 1 Timothy 3:16 and 2 Timothy 3:16. In the first there is an attack upon the deity of Christ, and in the second there is an attack upon the inspiration of the Scriptures of Truth. We know not when the storm will break, but we are persuaded that the enemy of Truth has singled out these two truths for special attack, and while time and opportunity remain, we desire, as unto the Lord, to make it plain where we stand on the vital issues involved.

For the moment we concentrate our attention upon 1 Timothy 3:16.

The Testimony of the Structure

It is possible to give so much 'proof' that the untrained mind may be bewildered rather than convinced. To avoid this, we first draw attention to the essential feature of the structure of the epistle.

A	1:17.	The King of the Ages, Incorruptible, INVISIBLE Honour and glory to the ages of the ages.
B	3:16.	GOD was manifested in the Flesh. SEEN.
A	6:15,16.	King of Kings. Immortal, UNSEEN Honour and might, age-lasting.

These are the great focal points of the epistle around which the remainder of the structure is grouped.

Many of our readers will be satisfied with the above; but in a matter of this character, where evidence is essential and where we must allow no advantage to the adversary, we must assume nothing but prove each point. We have, therefore, no option but to set out the structure of the whole epistle, although our appeal will be to the outline given above.

Instead of working out the members B and *B* we have placed the corresponding subjects in the same order in each section so that the parallel thoughts may be obvious without going minutely into detail. For example, 'the shipwreck' of 1:19 and 'the drowning' of 6:9 are an interesting parallel. It will be sufficient for our purpose if the simple outline given below is seen to be in line with the epistle as a whole and that both these important sections B and *B* are associated with a warning against heterodox teaching. The true doctrine is found in 1 Timothy 3:16, Section E, while the contrary, the doctrine of demons, is found in the greater apostasy of 1 Timothy 4:1-7, Section *E*. We can now confidently say that the structure of the epistle emphasizes the Mystery of godliness, in 1:17 and 6:15,16 where God is said to be invisible and unseen, and also points to 3:16 where it is stated that God has been manifested in the flesh and 'seen'. Here, therefore, we might pause and say, when the Word became flesh and dwelt among us, He manifested the invisible God and revealed the Father. In Him the mystery of God and of godliness find their exegesis.

1 Timothy

A 1:1,2. Salutation.

  B 1:3-20. *Hetero didaskaleo*, 'Teach no other doctrine' (1:3).
  The dispensation of God (1:4).
  Endless genealogies (1:4).
  Committed to trust (1:11).
  Aionion life (1:16).
  The King, incorruptible, invisible (1:17).
  This charge (1:18).
  Shipwreck (1:19).

    C 2:1-7. I exhort (2:1).
    The salvation of all men (2:4).
    Paul's ministry (2:7).

      D 2:8 to 3:15. These things I write (3:14).
      Men. Women. Adam. Eve (2:8 to 3:13).
      I hope to come shortly (3:14).

        E 3:15,16. The MYSTERY OF GODLINESS.
        Angels.

        E 4:1-8. The APOSTASY. Doctrines of demons.

    C 4:9-12. Command and teach (4:11).
    The Saviour of all men (4:10).
    Timothy s example (4:12).

      D 4:13 to 6:2. These things teach and exhort (6:2).
      Men: Women. Elders. Widows (5:1-17).
      Till I come (4:13).

  B 6:3-20. *Hetero didaskaleo*, 'Teach otherwise' (6:3).
  The good deposit (6:20).
  Profane and vain babblings (6:20).
  Committed to trust (6:20).
  Aionion life (6:12).
  King, immortal, unseen (6:15,16).
  I give thee charge (6:13).
  Drowning (6:9).

A 6:21. Salutation.

(4) THE MEANING OF 1 TIMOTHY 3:16

We now pass from the testimony of the structure to the text itself. Chapter 3 is largely devoted to the qualifications of bishops and deacons, and the apostle states that he has so written that Timothy may know how to behave himself in the house of God, which is the church of the living God. A question now arises from the last clause of verse 15. Is the *church* 'the pillar and ground of the truth'? If we use the word 'church' in its most spiritual meaning, we shall find no basis in Scripture for such an important doctrine. The case before us, however, is most certainly not '*the* Church' but 'a church', a church wherein there are bishops and deacons; in other words, a local assembly, and surely it is beyond all argument that the truth does not rest upon any such church as its pillar and ground. The reader will observe that in the structure, 3:15 is divided between D and E, and that the latter part of verse 15 belongs to verse 16. There is no definite article before the word 'pillar', and a consistent translation is as follows. Having finished what he had to say about the officers of the church and Timothy's behaviour, he turns to the great subject of the mystery of godliness with the words:

> 'A pillar and ground of truth and confessedly great is the Mystery of godliness'.

Here the teaching is that whatever or Whoever the Mystery of godliness shall prove to be, it or He, is the pillar and ground of truth. The Mystery of godliness is then explained as 'God manifest in the flesh' and He, we know, is the sure and tried Foundation.

We now come to the question of the true reading of 1 Timothy 3:16. The A.V. reads 'God', the R.V. reads 'He Who', and some versions read 'Which'. As it is not possible for us to depart from our practice, and use Greek type, we have prepared the following explanation to which the reader, unacquainted with the Greek or with the ancient manuscripts, is asked to refer as we proceed. Anyone who has examined an ancient Greek manuscript will have noticed the large number of abbreviations that are employed. For instance, the Greek word for God, *Theos*, is always contracted to THS. Now this contraction is only distinguishable from the relative pronoun HOS by two horizontal strokes, which, in manuscripts of early date, it was often the practice to trace so faintly that they can now be scarcely discerned. Of this, any one may be convinced by inspecting the two pages of Codex A which are exposed to view at the British Museum. An archetype copy, in which one or both of these slight strokes had vanished from the contraction THS, gave rise to the reading HOS, 'who', of which substituted word traces survive in only two manuscripts, Aleph and 17; not, for certain, in *one single* ancient Father, no, not for certain in *one single* ancient version. So transparent, in fact, is the absurdity of writing to *musterion hos* ('the mystery *who*'), that copyists promptly substituted *ho* ('which'), thus furnishing another illustration of the well-known property which a fabricated reading has of, sooner or later, begetting offspring in its own likeness. Happily, to this second mistake the sole surviving witness is the Codex Claromontanus of the sixth century (D): the only Patristic evidence in its favour being Gelasius of Cyzicus (whose date is A.D. 476): and the unknown author of a homily in the appendix to Chrysostom. Over this latter reading, however, we need not linger, seeing that *ho*, 'which', does not find a single patron at the present day.

Theos is the reading of *all the uncial copies extant but two*, and of *all the cursives but one*. The universal consent of the Lectionaries proves that *Theos* has been read in all the assemblies of the faithful since the fourth or fifth century of our era. At what earlier period of her existence is it then supposed that the Church availed herself of the privilege to substitute *Theos* for *hos* or *ho*, whether in error or in fraud? Nothing short of a conspiracy, to which every region of the Eastern Church must have been a party, would account for the phenomenon. We inquire for the testimony of the Fathers; and we discover that (1) Gregory of Nyssa quoted *Theos* no less than twenty-two times. That *Theos* is also recognized by (2) his namesake of

Nazianzus in two places; as well as by (3) Didymus of Alexandria; and (4) by pseudo-Dionysius of Alexandria. It is also recognized (5) by Diodorus of Tarsus, and (6) Chrysostom quotes 1 Timothy 3:16 in conformity with the Received Text at least three times. In addition there are twelve others, bringing the number up to eighteen.

We are indebted to Dean Burgon for these facts and would strongly recommend all who have any doubt as to the true reading to consult the masterly investigation contained in the Dean's book, *The Revision Revised.*

Some may suppose that whether we read the A.V., 'God was manifest', or the R.V., 'He Who was manifest', it comes to much the same thing, and question the necessity of the foregoing investigation. To such we would explain that the reasons for our concern are:

(1) We must resist, on principle, *any* tampering with the text, irrespective of its immediate effect.

(2) We must be on our guard against anything that would 'modernize' the teaching of the Word concerning the Person of the Lord Jesus.

(3) We must remember that, sooner or later, they who adopt *hos*, who, will slide into *ho*, which. They will feel unsettled until they cut out all reference to 'God' and translate the passage 'which was manifest'. Dean Burgon expressed his thankfulness that there were no patrons for the discredited reading 'which'. Yet we are sorry to say that this reading is being revived, as it suits the teaching that subordinates the 'Word' from His true place in the Godhead.

(5) THE ALEXANDRIAN MANUSCRIPT

A great deal of controversy has gathered around the Alexandrian manuscript which is to be seen in the British Library. Since this came to England 300 years ago the writing has faded considerably and we are not therefore to find our warrant for substituting *hos* for *Theos* by what can be seen today, but by what competent observers saw at the time of arrival of the manuscript.

That Patrick Young, the first custodian and collator of the Codex (1628-52) read *Theos* is certain. Young communicated the various readings of Codex A to Archbishop Ussher; and the latter, prior to 1653, communicated them to Hammond, who clearly knew nothing of *hos*. It is plain that *Theos* was the reading seen by Huish, when he sent his collation of the Codex (made, according to Bentley, with great exactness) to Brian Walton, who published the fifth volume of his *Polyglott* in 1657. Bishop Pearson who was very curious in such matters, says, 'we find not *hos* in any copy', a sufficient proof how *he* read the place in 1659. Bishop Fell, who published an edition of the New Testament in 1675, certainly considered *Theos* the reading of Codex A. Mill, who was at work on the text of the New Testament from 1677 to 1707, expressly declares that he saw the remains of *Theos* in this place. Bentley who had himself (1716) collated the MS. with the utmost accuracy, knew nothing of any other reading. Emphatic testimony on the subject is borne by Wotton in 1718. 'There can be no doubt (he says) that this MS. always exhibited *Theos*. Of this, *anyone may easily convince himself who will be at pains to examine the place with attention*' (Dean Burgon).

Two years earlier (we have it on the testimony of Mr. John Creyk, of St. John's College, Cambridge) 'the old line in the letter *theta* was plainly to be seen'. It was 'much about the same time' also (viz., about 1716), that Westein acknowledged to the Rev. John Kippax, 'who took it down in writing from his own mouth — that though the middle stroke of the *theta* has been evidently retouched, yet the fine stroke which was originally in the body of the *theta* is discoverable at each end of the fuller stroke of the corrector'. And Berriman himself (who delivered a course of lectures on the true reading of 1 Timothy 3:16 in 1737-8), attests emphatically that he had seen it also. *'If therefore'* (he adds), *'at any time hereafter the old line should become altogether undiscoverable there will never be just cause to doubt but that the genuine, and original reading of the MS. was* THEOS; and that the new strokes, added at the top and in the middle by the corrector were not designed to corrupt or falsify but to preserve and perpetuate the true reading, which was in danger of being lost by the decay of time' (Dean Burgon).

To this testimony must now be added that of modern photography. The camera has not only revealed the faded bar that proves that *Theos* is the true reading; it has also restored other faded parts of letters about which no controversy has arisen, but which might have become the basis of argument had the words been vital.

After reviewing the testimony of the different cursive copies of the epistles of Paul that are known, Dean Burgon says:

> 'Behold then the provision which the Author of Scripture has made for the effectual conservation in its integrity of this portion of His written Word. Upwards of eighteen hundred years have run their course since the Holy Ghost by His servant, Paul, rehearsed the "Mystery of godliness"; declaring *this* to be the great foundation fact, namely, that GOD WAS MANIFESTED IN THE FLESH. And lo, out of two *hundred and fifty-four* copies of St. Paul's epistles no less than *two hundred and fifty-two* are discovered to have preserved that expression. Such "consent" amounts to *unanimity;* and, unanimity in this subject-matter is conclusive.
>
> 'The copies of which we speak (you are requested to observe), were produced in every part of ancient Christendom, being derived in every instance from copies older than themselves, which again, were transcripts of copies older still. They have since found their way, without design or contrivance, into the libraries of every country of Europe, where, for hundreds of years, they had been jealously guarded. And, for what conceivable reason can this multitude of witnesses be supposed to have entered into a wicked conspiracy to deceive mankind?'

Such is the testimony of antiquity. This we must sum up, for the benefit of those who may not have cared to wade through the evidence.

The reading of 1 Timothy 3:16, 'God was manifest in the flesh' is witnessed by 289 manuscripts, by three versions and by upwards of twenty Greek Fathers. The relative pronoun *hos* should agree with its antecedent, yet *musterion* is neuter. Bloomfield in his Synoptica says, '*hos ephanerothe* is not Greek'. We would conclude with the calculated affirmation of our belief that the original reading of 1 Timothy 3:16 is, 'GOD was manifest in the flesh' and like Thomas of old, we bow in His Presence and say, 'My Lord, and my God'.

NATION. Greek *ethnos* occurs 164 times in the New Testament and is translated Gentiles (93); heathen (5); nation (64) and people (2). See articles under GENTILE[2]; PEOPLE (p. 174); and PEOPLE[9], for fuller details.

NEPHILIM. This word occurs three times in the original Hebrew, and is translated 'giants'. 'There were giants in the earth' (Gen. 6:4); 'There we saw the giants, the sons of Anak, which come of the giants' (Num. 13:33). These 'nephilim' were in the earth immediately before the flood, and 'after that' as Genesis 6:4 continues: 'And also after that, when the sons of God came in unto the daughters of men, and they bare children to them, the same became mighty men which were of old, men of renown'. The giants which the spies saw were evidently descended from those Nephilim that were in the earth after the flood. The word *Nephilim* does not of itself indicate gigantic structure, it rather looks to the height from which these beings have fallen. *Naphal* in Hebrew means 'to fall' and the *Nephilim* are 'fallen ones'. Genesis 3:15 contains not only a promise concerning the seed of the woman but a warning that there would be a seed of the serpent, and that the conflict between these two seeds would constitute the conflict of the ages.

By the time of, and as a countermove of Satan to Abraham's call, this evil seed were concentrated in the land of Canaan, and the sword of Israel was as necessary as the previous waters of the flood, if the purposes of grace were to prosper. Another name given to this evil seed is *the Rephaim* (Gen. 14:5) which is translated 'giants' in Deuteronomy 2:11,20; 3:11,13; Joshua 12:4; 13:12; 15:8; 17:15; 18:16 and 1 Chronicles 20:4,6, and 8. These *Rephaim* (Isa. 26:14 'deceased' in A.V.), have no resurrection. For the particular application to dispensational truth of this subject see the article entitled GIANTS[2].

NEW. The words translated 'new' in the New Testament are:

Agnaphos, unsmoothed, unfulled, used of cloth (Matt. 9:16; Mark 2:21).

Kainos, entirely new, not something recent but something different, something never seen before. This word occurs forty-three times.

Kainotes, 'newness', occurs twice, namely in Romans 6:4 and 7:6.

Neos means something young, something recently originated or lately established and occurs thirteen times, eleven occurrences being translated 'new', once 'new man' and once 'young woman'.

Dr. Bullinger has the following note in his Lexicon:

> 'When the two words are used of the same thing there is always this difference: thus, the *kainos anthropos* "the new man" (Eph. 2:15 and 4:24) is one who differs from the former; the *neos* (Col. 3:10), is one who is renewed after the image of Him that created him'.

Prosphatos, Hebrews 10:20, means something very recent. See the adverb in Acts 18:2.

When the Saviour said, 'I am the door of the sheep' (John 10:7), He followed that figure with another, saying, 'I am the good Shepherd: the good Shepherd giveth His life for the sheep' (John 10:11). By this door, if any man 'enter in' he shall be saved. Again He said, 'I am the way, the truth, and the life; no man cometh unto the Father but by Me' (John 14:6). In Hebrews 10:20 this 'way' is spoken of as 'new' and 'living'. The true meaning of John 14:6 is, 'I am the True and Living Way' even as Hebrews 10:20 reveals Him as 'the New and Living Way'. 'True' as contrasted with all the types and shadows of the law; 'new' as contrasted with all that pertains to the old covenant that, waxing old, must vanish away. *The Companion Bible* draws attention to the fact that *prosphatos*, the word translated 'new' literally means 'newly slain', and the reader may be forgiven if he should consequently stress the reference to 'sacrifice'. The word does not occur elsewhere in the New Testament except in the form of an adverb, where it reads of Aquila that he had 'lately' come from Italy (Acts 18:2). *Prosphatos* occurs in the LXX four times: Numbers 6:3 'fresh grapes', Deuteronomy 32:17, 'new and fresh gods', Psalm 81:9 (in LXX Psa. 80), 'new god', Ecclesiastes 1:9, 'no new thing'. The adverb occurs twice. Deuteronomy 24:5 (LXX verse 7), 'recently taken a wife', Ezekiel 11:3, 'houses newly built'. It will be seen that the idea of a sacrifice 'newly slain' finds no support. This idea of something new is contained also in the word 'consecrate' which is found in Hebrews 10:20. The Greek word so translated is *engkainizo*, composed of *en* 'in' and *kainos* 'new'. This word gives us *engkainia*, the name of a feast 'the feast of dedication', a feast that commemorated the dedication of the temple at Jerusalem at its *renovation* and purification, after being polluted by Antiochus Epiphanes, who had offered in sacrifice a swine upon the altar (Josephus, Ant. Book 12: Chap: v. 4).

> 'Then said Judas and his brethren, Behold our enemies are discomfited: Let us go up and cleanse and dedicate (*engkainizo*) the sanctuary ... then they took whole stones according to the law, and built a new (*kainon*) altar ... and new (*kainos*) holy vessels ... Now on the five and twentieth day of the ninth month, which is called the month of Casleu, in the hundred and forty and eighth year ... they offered sacrifice according to the law upon the new (*kainon*) ... the gates and the chambers they renewed (*engkainizo*) and hanged doors upon them' (1 Maccabees 4:36-57).

Parkhurst says of *engkainizo* 'to handsel, in a religious sense'. This term 'to handsel' is still in use in Scotland but may not be readily understood by many today, as it has dropped out of common use. The word means an earnest, the first act of a sale.

> 'The apostles term it the pledge of our inheritance, and the *handsel* or earnest of that which is to come' (Hooker, *Eccles. Polity*).

To handsel any house is to open it for the first time for use (Deut. 20:5); so to handsel any road is to open it for access (see Bloomfield). We are now placed a little nearer to the position which any intelligent Hebrew would have occupied, and read Hebrews 10:20 as it would have appeared in the eyes of those who knew the Maccabean history, kept the feast of dedication, and understood the ceremony of *handsel.* The old covenant waxed old and was vanishing away. The offerings of the law never touched the conscience. The priests never sat down in the course of their ministry, even the high priest needed to offer for his own sins before he offered for the people. Christ was a high Priest of good things to come. Just as He fulfilled the Passover, the Firstfruits and the day of Atonement, so He fulfilled the feast of Dedication. The new tabernacle has been entered, and dedicated, the old things give place to the new.

In direct antithesis to the old covenant, a covenant which waxed old (Heb. 8:13), is the heavenly reality of the Priesthood, Sacrifice and True Tabernacle of the Mediation of the Son of God, Who has by virtue of His one offering fulfilled and made more glorious than did the exploits of Judas Maccabæus, for His dedication opens not a temple on earth but heaven itself.

The dispensational use of this word, is set out in articles entitled MAN (p. 1) and PLEROMA (p. 197). In a number of passages, 'new' is associated with the idea that 'former things' must pass away and come into mind no more. It is this aspect that justifies the comment of Solomon in Ecclesiastes 1:9,10. He is considering the endless round that everywhere marks the way of the world. One generation passeth away and another generation cometh. The sun is no sooner risen than it seems to hasten to the place from which it arose. The wind whirls about continually and returns according to its circuits. All the rivers run into the sea, yet the sea is not full; unto the place from whence the rivers come, thither they return again. It is this endless round that is in contrast with that which is 'new' that gives the 'new' man and 'new' creation most of its wonder and blessedness. See also articles entitled BODY[1]; BOTH[1]; MIDDLE WALL (p. 12), for further application of this conception of newness.

NOAH. Peter speaks of Noah in both of his epistles, calling him the 'eighth person', and reminding us that there were 'eight souls' saved in the ark (1 Pet. 3:20; 2 Pet. 2:5). This association of the number 'eight' with Noah is not accidental. We find that the number 8 is attached to Noah and his sons by numerics, Noah, Shem and Japheth between them giving the total 888. For explanation of this statement, see the article entitled NUMERICS (p. 114). Eight is the octave, the number that makes a fresh start, and this feature is very marked in the typical position occupied by Noah in the record of Genesis.

The following parallels between Adam and Noah are sufficient to justify the teaching that Noah (the eighth person) sets forth in type the Second Adam.

Adam	Noah
A judgment in the background which left the earth without form and void (Gen. 1:2; Isa. 45:18).	A flood in the background that left the earth a ruin (Gen. 7:17-24).
(The parallel between these two passages is so close that commentators are divided as to which of them 2 Peter 3:5,6 refers).	
The dry land appears on the third day, grass and trees grow (Gen. 1:9-13)	The dry land appears in Noah's 601st year, and the pluckt olive leaf indicated to Noah that this was so (Gen. 8:11-13).
Living creatures are 'brought forth' from the water and from the earth, and God blessed them saying, 'Be fruitful and multiply, and fill the waters in the seas, and let fowl multiply in the earth' Gen. 1:20-25).	Living creatures are 'bought fourth' with Noah out of the ark that they may breed abundantly in the earth, and be fruitful, and multiply in the earth (Gen. 8:15-19).

Man made in the image of God to have 'dominion over the fish of the sea, and over fowl of the air, and over the cattle, and over all the earth, and over every creeping thing that creepeth ... and God blessed them, and God said unto them, Be fruitful and multiply and replenish the earth, and subdue it' (Gen. 1:26-28).	'And God blessed Noah and his sons, and said unto them, Be fruitful, and multiply, and replenish the earth, and the fear of you and the dread of you shall be upon every beast of the earth, and upon every fowl of the air, upon all that moveth upon the earth, and upon all the fishes of the sea, into your hand are they delivered'. 'In the image of God made He man' (Gen. 9:1,2,6).
Food ... 'Every herb bearing seed, which is upon the face of all the earth, and every tree, in the which is the fruit of a tree yielding seed; to you it shall be for meat' (Gen. 1:29).	Food ... 'Every moving thing that liveth shall be meat for you; even as the green herb have I given you all things', but not blood (Gen. 9:3,4).
The seventh day rest (Gen. 2:1-3).	Every flood date (except Gen. 8:5) is a Sabbath. (*Companion Bible note*) The ark rested in the seventh month, on the seventeenth day of the month, which was a Sabbath (Gen. 8:4).
Adam has three sons, Cain, Abel and Seth (Gen. 4:1.2.25).	Noah has three sons, Shem, Ham and Japheth (Gen. 5:32).
One son, Cain is cursed more than the earth, and becomes a fugitive and a vagabond (Gen. 4:12).	One son, Ham, the father of Canaan, is cursed, even though God had promised not to curse the ground any more, and Canaan becomes a servant of servants (Gen. 9:25; 8:21).
God curses Cain for shedding his brothers blood, but does not sanction vengeance by human hands (Gen. 4:10-15).	God will require the life blood from every beast and man, but now delegates the execution of judgment to man himself. 'Whoso sheddeth man's blood, by man shall his blood be shed' (Gen. 9:5,6).

The Lord sets a 'mark' (*oth*) to protect Cain (Gen. 4:15).	The Lord sets a bow in the cloud for a 'token' (*oth*) to assure all flesh (Gen. 9:13).
God planted a garden.	Noah planted a vineyard.
Nakedness and shame are linked together in connection with Adam.	Nakedness and shame are linked together in connection with Noah.
The fruit of the tree, and the fig (Gen. 2:8; 3:6,7,10).	The wine of the vineyard (Gen. 9:20-23).
The redemption of both man and his lost dominion is symbolized by the Cherubim (Gen. 3:24).	The redemption of both man and his lost dominion is symbolized by the animals preserved alive in the ark (Gen. 7:13-16; 8:1,17-19).
The serpent beguiled the woman and brought about the curse (Gen. 3:1-24; 2 Cor. 11:3).	The sons of God by their actions towards the daughters of men bring about the flood (Gen. 6:1-4).
All the days of Adam were 930 years (Gen. 5:5).	All the days of Noah were 950 years (Gen. 9:29).

The relation of the days of Noah with Peter's prophecy given in 2 Peter 3 is fully discussed in the article entitled PLEROMA, section 6 (p. 221), and the days of Noah and their foreshadowing of the days that precede the Coming of Christ will be included with other features in the article entitled SECOND COMING[4]. The reference to 'the sons of God' which is found in Genesis 6 will be dealt with in the articles entitled NEPHILIM (p. 104); and SONS OF GOD[4].

A word is called for in connection with Lamech the father of Noah, Lamech was 182 years of age when Noah was born. Sufficient time had passed for him to arrive at the conclusion that has been discovered by others since, viz., that 'all is vanity' apart from the restoring grace of the Redeemer.

In naming his son Noah, Lamech emphasized his felt need of rest. Noah is derived from *nuach* which means 'to be at rest', and occurs in Genesis 8:4, 'and the ark *rested* in the seventh month'. Again in Exodus 20:11, 'for in six days the Lord made heaven and earth, the sea, and all that in them is, and *rested* the seventh day'. When we read in Genesis 8:9, 'the dove found no *rest*', the word is *manoach*, or in 8:21, 'the Lord smelled a *sweet* savour' the word 'sweet' is *nichoach*, and literally the passage reads, 'a savour of rest'. Thus it will be seen that for *God* as well as *man* there is a place of rest, and that rest is Christ, of whom Noah and the ark are prophetic.

Lamech in naming his son said, 'this same shall comfort us (*nacham*, or, give us rest) concerning our work and toil of our hands, because of the ground which the Lord hath cursed'. The word rendered 'toil' is twice rendered 'sorrow' in Genesis 3 where the curse is first pronounced, 'I will greatly multiply thy sorrow', and 'in sorrow shalt thou eat of it all the days of thy life' (verses 16,17). The words 'work and toil' may be a figure, meaning very grievous work; the work and the toil are clearly specified as being the work and toil of the *hands*, and in connection with the *ground*, which under the curse yielded but thorns and thistles of itself, whereas bread only came by sweat of face. We read that Cain experienced a special pronouncement of this curse (Gen. 4:12), and he is the first builder of a city that is named in Scripture, possibly still acting in character, making an attempt to find some amelioration of the curse which Lamech refused.

We cannot help noticing the similarity of names that occur in the two lines of Adam's descendants. If there is an Enoch who walked with God, there is an Enoch born to Cain in the land of banishment. If there is a Jared in the line of Seth, there is an Irad in the line of Cain, which differs only in one letter in the original. Methuselah has a son named Lamech in the line of Seth, so Methusael has a son of the same name in the line of Cain. Both Lamechs have seven, and seventy and seven connected with them. They speak to us of the beginning of that parody of truth which Satan has so skilfully established and maintained, by taking advantage of similar sounding names, and of the confusion of tongues which we associate with Babylon and Babylonianism. (See *The Two Babylons*, by Hislop).

Lamech, 'the sixth from Adam', in the line of Cain, has three sons, one (Jabal) kept cattle, and so continued in the work of the ground, but Jubal was the father of all such as handle the harp and organ, and Tubal-Cain an instructor of every artificer in brass and iron. It would appear that *the veneer* which has spread over the curse, and which is variously named culture, civilization, progress, etc., today, was originated by the sons of Lamech of Cain's line. The Lamech who begat Noah, however, is in direct contrast, he does not appear to have attempted to evade the weary toil that must be experienced by those who, by sweat of face, eat the bread that is produced by the ground that is cursed. Lamech longed for rest, but he did not accept the vain substitutes of the line of Cain. There are many today who, surrounded by the comforts and inventions of man, would scarcely believe that there is truth in the record of the curse on the ground. The products of the earth and sea are brought to their door, no thought passes through their mind as to the sorrow and the toil that someone, somewhere, must endure to provide them with the necessities of life. Not all may be so crude as the little town-bred urchin who, when taken for the first time to a farm in the country, said, 'I don't want milk from a Cow. I want milk that comes from a SHOP', but something akin to this attitude is induced by the multiplication of 'push buttons' in the daily round. Lamech knew no such deadening influence; the toil of his hands was hard and wearying because of the ground that the Lord had cursed. A friend writing recently gave an unconscious echo of Lamech's words, saying, 'When one, from the back of the land, sees the toil of man and beast, there comes to the lips no more fitting words than, 'Even so, come, Lord Jesus'.

Harps and organs, however melodious and charming; brass and iron, modelled and designed into the most wonderful of machines and inventions, though they may 'prove' to the natural man the upward development of his attainments, afford no rest for those in whose hearts the truth of God abides. Rest for them is found in the true Noah, Whose witness and Whose experience testify of a safe passage through the flood of judgment, of the resurrection, and of a new heaven and a new earth wherein dwelleth righteousness.

See the article ATONEMENT[6].

'Now' IN Acts 26:17. Most scholars are agreed that the word 'now' in Acts 26:17, 'Unto whom now I send thee' is a gloss, an addition by a writer who sought either *to preserve* or *to enforce* what he conceived to be the import of the passage. Those who deny that Acts 28 constitutes a dispensational frontier have given undue emphasis to this omission. The present tense of the verb *apostello*, 'I send thee' can have no other meaning than I Now send thee, whether the preposition is included or omitted. It is impossible to translate Acts 26:17 :

> 'Unto whom I AM SENDING thee (in the present), some years ago (in the past), when I met thee on the road to Damascus'.

In Acts 22:17-21 we learn that Paul was in the temple and in a trance, and therefore this cannot be when he was on the road to Damascus, and there he heard the voice of the Lord saying:

> 'Depart: for I will send (future) thee far hence unto the Gentiles'.

Here we have the future *exapostello*, and of course here the word 'now' is impossible. In Acts 26:17 *that promise* to send Paul in the future was about to be fulfilled, and the word translated 'send' changes from the future to the present, it is 'now' as the ancient gloss indicated.

The Gentiles to whom Paul was to be sent were 'far off' but at the moment unidentified. Subsequently we learn that Rome was in view.

In Acts 19:21 Paul said, 'I must also see Rome'.

In Acts 23:11 the Lord said to Paul, 'So must thou bear witness also at Rome'.

And at Rome Paul announced, consequent upon the rejection for a season of Israel, that:

> 'The salvation of God is sent' (or "was sent" as already revealed in Acts 26:17) unto the Gentiles (far off ones at Rome)' (Acts 28:28).

There is no need for the reader to stampede, because some, who are antagonistic to the Acts 28 position have seized upon these Scriptures for their own ends. We want them, just as they are written, unaltered. The only difference in the two readings of Acts 26:17 is that of *emphasis*. In one, the reading 'now' is expressed, in the other the word 'now' is implicit in the present tense of the verb.

NUMERICS. Number in Scripture is presented in two forms. First there is the significance of any number, secondly the numerical value of the letters forming any particular word.

Thus:

ONE	denotes unity.
TWO	difference.
THREE	completeness.
FOUR	creation.
FIVE	denotes grace.
SIX	is the number of man.
SEVEN	spiritual perfection.
EIGHT	the octave, the first of a new series and dominion.
NINE	often indicates finality of judgment.
TEN	ordinal perfection.
ELEVEN	disorder.
TWELVE	governmental perfection, and is especially related to Israel.
THIRTEEN	denotes rebellion.

Another and suggestive characteristic of Bible Numerics is that which is related to the numerical value of the letters of the Hebrew and Greek alphabets. It must be understood that figures are not used in either the Hebrew or Greek originals of the Scriptures, letters of the alphabet being used instead. In Hebrew *Aleph* (A) = 1, *Beth* (B) = 2, *Gimel* (G) = 3, and in Greek *Alpha* (A) = 1, *Beta* (B) = 2, *Gamma* (G) = 3, and so on. It must be remembered, however, that these ancient alphabets do not conform either with one another in the names or order of their letters, neither does the English alphabet conform to either the Hebrew or the Greek. Before, therefore, the reader can arrive at the numerical value of any word he must have the whole alphabet together with the numerical value of each letter before him. However from what we do know we can easily see that the numerical value of the Hebrew word ABBA (Father) is SIX.

Thus A + B + B + A = 1 + 2 + 2 + 1 = 6.

As an illustration of the significance of these numerics we give instances of EIGHT and THIRTEEN.

Eight, the Number of Lordship

The numerical value of the name 'Jesus', which in Greek is Iesous is 888, can be set out thus.

J	I	10
E	E	8
S	S	200
U	O	70
S	U	400
	S	200
		888

This must be set over against the number of the name of the Beast of Revelation 13:18 which is given as 666.

Kurious 'Lord' is 800, Christ and Messiah are multiples of 8.

The names of Noah, Shem, Ham and Japheth amount to 936, but if we remove the name of Ham, which is 48, we leave the total 888 once again. The total 936 is a multiple of thirteen, rebellion. This significance can be seen in both the Hebrew and Greek names of Satan.

Satan in Hebrew	364	(13 x 28)
Satan in Greek	2197	(13 x 13 x 13)
Dragon in Greek	975	(13 x 75)
Serpent in Greek	780	(13 x 60)

Daniel and his four companions, Daniel, Hananiah, Mishael and Azariah = 95, 120, 381 and 292 respectively, giving the total once more 888.

There is always a danger that such a feature as this will be abused by some whose zeal outruns their discretion, but enough we trust has been exhibited to enable the student to observe and appreciate this remarkable feature of Holy Scripture.

OLIVE TREE, see ROMANS[4]. The section dealing with 'The Olive Tree and Israel's National Position (Rom. 11:11-32).

ONE. The unity of the Spirit, entrusted to the believer to 'keep' is a sevenfold unity, which can be likened to the candlestick made for the tabernacle. It will be very evident to the reader, that unless we know what this unity of the Spirit comprises, we shall not be able to keep it; consequently the apostle proceeds to give the details of this blessed trust. There are six parts in this unity arranged in the structure in two groups on either side of the ascended Lord. The arrangement may be presented to the eye in the form of the six-branched lampstand used of old. We trust no reader will be misled, as one of our critics was, into believing that we teach that this unity of the Spirit was *actually* set forth in the tabernacle of old. How could it be set forth then if it was a mystery 'hid in God'? While making this clear, we need not be robbed of any help that such an illustration may give.

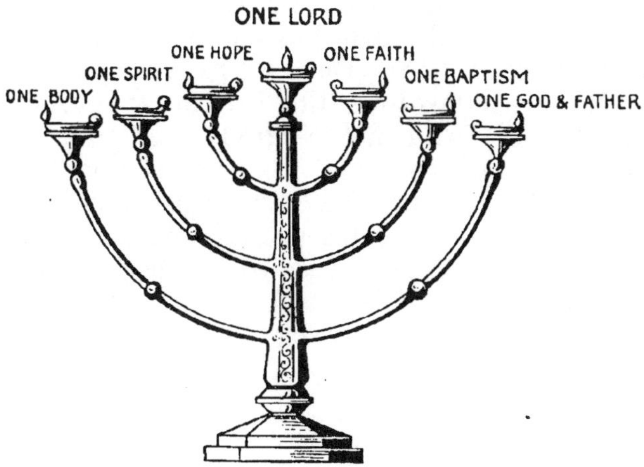

The central feature is the 'One Lord'. Without the ascended Christ there would be no Head, and so no Body;

no Chief Corner Stone, and so no Temple; no hope, no faith and no love. With the risen and ascended Lord we have both hope and faith. The hope is the 'one hope of your calling'. Hope and calling are inseparable; what our calling is here and now, our hope when realized, will be in the future. The prayer of Ephesians 1:18 has the knowledge of this hope as its central petition: 'That ye may know what is the hope of His calling'.

Other callings have other phases of hope; among them 'the hope of Israel', which covers the whole period of the Acts of the Apostles (Acts 1:6 to 28:20). The Second Coming of Christ as set forth in Matthew 24, 1 Thessalonians 4, 1 Corinthians 15 and in the epistles of Peter, James, John and Jude presents phases and aspects of the hope that was entertained by both believing Jews and Gentiles before the revelation of the Mystery. While Christ and His glory are, and ever must be, at the centre of the hope of all His own, the hope of each calling will be related to its own sphere of blessing.

The bond of peace is specific. It definitely refers to Ephesians 2. It is really 'the bond of *the* peace', for the article is used, and so indicates *that* peace connected with 'the creation of the two into one new man, so making peace' (Eph. 2:14,15). There we have the creation of the One Body, and this is the first item in the sevenfold unity of the Spirit. To attempt to introduce 1 Corinthians 12 in face of 1 Corinthians 13:10 ['in part', (1 Cor. 13:10), and 'in particular', (1 Cor. 12:27), are translations of the same word], is to introduce the passing and partial things of childhood into the experience of 'the perfect man' (Eph. 4:13). This 'peace of God' is to act as 'umpire' (not 'rule', Col. 3:15), and is inseparable from the 'calling' of the 'One Body' as it is written:

> 'Let the peace of God be as the umpire in your hearts, to the which also ye are called in one body'.

To allow any tampering with the sevenfold unity of Ephesians 4 either to add to, to subtract from, or to agree to differ about its terms, is not allowing the peace of God to be umpire, but submitting to our own ideas of fellowship, and a compromising for the sake of usefulness, charity, etc. To deny the One Body, its one baptism and its one hope of glory, for the sake of 'peace' is to decide against the 'ruling' of this very peace of God, and shatters all semblance of true unity.

There are no more two baptisms or two hopes in this unity than there are or can be two Lords. To us has been committed a sacred trust, a 'good deposit' (1 Tim. 6:20; 2 Tim. 1:12-14; 2:2). It is required in stewards that a man be found *faithful* — peaceable, useful, charitable by all means, so long as the first element of stewardship be untouched, but *faithful* he must be. Keeping the unity of the Spirit is an essential part of walking worthy of our calling (Eph. 4:1-6) and indeed is listed first. Let us not be tempted to 'come down' from our glorious position (Neh. 6:2,3), but humbly, yet resolutely, set ourselves by the grace given us and by the power that worketh in us to 'endeavour to keep as a sacred trust the unity of the Spirit in the bond of peace'. The unity of the Spirit, of Ephesians 4, keeps it in the bond of peace already made. The going on to the perfect man of Ephesians 4, is but the realization of the 'one new man' of Ephesians 2.

OUT-RESURRECTION. See PRIZE (p. 305); PHILIPPIANS (p. 196); HEBREWS[2]; and RESURRECTION[4,7].

OVERCOMER. Three Greek words are translated overcome in the New Testament, *hettaomai* (2 Pet. 2:19,20), *katakurieuo* (Acts 19:16) and *nikao*. The only word which is of dispensational consequence is *nikao*. *Nikao* 'to conquer, overcome, get the victory' occurs twenty-eight times; 'conquer' twice, 'get the victory' once, 'prevail' once and 'overcome' twenty-four times. *Nikos* and *nike* are translated 'victory'; the believer is said to be 'more than conqueror' (Rom. 8:37), and the word enters into eight names in the New Testament: Nicopolis, Nicanor, Nicolas, Nicolaitan, Nicodemus, Bernice, Eunice and Andronicus. Seventeen of the twenty-eight occurrences of *nikao* are found in the book of the Revelation and it is the association of the overcomer with that book that we are to consider.

Although the range of the Apocalypse is from heaven above to the bottomless pit, although it takes in its prophetic embrace, Satan, Archangel and demon, kings, armies and the habitable earth; although it speaks of the four living creatures, Apollyon, the great white throne, the day of judgment, the millennial kingdom, the new Jerusalem and the new heaven and the new earth, we shall fail to appreciate its message and understand its method if we forget that these vast and overwhelming subjects form after all *a background against* which the little band of overcomers fight the good fight and 'overcome because of the blood of the Lamb, and because of the word of their testimony' (Rev. 12:11).

Each of these seven churches, to which this book is addressed, is given a special promise to the overcomer:

Ephesus	The promise	'To eat of the tree of life' (Rev. 2:7).
Smyrna	The promise	'Not to be hurt of the second death' (Rev. 2:11).
Pergamos	The promise	'To eat of the hidden manna' (Rev. 2:17).
Thyatira	The promise	'Power over the nations' (Rev 2:26).
Sardis	The promise	'Clothed in white raiment' (Rev. 3:5).
Philadelphia	The promise	'Made a pillar in the temple' (Rev. 3:12).
Laodicea	The promise	'To sit with Christ in His throne' (Rev. 3:21).

In the last reference, Revelation 3:21, Christ Himself is set forth as the Great Overcomer. 'Even as I also overcame'.

The remaining references to the overcomer, divide into two groups.

(1) The True Overcomer. This includes both the Lord and His people.

(a) The Lord. 'The Lion of the tribe of Judah, the Root of David, *hath prevailed* to open the book' (Rev. 5:5).
'The Lamb shall overcome them' (Rev. 17:14).

(b) His People. 'They overcame him by the blood of the Lamb' (Rev. 12:11).
'Them that had *gotten the victory* over the beast' (Rev. 15:2).
'He that overcometh shall inherit all things' (Rev. 21:7).

(2) The False Overcomer.
'He went forth conquering and to conquer' (Rev. 6:2).
'The Beast ... shall overcome them' (Rev. 11:7).
'To make war with the saints, and to overcome them' (Rev. 13:7).

There are many things that one might have expected to find in the Revelation which are not there; that expectation arises out of a false conception of the scope of the book. It is not written to explain universal history, it was sent as a message of encouragement to seven churches, and with particular regard to the 'overcomer'.

For a fuller analysis of the Revelation, and the relation of the seven churches with the book as a whole, see LORD'S DAY[2]; REVELATION[4]; and MILLENNIAL STUDIES[9].

OVERTHROW This translation of the Greek word *katabole* which occurs in the phrase 'before the foundation of the world' is fully discussed in article EPHESIANS[1], which should be consulted.

PARABLE

As the student of Scripture grows in grace and knowledge of the truth, things which once seemed trivial appear of great importance; passages which once he thought he 'knew all about' are approached with deepening humility, to be re-read and learned afresh. Among our earliest recollections, either as scholars in Sunday Schools or as members of churches, will be those passages of Scripture known as 'The Parables'. The time worn definition, 'an earthly story with a heavenly meaning' is doubtless familiar to us all. Do we not begin to realize, however, that these parables contain teaching which some of our teachers never saw, and that the dispensational key, which has turned the lock of so many difficulties and opened doors into such treasuries may be profitably applied to these 'dark sayings'?

The first thing to do is to be sure of the meaning of the word. The word 'parable' has been taken over into the English tongue from the Greek word *parabole. Para* means 'near' or 'beside' and *bole is* from *ballo,* 'I cast' or 'throw'. Literally it signifies something 'cast beside' another, and as applied to discourse it means a method of teaching which demands the use of similitude or comparison. A good example of this 'throwing beside' is the interpretation of the 'Tares' (Matt. 13:36-43).

He that soweth	is	the Son of man.
The field	is	the world.
The good seed	are	the children of the Kingdom, etc.

All the parables of Scripture are weighty and wise sayings. This may be gathered from the words of the proverb, 'the legs of a lame man are not equal, so is a parable in the mouth of fools' (Prov. 26:7). *The Companion Bible* gives the meaning, 'the clothes of a lame man being lifted up expose his lameness, so a fool exposes his folly in expounding a parable'. (See also Prov. 26:9).

An American writer has given a very helpful translation of Proverbs, chapter 1:2-6 which reads thus:

> 'To know wisdom and admonition: to put a *distinct* meaning into *discriminated* speeches: to accept clear-sighted admonition is righteousness and judgment and right behaviour.
>
> "In order to give subtlety to the simple; to the child, knowledge and thorough thought. The wise man will hear and increasingly acquire, and a man already become discerning will gain in capability to guide.
>
> "For putting a distinct meaning into a proverb or an enigma; into the words of the wise and their intricate sayings;
>
> "The fear of the Lord is the main knowledge, a wisdom and a discipline that fools despise"'.

It is in this frame of mind that we approach these 'dark sayings' in the fear of the Lord to learn their 'secrets'.

In Matthew 13:35 the Lord quotes from Psalm 78:2 in relation to His speaking in parables, and therefore we may expect to find some help in that Psalm to guide us to the right understanding of the purpose of parables. The heading of the Psalm is 'Maschil of Asaph'. The Hebrew word *maschil* is from the word *sakal*, which means, 'to look at', 'to scrutinize', and the term *maschil* means, 'an understanding arising from a deep consideration' (Neh. 8:8).

> 'Give ear, O My people, to My law:
> Incline your ears to the words of My mouth.
> I will open my mouth in a *parable*:
> I will utter dark sayings of old'.

The remaining portion of the Psalm is a rehearsal of the history of Israel from Moses to David, showing the inner reasons of their failures. Take for example verses 9 and 10:

> 'The children of Ephraim, armed, carrying bows,
> Turned back in the day of battle'.

Why?

> 'They kept not the covenant of God,
> And refused to walk in His law'.

From this we may infer that a parable urges us to consider deeply the ways of God with His people, and to look for the hidden causes, and workings which are veiled from the eyes of the uninstructed.

That a parable has some connection with a secret, a reference to Matthew 13 will prove. There for the first time in the New Testament do we read the word 'mystery' or 'secret' and there for the first time occurs the word 'parable'. Further, the Lord Jesus translates the words, 'I will utter dark sayings of old', by the words, 'I will utter things which have been kept *secret* since the overthrow *(katabole)* of the world' (Matt. 13:35).

The first parable of the Bible is one which concerns the people of Israel in relation to their separate calling as a distinct nation and peculiar people:

> 'And he took up his parable, and said, Balak the king of Moab hath brought me from Aram, out of the mountains of the east, saying, Come, curse me Jacob, and come, defy Israel. How shall I curse, whom God hath not cursed? or how shall I defy, whom the LORD hath not defied?' (Num. 23:7,8; *so also* 23:18; 24:3,15).

In Hebrews 9:9 and 11:19 we find the word translated, 'a figure'. A parable and a proverb are much alike. The parable of Matthew 15:13-15 might be termed a proverb. Indeed the word translated 'proverb' in Luke 4:23 is really 'parable'. The words, 'Physician, heal thyself' are called in the original a 'parable'. That a 'proverb' carried the same hidden teaching as did the 'parable and dark saying' can be seen by referring to John 16:25 and 29:

> 'These things have I spoken unto you in proverbs: but the time cometh, when I shall no more speak unto you in proverbs, but I shall shew you *plainly* of the Father'.

In the Old Testament we have 'type'; in the Gospels we have 'parable', and in the epistles we have 'doctrine', as the more prominent features. The parables lead us to contemplate *the hidden causes* of the failure of Israel in relation to the kingdom that had been proclaimed and look forward to the time when all will be put right at the Coming of the Lord in glory.

The first occurrence of a word very often suggests its fundamental meaning. The first occurrence of the word parable in the New Testament is Matthew 13:3. It follows that chapter wherein the rejection of the Messiah by the people in the land became evident. He had been heralded as their Messiah and King. He had vindicated His claims by the fulfilment of numerous prophecies, both with regard to His person and His works, and in chapter 12:6,41 and 42, although greater than the *temple,* greater than the *prophet Jonah,* and greater than *king Solomon,* He is 'despised and rejected'.

> 'The same day went Jesus out of the house, and sat by the sea side ... And He spake many things to them in parables ... And the disciples came, and said unto Him, Why speakest Thou unto them in parables? He answered and said unto them, Because it is given unto you to know the *mysteries of the kingdom of the heavens* ... Therefore speak I to them in parables: because they seeing see not; and hearing they hear not, neither do they understand. And in them is fulfilled the prophecy of Isaiah, which saith, By hearing ye shall hear, and shall not understand; and seeing ye shall see, and shall not perceive: for this people's heart is waxed gross, and their ears are dull of hearing, and their eyes they have closed; lest at any time they should see with their eyes, and hear with their ears, and should understand with their heart, and should be converted, and I should heal them. But blessed are your eyes, for they see: and your ears, for they hear. For verily I say unto you, That many prophets and righteous men have desired to see those things which ye see, and have not seen them; and to hear those things which ye hear, and have not heard them' (Matt. 13:1-17).

The reader should observe that these parables of Matthew 13 ARE NOT about 'The Kingdom of Heaven' pure and simple, but about 'The *mysteries* of the Kingdom of Heaven', a very different aspect of truth.

Such is the setting of the first occurrence of the word parable in the New Testament. The parables were used when Israel manifested that the prophecy of Isaiah 6:10 was fulfilled in them. The parables veiled the teaching from the majority whose eyes were judicially closed. The parables relate to 'the secrets' of the kingdom. They teach things hitherto 'kept secret since the overthrow of the world' (Matt. 13:35). Prophets desired to see and hear these things, as Matthew 13:17 and 1 Peter 1:10-12 tell us:

> 'Searching what, or what manner of time the Spirit of Christ which was in them did signify, when it testified beforehand the sufferings of Christ, and the glory that should follow' (1 Pet. 1:11).

Here, as in the majority of Old Testament prophecies, no break is made between the sufferings and the glory. No interval is allowed between 'the acceptable year of the Lord, and the day of vengeance of our God' (Isa. 61:2, but cf. Luke 4:19). The rejection of God's King was only partly seen; *the abeyance of the kingdom was a secret.* Thus we may place the two passages together:

> 'I will open My mouth in parables; I will utter things which have been kept secret since the *overthrow* of the world' (Matt. 13:35).
>
> 'Why speakest Thou unto them in parables? ... Because it is given unto you to know the secrets of the kingdom of the heavens, but to them it is not given' (Matt. 13:10,11).

Everything leads us to expect that, just as in Psalm 78, we shall find in these parables some of the inner working of God's counsels relative to His purpose in Israel, and that to introduce the doctrinal teaching of the gospel of the grace of God, or the dispensational teaching of the Mystery which is not a subject of revelation until over thirty years later (Eph. 3:1-10), or to attempt to make them speak of the millennial kingdom, will be to confound things which differ, and signally to fail rightly to divide the Word of Truth.

The parables are particularly *dispensational* in character. Their object is not to provide a moral lesson or a text for a gospel address. How many have gone astray by reason of this mischievous practice! The parable of the Prodigal Son serves those who have no desire for the retention of the Atonement with a 'proof' text for the universal Fatherhood of God, and the reception by Him of all who come, irrespective of the one way of acceptance, the mediation of Christ. The parable of the Unforgiving Servant is made to teach, in direct opposition to the doctrine of the epistles, that sins once forgiven may be re-imputed, or that a sinner once saved by grace can fall away again !

Let us remember the Scriptural settings of these parables, the reasons which drew them from the Lord Jesus, the dispensation in which they were uttered, and the people and the kingdom about which they speak; we shall then have no need to be ashamed of our testimony.

Thus far we have sought to clear the way for the study of these parables. We shall next endeavour to present to the reader the arrangement of the parables of Matthew 13 and to enter into the teaching of these parables of *the secrets* of the kingdom of the heavens. While all the parables of the New Testament have a dispensational setting that must be perceived before their true teaching can be discovered, the parables of Matthew 13 are peculiarly important, so that we supplement these introductory notes on parables generally, with a fuller exposition of the parables of this chapter.

Before we examine the parables in detail, we must examine them together. Some of our readers may be surprised to find us speaking of the EIGHT parables of Matthew 13. It has become almost sacred to prophetic students to speak of the seven parables of Matthew 13, so that we shall have to set out the complete arrangement in order to demonstrate the fact that the Lord gave eight parabolic or figurative utterances in connection with the 'mysteries (or secrets) of the kingdom'.

Structure of Matthew 13

The Eight Parables

A 1-9. The SOWER The sowing of the seed into four kinds of ground.

They (Israel) did *not* understand.

B	24-30.	The TARES	Good and bad together. Separated at the harvest (the end of the age); the bad are cast into a furnace of fire, there shall be wailing and gnashing of teeth.	The first four parables spoken outside the house to great multitudes.
C	31,32.	The MUSTARD TREE	One tree.	
D	33.	The LEAVEN	Hid in three measures of meal.	
D	44.	The TREASURE	Hid in a field.	
C	45,46.	GOODLY PEARLS	One pearl.	
B	47-50.	The DRAG NET	Good and bad together. Separated at the end of the age; the bad are cast into a furnace of fire, there shall be wailing and gnashing of teeth.	The last four parables spoken inside the house to the disciples.

They (disciples) *did* understand.

A 51,52. The SCRIBE The treasure opened to those in the house.

The harmony that exists between the component parts of this structure is quite evident to all. If we can see the disposition of any passage of Scripture, we are in possession of a help to its interpretation. Sometimes a word may have more than one meaning, and the balance in favour of either rendering may be fairly equal. If we can find its place in the structure, we shall often, by so doing, fix its meaning also.

Look at the central pair of parables. The Leaven 'hidden' in three measures of meal in the parables spoken outside the house finds its corresponding member in the contrasted Treasure 'hidden' in the field which was spoken to the disciples only. The parable of the Tares finds its complement in the parable of the Drag Net. The parable of the Sower is balanced by that of the Scribe, and the Mustard Seed by the Pearl.

THE SOWER

Matthew 13:1-9,18-23

We now approach the consideration of this initial parable. Initial not only because it is the first in order of utterance, but because its interpretation supplies a model for the interpretation of all parables, 'Know ye not this parable? and how then will ye know all parables?' (Mark 4:13).

John tells us that although he has recorded eight 'signs' to support the particular purpose of his gospel (John 20:31), yet the number actually wrought by the Lord far exceeded this, so much so that 'if they should be written every one, I suppose that even the world itself could not contain the books that should be written' (John 21:25). What is true concerning the Lord's works is also true concerning His words; each Gospel narrative gives a divinely inspired selection of his wonderful teaching. If this is so, what importance must be placed upon that miracle, parable or discourse which is repeated twice or even thrice! The parable of the Sower occurs in the three Synoptic Gospels (Matt. 13:1-9; Mark 4:1-9; Luke 8:4-8). In each record we read of the four sowings, on four kinds of ground.

One of the differences between Matthew's account and that of Mark is that Matthew speaks always in the plural, 'they', 'them', whereas Mark speaks of the seed in the singular, 'it'. Luke adds the words, 'and it was trodden down', in the first sowing, and omits the reference to 'no depth of earth' and the effect of the sun, telling us that it withered because it lacked moisture. The addition of the words, 'with it', in Luke's account of the thorns is also suggestive.

Parallel with this teaching of the Sower is the witness of the same truth in the parable of the Fig Tree (Luke 13) and the Great Supper (Luke 14). The primary teaching of these parables is not merely to supply a moral or spiritual lesson, but to depict the secret course of the mysteries of the kingdom on through its apparent defeat at the rejection of the King, to its glorious close.

It will not be possible to analyse all the parables in this fashion, the interested reader is referred to the book by the Author, entitled, *Parable, Miracle and Sign.*

We sum up the remaining parables for the guidance of the student thus:

THE SOWER

The ministries of John the Baptist, the Lord Jesus, and the apostles during the 'Acts' were to a large extent, externally, failures, but there is yet to be a gloriously fruitful sowing when the time comes for the New Covenant to be put into operation (Jer. 31:27).

THE TARES

The reason for the delay in the setting up of the kingdom is discovered in the fact that an enemy is at work, and side by side with the true children of the kingdom are the children of the wicked one, but these are not removed until the end of the age (see articles SEED[4] and GIANTS[2]).

THE MUSTARD TREE

The next reason for the delay is that whereas the small seed of Israel should have flourished and filled the earth with fruit, the sovereignty changed hands and was deposited with the Gentiles, beginning with Nebuchadnezzar, 'until the fulness of the Gentiles come in'. This stage is marked by the words, 'it becometh a tree, and the fowls lodged in its branches' (see Daniel 4). That which should have been pre-eminently the kingdom of righteousness, becomes the habitation of Satan and his angels.

THE LEAVEN

The third reason for delay is that the leaven of evil has been put into the meal of God's truth. This will work its course until the rise of Antichrist, and the complete corruption of the visible witness for God (see use of leaven, Matt. 16:6,12).

Thus we see that the Lord Jesus had no idea of the gradual uplifting of the masses, and the permeating influence of the gospel. He saw that man had corrupted his way upon the earth, even as it was in the days of Noah. Hence it is that He uses the same words to represent the end. Blessed be God, that out of all this corruption and apostasy He will yet bring His treasure and display His grace.

We have considered the first four parables and discovered something of their bearing upon the course of the rejected kingdom of the heavens. A division is now observable, emphasized alike by the structural arrangement, the teaching, and the different place in which they were spoken.

THE TREASURE

After the parable of the Leaven the Lord dismissed the multitude, and went into the house. There He explained the parable of the Tares, and then proceeded to unfold the *inner* or *Godward* aspect of the kingdom in the four parables that followed. Their relation to each other may be summarized thus:

A THE TREASURE IN THE FIELD:
The nation of Israel as distinct from the nations.
B ONE BEAUTIFUL PEARL:
The remnant of Israel as distinct from the nation.
B THE MANY FISH:
The Gentile nations as distinct from Israel.
A THE TREASURE HID IN THE HOUSE:
Israel, viewed as a missionary nation sent to the nations.

The group of parables that come after the great dividing line of Matthew 16 'From that time forth' are linked with those of Matthew 13 by the parable of Matthew 15:10-20. The second group of parables in Matthew is contained in chapters 18 to 25 (see structure opposite).

Sufficient we trust has been exhibited to prove beyond a doubt that these parables are of paramount importance in the realm of Dispensational Truth, and a comprehensive acquaintance with them is incumbent upon all who would attempt to teach. These parables are given a thorough exposition in the volume, *Parable, Miracle and Sign*, and this is commended to the earnest student.

The Parables of Matthew 18 to 25

A 18:23-35. THE UNFORGIVING SERVANT ('The reckoning' *sunairo**).
Delivered to tormentors.

B 20:1-16. THE HOUSEHOLD AND VINEYARD.
The Call of the Labourers:

1. Early.	Many
2. Third hour.	called,
3. Sixth and ninth hours.	but few
4. Eleventh hour.	chosen.

C 21:28-32. TWO SONS AND VINEYARD.
Lesson, publicans and harlots enter the kingdom while many who claimed entrance were kept outside.

C 21:33-46. WICKED HUSBANDMEN AND VINEYARD.
Lesson, kingdom taken from them and given to a fruitful nation.

B 22:1-14. THE MARRIAGE OF KING'S SON.
The Call to the Guests:

1. Bid those who were bidden.	Many
2. Again tell them.	called,
3. Go therefore to highways.	but few
4. The wedding garment.	chosen.

A 24:32 to 25:30. TWO KINDS OF SERVANTS.

a 24:32-44. The Fig Tree. 'Noah'.—
Coming as a thief while the good man slept.
'Ye know not what hour your Lord doth come'.

b 24:45-51. The faithful and evil servants.—
The one made ruler, the other has his portion with the hypocrites.

'Weeping and gnashing of teeth'.

a 25:1-13. The wise and foolish virgins.—
'Ye know neither the day nor the hour'.

b 25:14-30. The faithful and unprofitable servants ('the reckoning' *sunairo**). The one made ruler, the other cast into outer darkness.

'Weeping and gnashing of teeth'.

---

* The only occurrences of *sunairo* in the New Testament.

BEREAN MATTHEW CHARTS
No 9.
The Goshel of the King-Priest.
A BIRTH
B BAPTISM
Born King of the Jews.
C THREEFOLD TEMPTATION OF KING
KING
D. THE SON OF DAVID
iii.17. The VOICE
xvi.16. Confession by PETER (an Israelite)
"From that time forth began" iv.17.
Sermon on Mount
Rules during Rejection
Parables of xiii.
Mystery during Rejection
Su eihas
xvi.18. "Thou hast said".
Dividing line at Matthew xvi verse 20.
PRIEST
D. THE SON OF ABRAHAM
xvii.5 The VOICE
xxvii.54. Confession by CENTURION (a Gentile)
"From that time forth began" XVI.21.
Parables of Absence
Reckoning with servants
Prophecy of Presence
After Tribulation
Su eihas
xxvi.64. "Thou hast said".
C THREEFOLD AGONY OF PRIEST
B BAPTISM
A RESURRECTION
Died King of the Jews.
C.H.W. 34.

PARENTHESIS. The recognition of a parenthesis is important when translating the Scriptures; two instances may be useful here.

2 Peter 1:19 *as it stands* favours the idea that the Second Coming is not personal, but occurs when one receives the Saviour in the heart.

Ephesians 6:12 *as it stands* teaches that there, even where Christ sits in 'heavenly places' war is still being waged. The truth in each passage is revealed by the observance of the parenthesis.

'Whereunto ye do well that ye take heed	{ *as unto a light ...* *until the day star* *arise* }	in your heart.
'For we wrestle not with flesh and blood	{ *but with* *principalities* *... of this world* }	in heavenly places'.

In each case the central portion of the sentence can be omitted, leaving the simple sentence:

'Whereunto ye do well that ye take heed in your hearts'.

'For we wrestle not with flesh and blood in heavenly places'.

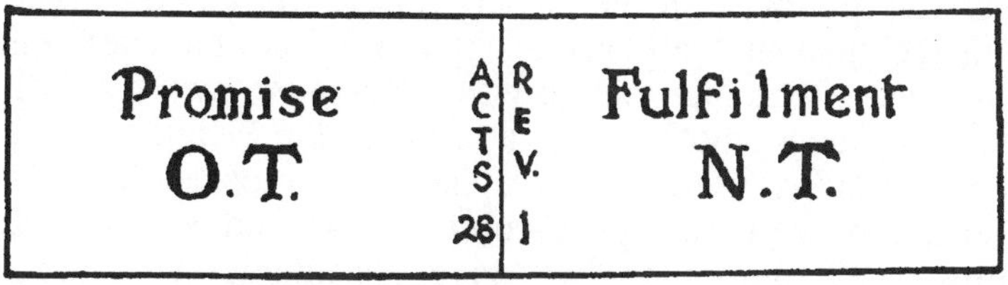

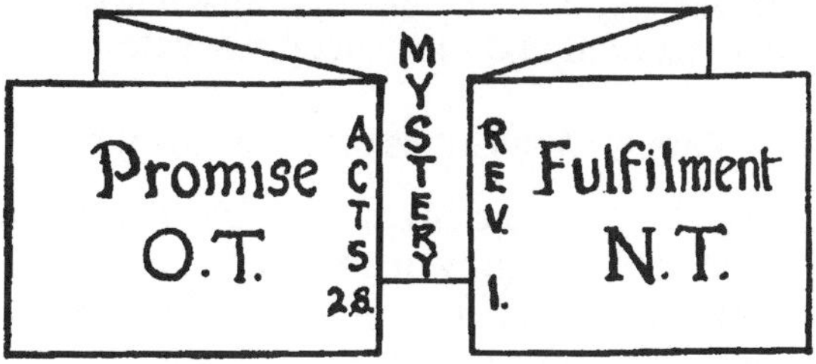

We are, however, not so concerned here with a *grammatical* parenthesis as to make sure that the reader understands a remark that occurs more than once in our articles, namely that the present *dispensation* is parenthetical. The idea is that the promise made to Abraham and the fulfilment in the age to come, can be likened to the two outside positions of the sentence shown above, while the Mystery finds its place between the break which occurred at Acts 28 and the resumption of the promise to the Fathers that will mark the close of the present dispensation. We give a drawing above of a method often adopted to exhibit this feature.

PAROUSIA — see SECOND COMING[4] — terms used.

PAUL

The conversion and commission of Paul, his apostleship to the Gentiles, and his stewardship of the Mystery as the Prisoner of Jesus Christ, are dealt with in articles, entitled ACTS OF THE APOSTLES[1]; APOSTLE[1]; DISPENSATION[1]; GALATIANS[2]; GOOD DEPOSIT[2]; MYSTERY (p. 59); and PRISON EPISTLES (p. 160). In the present article we are concerned with the man himself, his background, his character, his equipment. The fact that he was a Roman citizen by birth has an influence both on his attitude to the Gentile world, to illustrations used in his epistles, and particularly in connection with his appeal unto Cæsar and his trial at Rome. We will, therefore, give consideration to these backgrounds, hoping that the apostle himself will be all the more clearly discerned and more deeply loved.

(1) PAUL'S APPREHENSION AT JERUSALEM

The second half of the Acts devotes a great deal of space to an account of Paul's apprehension and subsequent trials, culminating in his imprisonment for two years at Rome. When the apostle arrived at Jerusalem with the contribution for the poor saints there, he was obliged to meet the charge made against him, that he taught all the Jews that were among the Gentiles to forsake Moses. In order to refute this charge publicly, he associates himself with some men who had taken upon themselves the Nazarite vow. While thus engaged, he is recognized by some Jews from Asia, who raise the cry that he has defiled the Holy Place by taking Trophimus into the sacred enclosure. The Romans had given power to the Jews to inflict the death penalty for this act of sacrilege, and the marble slab warning any intruder of the consequences of such an act may still be seen in the office of The Palestine Exploration Fund. See article entitled MIDDLE WALL p. 12.

The following extract from Josephus' *Wars of the Jews* will show how serious was the apostle's position.

> 'Now Titus was deeply affected with this state of things, and reproached John and his party, and said to them,— "Have not you, vile creatures that you are, by our permission, put up this partition-wall before your sanctuary? Have not you been allowed to put up the pillars thereto belonging, at due distances, and on it to engrave in Greek, and in your own letters, this prohibition,— That no foreigner should go beyond that wall? Have not we given you leave to kill such as go beyond it, though he were a Roman?"' (Josephus, *Wars*. vi. ii. 4).

Riots over this and similar things were a constant source of anxiety to the Roman Governor. Under Cumanus, who preceded Felix, there had been a riot which had resulted in the death of a thousand Jews. And so we read in Acts 21:

> 'All the city was moved, and the people ran together: and they took Paul, and drew him out of the temple' (Acts 21:30).

The tumult had by this time attracted the attention of the authorities, and the Temple guard immediately closed the great gate that secured the inner shrine from profanation. They then closed the other three gates, or, as Acts 21:30 puts it: 'and forthwith the doors were shut'.

Paul was now outside the sacred enclosure, and the mob was therefore free to shed his blood without defiling the Temple. From their stations on the roof of the cloisters, however, the Roman guard had seen what was going on, and tidings were conveyed to the Captain 'that all Jerusalem was in an uproar'. The Captain evidently did not underestimate the violence of the people, for we read that he 'took soldiers and centurions', which means that several hundred soldiers were employed, and ran down the steps connecting the castle with the court. And 'when they saw the Chief Captain and the soldiers, they left beating of Paul'. Paul is now immediately bound with 'two chains', that is, he is handcuffed to two soldiers, one on either side of him, and the Captain seeks to discover the cause of the tumult, asking him 'who he *was,* and what he had *done'*.

As the uproar continues, however, the Captain orders him to be removed to the castle. Fearing that they may lose their prey, the mob now rush for the stairs, and their violence is so great that the soldiers are obliged to 'carry' the apostle. Paul is now under arrest *without warrant.*

According to Septimus Buss there were three kinds of custody under Roman law.

(1) *Custodia Publica*, when the prisoner was committed to gaol, as in the case of Paul and Silas at Philippi.

(2) *Custodia Libera*, when the accused was placed under surveillance either in his own house, or in the house of a magistrate, who became responsible (*sponsor*) for his production in court on the day of trial, and gave a legal promise for that purpose.

(3) *Custodia Militaris*, when the accused were given in charge to a guard of soldiers.

Lysias, the Captain, is surprised when Paul addresses him in good Greek, for he evidently thought he had captured an Egyptian who had led over 4,000 assassins into the wilderness. A second riot threatens to follow the apostle's speech from the stairs, and so the prisoner is taken into the castle, and examined. Lysias now commands that Paul shall be scourged as a means of extracting a confession from him, but while he is being bound and 'bent forward' (*proteinan*), he quietly says to the Centurion:

> 'Is it lawful for you to scourge a man that is a *Roman*, and *uncondemned*?' (Acts 22:25).

To apply the *flagellum horribile* at the very outset was in itself illegal: and much more so in the case of a Roman citizen. And so we read:

> 'When the centurion heard that, he went and told the chief captain, saying, Take heed what thou doest: for this man is a Roman' (Acts 22:26).

Lysias had first of all mistaken Paul for an Egyptian, and now, learning that he claimed to be a Roman citizen, he hurries back to make sure, saying:

> 'Tell me, art thou a Roman? He said, Yea. And the chief captain answered, With a great sum obtained I this freedom. And Paul said, But I was free born. Then straightway they departed from him which should have examined him: and the chief captain also was afraid, after he knew that he was a Roman, and because he had bound him' (Acts 22:27-29).

Lysias could not retain the prisoner in custody without some charge being laid against him, and so we read:

> 'He loosed him from his bands, and commanded the chief priests and all their council to appear, and brought Paul down, and set him before them' (Acts 22:30).

At this meeting, the difference of opinion between the Sadducees and the Pharisees was so strong, that Paul once again has to be rescued from their violence by the Roman soldiers. When Lysias hears of the conspiracy against the apostle's life, he determines to send him 'safe to Felix'. Accordingly he calls out two hundred soldiers, seventy horsemen, and two hundred spearmen, and bids them be ready by nine o'clock at night for the start to Caesarea. The number of soldiers decided upon to escort one man a distance of sixty miles, is eloquent testimony to the turbulent character of the people. The letter which Lysias sent to Felix follows the usual form, but skilfully covers up his error. It implies that Paul was rescued from the Jews *after* Lysias had learned that he was a Roman.

Closely allied with the subject just considered is that of Roman citizenship. To this subject, therefore, we now devote our attention.

(2) CIVIS ROMANUS SUM

Paul and Roman Citizenship

The Jew regarded the world as made up of 'the circumcision' and 'the uncircumcision' — his own were the 'favoured nation', and the rest of the world 'Gentile dogs'. The Greek, on the other hand, divided the world up into 'Greeks' and 'barbarians' (Rom. 1:14), while the Roman viewed it as being composed of freemen and slaves. A 'freeman' in the Roman sense might either be *civis* (a Roman citizen), or *peregrinus* (a foreigner, though free). A 'freeman' could either be *born free* or could *become free.*

In contrast with the position of the 'freeman' the slave was devoid of all rights of liberty, citizenship and position in a family. *Nullum habet caput.* Up to A.D. 61, a slave could be ordered to fight in the arena with gladiators or wild beasts, and until the time of Claudius, his master could punish him with death at will. There was one well-known case of Vedius Pollio, in the reign of Augustus, who cast his slave into the ponds to feed his lampreys. The only penalty Pollio suffered was the loss of his fish ponds.

A slave who committed murder was punished with great severity, and we read that 400 slaves were executed to avenge the murder of Pedanius Secundus. Torture by whip or fetters was also inflicted for the slightest offences, and most of the large Roman houses contained an *ergastulum*, or private prison, where the slaves worked in chains.

A slave could become free by the process of 'manumission'. The actual form of this enactment has come down to us from Delphi and reads as follows:

> 'Date. Apollo, the Pythian *bought* from Sositus of Amphia, for freedom, a female slave, whose name is Nicæa, by race a Roman, *with a price* of three and a half minæ of silver. Former seller according to law: Eumnastus of Amphissa. The price he hath received. The purchase, however, Nicala hath committed unto Apollo, for freedom'.

The reader will not fail to see the parallel here with the apostle's words, 'bought with a price', and the literal rendering of Galatians 5:1 'for freedom did Christ set us free'.

In numerous records of manumission the enfranchised person is said to be allowed henceforth to 'do the things that he will', an obvious parallel with Galatians 5:17. Moreover, many manumission orders contain the clause that the freed person shall never 'be made a slave again', a phrase which finds an echo in such passages as Galatians 5:1 and 1 Corinthians 7:23.

The 'freeman' (*liber*) might be born free (*ingenuus*), or he might be made free (*libertinus*). In the first case (*ingenuus*) he could either be a citizen (*civis*) or a *latinus* — i.e. one occupying a position intermediate between that of the true-born Roman (*civis*) and the foreigner (*peregrinus*).

The privileges of the full citizen were as follows:

POLITICAL RIGHTS

(1) The right of voting in the *comitia* (*Jus Suffragii*).

(2) Eligibility for all public offices and magistracies (*Jus Honorum*).

(3) The *Jus Provocationis*, or right of appeal.

CIVIL RIGHTS

(1) *Conubium*, the power to contract a legal marriage, with power of life and death over the family.

(2) *Commercium*, the right to acquire, hold or transfer property, and to make contracts.

The apostle himself was a full Roman citizen *(ingenuus*, or 'free born'), for his father had been a citizen before him. We do not know how Paul's father had acquired this coveted privilege, but it was so ordered, in the wisdom of God, in order that His messenger to the Roman world should be fully equipped. He was a Tarsian, 'a citizen of no mean city'; he was also a Roman, a Jew, a Pharisee and one trusted by the Sanhedrin.

'How often', says Cicero, 'has this exclamation *Civis Romanus sum* ("I am a Roman citizen") brought aid and safety even among Barbarians in the remotest parts of the earth' (*Cic. Verr. v.* 57). The reader will remember how scared the Philippians were when they discovered that Paul and Silas were Roman citizens (Acts 16:37-39). They had probably heard of the punishment in A.D. 44 of the inhabitants of Rhodes, whom Claudius had deprived of their freedom for putting a Roman citizen to death.

The trial of the apostle before Nero demands some space here, and the following notes may be of help. The Roman courts required the personal presence of the prosecutor. The crown was not the prosecutor, as in English law. We learn from Josephus that at about this same time two embassies set out from Jerusalem for Rome, one, to impeach Felix for his conduct while Governor (we remember how, upon his recall, he sought to placate the Jews by leaving Paul bound, Acts 24:27), the other, to intercede with Nero on the subject of Agrippa's palace, which overlooked the Temple. As the High Priest himself was included in this latter embassy, he may also have been entrusted with the prosecution of Paul.

'The law's delays' are no modern evil. Josephus tells us of three Jews who had languished in prison for three years without a hearing, and who were finally released upon his appeal to Poppaea. It was Nero's custom to consider separately each charge against a prisoner (*Suet,*

Nero, 15), and in the case of Paul we have seen that there were three counts against him. A further source of delay was that proceedings would be adjourned from time to time to suit the Emperor's convenience. Eusebius, in his *Ecclesiastical History is* the only authority that we have for the opinion that Paul was tried on the occasion of this first imprisonment, for the Acts does not record the trial. Eusebius says:

> 'After defending himself successfully, it is currently reported that the apostle again went forth to preach the gospel, and afterwards came to Rome a second time'.

The apostle's statement in Philippians 1:12-14,25 and 2:23,24 suggests that a trial is nearing its end, and that the result is a foregone certainty. Tiberius and Claudius followed the ancient custom of hearing causes in the Forum, but Nero sat for this purpose in his palace. Standing before the tribunal, the apostle's bonds would become manifest in the whole Prætorium (Phil. 1:13). The preliminaries of the trial had already taken place under Felix and Festus, the prisoner being therefore already in a state of accusation. The termination of the proceedings was announced by a crier proclaiming '*dixerunt*' (they have spoken). The jury then voted by depositing in an urn, wax tablets bearing the letter A for *absolvo, C, condemno* or N.L., *non liquet* (a new trial).

At his second arrest Paul did not receive the humane treatment that characterized the first. He now suffered as an 'evil doer'. His place of detention is no longer the house of a friend or his own hired house, but a dungeon, so damp and cold that he asks Timothy to bring with him, when he comes, his cloak that had been left behind at Troas.

The trial fell into two parts, for he speaks of his 'first defence' (2 Tim. 4:16). Evidently he had been remanded; the presiding judge having pronounced the word *amplius*, an adjournment had taken place, and the apostle seized the opportunity to write his last letter to his beloved son Timothy. Hatred of the Christians now ruled men's minds, and a charge of treason, from which there would be no hope of acquittal, would be laid against the apostle.

Somewhere outside the city walls, along the *Via Ostiensis*, where now stands the church of *San Paolo fuori le mura*, the apostle was led forth from his dungeon to execution. In the days of the Republic this would have been effected by the lictor's axe, but under Nero, it was accomplished by the sword. It is not for us to follow the traditions of men as to what became of Paul's body after his death. He had finished his course, he had kept the faith, he was assured that there awaited him 'at that day' a crown. We can rejoice that what seemed most like defeat, was victory. He was 'more than conqueror' through Christ Who loved him.

(3) PAUL THE ZEALOT

The apostle has referred to his early days, how that he was a Pharisee, and a zealot for the traditions of his fathers, and these terms should be understood if we are to possess a true portrait of this apostle of grace. His entry into the pages of Scripture is not at his conversion but at the stoning of Stephen.

The infuriated Jews who stoned Stephen for his faithfulness found a champion for their traditions in the young man, Saul of Tarsus:

> 'The witnesses laid down their clothes at a young man's feet, whose name was Saul. And they stoned Stephen ... And Saul was consenting unto his death' (Acts 7:58 to 8:1).

What sort of man was this who would consent to the death of such a saint? The secret of his blind cruelty was 'a zeal for God, but not according to knowledge'. Many of the Pharisees knew that Jesus was the Christ. They had said, 'this is the heir, come, let us kill him'. Paul, however, tells us that what he did, he did 'ignorantly and in unbelief ' (1 Tim. 1:13).

To the English reader, separated by centuries from the period of the Gospels, the term 'Pharisee' has taken upon itself a colouring more or less traditional. All Pharisees were not alike, however, even as all Scribes or all Priests were not alike in their zeal or character. The Talmud tells us of seven classes of Pharisees. It speaks of the *Shechemite* Pharisee, who obeyed for self-interest; the *tumbling* Pharisee (*nifki*), who paraded humility; the *bleeding* Pharisee (*kinai*), who, rather than risk outraging his modesty by seeing a woman, risked a broken skull by walking with his eyes shut; the *mortar* Pharisee (*medukia*), who covered his eyes, as with mortar, for similar reasons; the *timid* Pharisee, who was actuated by motives of fear; the *tell-me-another-duty-and-I-will-do-it* Pharisee; and the seventh class, the *Pharisee from love.* Saul of Tarsus was of the sixth order enumerated above, for in Galatians 1:14 we read:

> 'I was going ahead (a metaphor taken from a ship at sea), in Judaism above many of my contemporaries in mine own nation, being more vehemently a zealot for the traditions handed down from my fathers'.

The choice of the word *zelotes* confirms this. The *Zelotai* were a sect which professed great attachment to the Jewish institutions, and undertook to punish, without trial, those guilty of violating them. It was this bigoted or fanatical temper which moved the young man Saul to associate with the murderers of Stephen, and to personally conduct a campaign, with the idea of exterminating the heresy of the Nazarenes. Such was the character of the 'chosen vessel' who was destined, by grace, to shake traditionalism and legalism to their fall, and to stand alone with God, preaching 'the faith which once he destroyed' (Gal. 1:23).

To stay here, however, would be but to give a one-sided view of the character of Saul of Tarsus. Writing by inspiration of God, in the full light of his acceptance in the Beloved, he says concerning his past, 'touching the righteousness which is in the law, *blameless*' (Phil. 3:6).

According to the teaching of the rabbis, there were 248 commands and 365 prohibitions of the Mosaic Law, which formed part of the 'hedge of the law'. These laws and prohibitions, without exception, in letter as well as spirit, and with the almost infinite number of inferences which were deduced from such laws, were to be obeyed. The belief was current that if only one person could attain unto this perfection for but one day, the Messiah would come, and the glory of Israel be ensured. This hope then, together with a nature which must spend and be spent upon that to which for the time being the possessor is attached, was the force which actuated Saul of Tarsus, and through him breathed out threatenings and slaughter.

In eight separate passages does Scripture refer to the terrible persecutions with which Saul of Tarsus was prominently associated. It is written, 'he made *havoc* of the church' (Acts 8:3). The word used here is that used in the LXX of Psalm 80:13 of the uprooting by wild boars. He dragged men and women to judgment and prison; he *devastated* in Jerusalem those that called upon the name of Jesus. In the epistle to the Galatians the apostle tells us how he persecuted the early saints beyond measure (Gal. 1:13). To the Corinthians (1 Cor. 15:9) and to the Philippians (Phil. 3:6), he recounts with sorrow how he *persecuted the church.* To the day of his death he never forgot that grace which had changed a blasphemer, a persecutor, and an injurious bigot (1 Tim. 1:13), the very chief of sinners, into the chiefest of the apostles. Truly, he 'persecuted this way *unto the death*' (Acts 22:4).

How fully he was permitted to enter into the sufferings and afflictions of the faith the Scriptures amply testify. Alone, forsaken by all earthly friends, he was permitted to drain to the dregs the bitter cup of religious persecution. Stoned and left for dead, beaten with rods on five occasions by the order of some ruler of the synagogue, imprisoned, betrayed, suffering the anguish of hunger, thirst, nakedness, shipwreck, and finally martyrdom, he fulfilled the opening words of his commission, 'I will shew him how great things he must *suffer* for My Name's sake' (Acts 9:16).

As Saul of Tarsus, or Paul the apostle, this man was not content to do things half-heartedly. His zeal for the time at least stamped out the activity of the heresy of the Nazarene in Jerusalem, but from other cities news arrived that this pernicious weed had taken root. Unsatiated by the blood of the saints shed in Jerusalem, he desired to vindicate his Pharisaic claims by up-rooting the Christian faith in the distant city of Damascus. Armed with the necessary warrant from the high priest, the persecutor started upon his journey of 150 miles in a frame of mind expressed in the unparalleled term, 'breathing out threatenings and slaughter'. How long the journey took we do not know; but taking the nature of the roads, the climate, and the Eastern method of travelling, authorities have estimated that it occupied the better part of a week.

What were the thoughts of this man during this week's travel? Nothing is recorded in the Scriptures to tell us, except the words of the Searcher of the hearts, 'It is hard for thee to kick against the pricks' (or ox goads). Saul, during that fateful journey, had been 'kicking against the goads', as the rebellious oxen do in the plough. The whirl of the city, the excitement of the persecutions and scourgings gave place to the isolated meditation of the Damascus journey. The ox goads against which Saul had kicked were of a similar nature, though perhaps of much deeper intensity, than those which many believers and readers of this little witness have had, when faced with the claims of dispensational truth, and balanced by the opinions of men, and liability of being 'put out of the synagogue'.

Could it be possible that such men as Peter and Stephen were right, and he with the whole Sanhedrin were wrong? Pride rose against such a thought; those who spoke against the law and the temple must certainly be accursed. Thus would he reason; he could not give expression to these ideas to those with him, for that would be suicidal. Did the angel face of Stephen haunt his steps along the road? We know not. Was Gamaliel, his teacher, right in even suggesting that such action as his *might* prove to be fighting against God? We cannot tell. What we do know is this. Spurred on by the goads of an uneasy conscience, Saul urged his followers to abandon the wonted noon-day rest and press on to the city of their desires.

Then, suddenly, the persecutor was changed into the preacher, the infuriated bigot into the apostle of grace. A light, which eclipsed the noon-day sun, as the gospel did the traditions so tenaciously held by Saul, shone about them. He was struck to the earth; something awful had happened. One man alone knew its solemn meaning and intelligently heard the words from heaven; into the darkened heart of Saul of Tarsus had entered 'the light of the knowledge of the glory of God, in the face of Jesus Christ'. God had revealed His Son in him. That was the turning-point of his life, for he had seen the Lord.

After the blinding flash of heavenly light there came a Voice from heaven speaking in the Hebrew tongue, saying, 'Saul, Saul, why persecutest thou Me, it is hard for thee to kick against the goads!' In answer to the trembling cry, 'Who art Thou, Lord?' the Voice replied, 'I am *Jesus of Nazareth*, whom thou persecutest'. Oh wondrous revelation! Had the Voice said, 'It is Israel's Messiah you are persecuting', the apostle would have denied the charge, but in the revelation from the heavenly glory that he was persecuting 'Jesus of Nazareth', and that He indeed was the Lord, the Messiah of Israel, all his hopes, his pride, his tenacious hold upon the traditions of the elders, his self-righteousness and meritorious zeal, vanished and left him naked and destitute.

What are the first words which Saul as a believer shall utter? They form a keynote to his after life, 'Lord, what wilt *Thou* have me to do?' From henceforth he served the Lord Christ; from this time onward for him to live was Christ. He had fallen to the earth a proud, persecuting fanatic; he rose a humble and gracious follower of Christ. How different to what he had dreamed was his actual entry into Damascus and departure therefrom. No longer breathing threatenings and slaughter, but breathing prayers and supplications, for it is written, 'Behold he prayeth!' Not leaving the city with the trophies of his inquisition and the applause of the orthodox, but let out of the city by stealth, in a basket from the wall! After the darkness and the visit of Ananias came the light, for 'there fell from his eyes as it had been scales'. Something of the character of this apostle can be gleaned from the following extract of an able writer:

> 'It was, throughout life, Paul's unhappy fate to kindle the most virulent animosities, because, though conciliatory and courteous by temperament, he yet carried into his arguments that intensity and downrightness that awakens dormant opposition. A languid controversialist will always meet with a languid tolerance, but any controversialist whose honest belief in his own doctrines makes him terribly in earnest, may count on a life embittered by the anger of those on whom he has forced the disagreeable task of reconsidering their own assumptions ... . Out of their own Scriptures, by their own methods of exegesis, in their own style of dialectics, by the interpretation of prophecies of which they did not dispute the validity, he simply confounded them. He could now apply the same principles which in the mouth of Stephen he had found it impossible to resist'.

(4) THE SELF-DRAWN PORTRAIT OF THE APOSTLE PAUL

The Portrait as a Whole

Most students of Scripture have at some time or other used Conybeare and Howson's *Life and Epistles of St. Paul.* In the introduction to Vol. I, there occurs one of the longest sentences to be met with in ordinary literature — a sentence containing more than 500 words.

The introduction opens as follows:

'The purpose of this work is to give a living picture of St. Paul himself, and of the circumstances by which he was surrounded'.

Later on in the introduction we read:

'We must listen to his words, if we would learn to know him ... In his case it is not too much to say that his letters are himself — a portrait painted by his own hand, of which every feature may be 'known and read of all men'.

'Here we see that fearless independence with which he 'withstood Peter to the face' — that impetuosity which breaks out in his apostrophe to the 'foolish Galatians' — that earnest indignation which bids his converts 'beware of dogs', 'beware of the concision' and pours itself forth in the emphatic 'God forbid' which meets every Antinomian suggestion — that fervid patriotism which makes him 'wish that he were himself accursed from Christ for his brethren, his kinsmen according to the flesh, who are Israelites' — that generosity which looked for no other reward than 'to preach the Glad Tidings of Christ without charge' and made him feel that he would rather 'die than that any man should make this glorying void' — that dread of officious interference which led him to shrink from 'building on another man's foundation' — that delicacy which shows itself in his appeal to Philemon, whom he might have commanded, 'yet for love's sake rather beseeching him, being such an one as Paul the aged, and now also a prisoner of Jesus Christ' and which is even more striking in some of his farewell greetings as (for instance) when he bids the Romans salute Rufus, and '*his mother who also is mine*' — that scrupulous fear of evil appearance which 'would not eat any man's bread for nought, but wrought with labour and travail night and day, that he might not be chargeable to any of them' — that refined courtesy which cannot bring itself to blame till it has first praised, and which makes him deem it needful almost to apologize for the freedom of giving advice to those who were not personally known to him; — that self-denying love which 'will eat no flesh while the world standeth, lest he make his brother to offend' — that impatience of exclusive formalism with which he overwhelms the Judaizers of Galatia, joined with a forbearance so gentle for the innocent weakness of scrupulous consciences — that grief for the sins of others, which moved him to tears when he spoke of the enemies of the cross of Christ — 'of whom I tell you even weeping'

— that noble freedom from jealousy with which he speaks of those who, out of rivalry to himself, preach Christ even of envy and strife, supposing to add affliction to his bonds; 'What then? notwithstanding, every way, whether in pretence or in truth, Christ is preached; and I therein do rejoice, yea, and will rejoice' — that tender friendship which watches over the health of Timothy, even with a mother's care — that intense sympathy in the joys and sorrows of his converts, which could say, even to the rebellious Corinthians, 'Ye are in our hearts, to die and live with you' — that longing desire for the intercourse of affection, and that sense of loneliness when it was withheld, which perhaps is the most touching feature of all, because it approaches most nearly to a weakness, 'When I had come to Troas to preach the Glad Tidings of Christ, and a door was opened to me in the Lord, I had no rest in my spirit, because I found not Titus, my brother; but I parted from them, and came from thence to Macedonia'. And 'when I was come into Macedonia, my flesh had no rest, but I was troubled on every side; without were fightings, within were fears. But God, Who comforts them that are cast down, comforted me by the coming of Titus'. 'Do thy utmost to come to me speedily, for Demas hath forsaken me, having loved this present world, and is departed to Thessalonica; Crescens to Galatia, Titus to Dalmatia; only Luke is with me'.

Under the heading, 'The Self-drawn Portrait of the Apostle Paul', a series of fourteen studies ran through *The Berean Expositor*, in Volumes 31 to 34, a series too bulky to reproduce here; all that we can do is to draw the reader's attention to the series, in the hope that where fuller light upon the apostle's character is sought, those articles may make their contribution.

We conclude with a few opinions of Paul culled from modern writers. 'He is difficult to comprehend, not because he conceals himself, but because he reveals so much of himself in his epistles'... Deissmann (*St. Paul* 62 ff). Deissmann notes his ailing body and his tremendous powers for work, his humility and his self-confidence, in periods of depression and of intoxication with victory, his tenderness and his sternness: he was ardently loved, and furiously hated; he was an ancient man of his time, but he is cosmopolitan and modern enough for today. Findlay adds that he was a man possessed of dialectical power and religious inspiration. He was keenly intellectual and profoundly mystical (cf. Campbell, *Paul the Mystic*, 1907). He was a theologian and a man of affairs. He was a man of vision with a supreme task to which he held himself. He was a scholar, a sage, a statesman, a seer, a saint (Garvie, *Studies in Paul and his Gospel*, 68-84). He was a man of heart, of passion, of imagination, of sensibility, of will, of courage, of sincerity, of vivacity, of subtlety, of humour, of adroitness, of tact, of genius for organization, of power for command, of gift of expression, of leadership — 'all these qualities and powers went to the making of Jesus Christ's apostle to the nations, the master builder of the universal church and of Christian theology'. (Findlay, H. D. B., see *St. Paul the Master Builder*, 1905; and M. Jones, *St. Paul the Orator*, 1910). Extract from *International Standard Bible Encyclopædia.*

Speaking of Paul's Gospel the same article says:

> 'He insisted strongly on the spiritual experience of Christ as the beginning and the end of it all, as opposed to mere ritualistic ceremonies which had destroyed the life of Judaism. But all the more Paul demanded the proof of life as opposed to mere profession. (See Romans 6 to 8 in particular). Mystic as Paul was ... he was the rarest of moralists, and had no patience with hypocrites and licentious pietists or idealists who allowed sentimentalism and emotionalism to take the place of righteousness'.

The underlying truth expressed by the poet in the lines:

> 'What do they know of England
> Who only England know?'

leads us to realize that we shall not have a true portrait of the apostle unless we include some of his friends and fellow workers. He valued and stressed fellowship in service, and such as Ananias, Barnabas, Silas, Timothy,

Luke, Aquila and Priscilla, show by their concern, their friendship, their loyalty and their endurance, aspects of the apostle's character that would not otherwise be appreciated. Eight articles under the title, PAUL AND HIS COMPANIONS, will be found in *An Alphabetical Analysis* Part 10, and in *The Berean Expositor* Vol. 26, to which the reader is directed. The limitations of space make it impossible to reproduce them here, but the reader may appreciate the closing article, as a sample of the rest.

(5) PAUL AND HIS COMPANIONS, AQUILA AND PRISCILLA, or 'GREATER LOVE HATH NO MAN THAN THIS'

Some of the apostle's companions were definitely called by the Holy Spirit and acknowledged by the Church, as was Barnabas (Acts 13:2,3). Some possessed qualifications which practically forced them into the breach that opened before them, as Silas (Acts 15:26, 27,32,40). In the case of Aquila and Priscilla two very different and remote causes worked together for their good, for the apostle's consolation and our lasting benefit. These were the edict of a Roman Emperor, and the teaching of the Talmud.

> 'After these things Paul departed from Athens, and came to Corinth; and found a certain Jew named Aquila, born in Pontus, lately come from Italy, with his wife Priscilla; (because that Claudius had commanded all Jews to depart from Rome:) and came unto them' (Acts 18:1,2).

Suetonius, a Latin historian, says that Claudius expelled the Jews from Rome because of the tumults among them stirred up by one, *Chrestus*. Whether *Chrestus* was the actual name of some disturber of the peace, or, as some believe, an ignorant misreading of the name Christ, cannot now be determined. We know that there were pious Jews from Rome who heard Peter's message on the day of Pentecost, just as there were Jews from Pontus, the birthplace of Aquila. Whatever the fact may be, one result of this edict was the migration of Aquila to Corinth, and there the apostle found him. There is nothing in the narrative to suggest that Paul was acquainted with Aquila and sought him out. The narrative rather suggests that he looked for suitable shelter in the Jewish quarter of Corinth, and that he was guided by the Lord unknown to himself. However, the narrative continues:

> 'And because he was of the same craft, he abode with them, and wrought: for by their occupation they were tentmakers' (Acts 18:3).

A harmful affectation sometimes assumed by those having a literary bent, or who pose as scholars, is to boast of their uselessness in manual work and their inability to distinguish between a chisel and a screwdriver! Paul needed no such pretension to bolster up his dignity. He was as great, while stitching his tents, as when he wrote Ephesians, for in both he was doing the will of the Lord. It is written in the Talmud:

> 'What is commanded of a father towards his son? To circumcise him, to teach him the law, to teach him a trade'.

Gamaliel said:

> 'He that hath a trade in his hand, to what is he like? He is like a vineyard that is fenced'.

There are several references by Paul in his writings to the fact that he supported himself by his own manual labour. He did so at Ephesus (Acts 20:34), at Corinth (1 Cor. 9:12; 2 Cor. 7:2), and Thessalonica (1 Thess. 2:9; 2 Thess. 3:8), and no doubt these are but typical instances of his habit.

Because *cilicium*, a hair cloth, was in common use at the time, it has been assumed that the tents made by Aquila and Paul must of necessity have been of goats' hair. Chrysostom, however, who was born at Antioch, and died in A.D. 407, says on this subject:

> 'St. Paul, after working miracles, stood in his workshop at Corinth, and stitched hides of leather together with his own hands, and the angels regarded him with love, and the devils with fear'.

We find that after maintaining a witness at Corinth, extending over a period of eighteen months, Paul set sail for Syria, Priscilla and Aquila accompanying him. On the journey they touched at Ephesus, and there Paul parted from Aquila for a time (Acts 18:18-28). It was at Ephesus that these two companions of Paul did such splendid service in that they took Apollos with them and expounded unto him the way of God more perfectly. The apostle mentions these companions in three epistles:

> 'Greet Prisca (R.V.) and Aquila my helpers in Christ Jesus: who have for my life laid down their own necks: unto whom not only I give thanks, but also all the churches of the Gentiles. Likewise greet the church that is in their house' (Rom. 16:3-5).

The R.V. here rightly reads 'Prisca', as does the A.V. in 2 Timothy 4:19. The form of the name is probably an affectionate diminutive, and the use of it opens for a moment a door into the private life and homely affections of the great apostle. The genuineness and reality of the apostle's character was such that he had no need as we say, 'to stand on his dignity' and could indulge in a little playfulness without detracting from the solemnity of his message.

With regard to the passage quoted from Romans 16 it is written: 'Greater love hath no man than this, that a man lay down his life for his friends' (John 15:13). So Aquila and Priscilla had shown the apostle the highest quality of love this world affords. How? where? and precisely what? were all the circumstances which brought out this manifestation of love we do not know. The narrative of the Acts abounds with accounts of riots, plots and murderous attacks upon the apostle, and at least on one of these dangerous occasions the intervention of this homely couple saved the life of the apostle, for which it may truly be said, not Paul only, but the churches of the Gentiles ever since, give thanks.

Aquila and Priscilla join the apostle in sending salutations to the Church at Corinth, and it is noticeable that while they have evidently removed from one city to another, they still have a church in their house (1 Cor. 16:19). The faithful fellowship and affectionate nearness of these companions of Paul continued to the end. 'Salute

Prisca and Aquila', wrote the apostle on the eve of his martyrdom. At last he was to lay down his neck for the truth he held dearer than life itself, and he cannot forget those whose love was instrumental, under God, in enabling him to finish his course. Apart from the important instance recorded in Acts 18 in connection with Apollos, we do not associate Aquila or Priscilla so much with teaching as with that equally important ministry of hospitality and loving service, even unto death. What a sanctifying of life for man and wife and home, thus to be consecrated to the Lord! On every hand there are indications that before this dispensation ends the 'church' will once more be in 'the house' of such believers. What glory may be awaiting some readers of these lines!

May the Lord use the message to accomplish His purposes of grace and prepare His Aquilas and His Priscillas for service in these closing days.

(6) PAUL – AN HEBREW OF THE HEBREWS

Paul was a Hebrew of the Hebrews. He spoke Greek. He was a Roman citizen. In his writings we find that he draws upon these three sources for his analogies and types. The following list does not pretend to be exhaustive, but it is a fair sample.

Hebrew	**Greek**	**Latin**
Circumcision	Adoption	Sign, seal, earnest
Mercy Seat	Spectacle	Adoption
Tabernacle	Offer to idols	Slave
Potter and clay	Race, Prize, Crown	Liberty
Trap	Mirror	Olive culture
Redemption	Bema	Weapons
Passover	Ambassador	Armour
Leaven	Letter of commendation	Cross
Muzzle ox	Athlete	Prisoner
Trumpet	Spoil	Clothing
Firstfruits	Rudiments	Triumph
Veil	Under-rower	Citizenship
Tree	Pattern	Garrison
Middle Wall	Vessel	Soldier
Sweet smell	Parousia	Farmer
Offered	Church	
Dogs	Deposit	
Earnest		

PAUL THE PRISONER. A note on an objection.

A serious and reverent examination of the teaching that Acts 28:28 is the Dispensational Boundary, has included in its objections two terms, used in Acts 28:30 and 31, which it is incumbent upon us to examine.

> 'The direct evidence of Scripture indicates that Paul was neither in prison nor in bonds during the time covered by Acts 28:30,31'.
>
> 'The first objection is based upon the words "his own hired house", the second on the words, "no man forbidding him"'.

There is 'direct evidence' that Paul *was* a prisoner when he reached Rome. 'I was delivered prisoner from Jerusalem into the hands of the Romans ... I was constrained to appeal unto Cæsar ... for the hope of Israel I am bound with this chain' (Acts 28:17-20). While Paul was in *this* condition, he received a deputation of Jews to his 'lodging'.

What difference we may well ask is there between a 'lodging' and 'an hired house'? Is it outside the realm of possibility that Acts 28:23 and 30 are two ways of speaking of the same place?

How is it possible to argue that Paul could be a prisoner and bound with a chain in his 'lodging', but that he must, of necessity be conceived of as being free, if he receives visitors in his own 'hired house'? The lodging *xenia*, means a place for the accommodation of strangers, and *xenizo* is used in Acts 28:7 where we read that Paul was 'lodged' for three days courteously. If an 'hired house' makes prison impossible then most certainly Paul was never a prisoner in Rome at all! But if a Roman prisoner could have a 'lodging' then he could also have an 'hired house', the two passages stand or fall together. It will be observed in Acts 28:16 that:

> 'Paul was suffered to dwell by himself *with a soldier* that kept him',

'which' Lewin comments 'indicates a private residence; and accordingly *after this*, mention is made of the *xenia* (verse 23), and again of *idion misthoma*, which express only what had before been less precisely expressed'. Further there is no 'house' mentioned, but merely a suite of apartments, see Wetstein on Acts 28:30. It will be seen that the attempt to 'prove' from the words, 'in his own hired house' that Paul was no longer a prisoner is invalid; it proves too much, for it would exclude the 'lodging' and the dwelling by himself (Acts 28:16,23) as well.

The second ground of objection is the word translated 'no man forbidding him', the Greek *akolutos*. It is amazing that a writer, who in the examination of the Greek terms used, shows much acumen and industry, should have *passed over* the way in which this term 'unhindered' is used.

The following extract from ACTS 28, DISPENSATIONAL BOUNDARY[1], will show that 'unhindered' has no bearing upon whether Paul was or was not a prisoner at the time, but that it indicates that with the dismissal of Israel, the hindrance offered by that people to the preaching to the Gentiles had ceased.

> 'Acts 28 ends with the apostle dwelling for two years in his own hired house preaching and teaching, "no man forbidding him"'.
>
> 'During Paul's early ministry, the Jew had consistently opposed the preaching of the gospel to the Gentiles, and this, said the apostle, was their climax sin.
>
> 'They "killed the Lord Jesus" but forgiveness was given and a new opportunity to believe and repent was granted. They had earlier "killed their own prophets" and had more recently "persecuted" the apostle and his helpers "forbidding us to speak to the Gentiles that they might be saved", reaching however a climax "TO FILL UP their sins alway: for the wrath is come upon them to the uttermost" (1 Thess. 2:15,16).
>
> '"To the bitter end", reads Moffatt. "In its severest form", reads Weymouth. The same word "forbidding" found in 1 Thessalonians 2:16 is the word used of Paul, "no man forbidding him". Israel the opposer had gone. They had filled up their measure of sin to the brim, and the very Gentiles that they had 'forbidden' now entered into blessings hitherto unrevealed" (See THREE SPHERES OF BLESSING[5])'.

To which we add:

Peter's ministry in the Acts concluded with the words 'forbidding' and 'withstand' both translations of the Greek word *koluo* (Acts 10:47; 11:17). Paul's ministry concludes with the words, 'no man forbidding' (Acts 28:31) where the Greek word is *akolutos*. Peter maintained this attitude up to the tenth chapter of the Acts, he would have 'forbidden' both Cornelius and God, for the word "withstand" in Acts 11:17 is *koluo*'.

The upshot of this work at Cæsarea was that even Peter was called upon to give an account of himself.

> 'The apostles and brethren that were in Judæa heard that the Gentiles had also received the word of God. And when Peter was come up to Jerusalem, they that were of the circumcision contended with him, saying, Thou wentest in to men uncircumcised, and *didst eat with them*' (Acts 11:1-3).

We find no remonstrance from Peter to the effect that seeing that the Church began at Pentecost, the conversion of Cornelius should have been anticipated and be a matter for rejoicing. No; Peter patiently, and humbly, and apologizingly, rehearsed the matter, even to the pathetic conclusion: 'What was I, that I could *withstand God*?'

Why should Peter ever think of withstanding God, if he knew that the Church began at Pentecost? It is abundantly evident that neither Peter, the other apostles, nor the brethren at Jerusalem had the remotest idea of any such thing.

> 'When they heard these things, they held their peace, and glorified God, saying, THEN HATH GOD ALSO to the Gentiles granted repentance unto life' (Acts 11:18).

Neither the 'hired house' nor the word 'unforbidden' can have the slightest bearing, one way or another, as to whether Paul was, or was not, at the time of Acts 28:28, 'the prisoner of the Lord for us (you) Gentiles'.

THE PRISON EPISTLES

STRUCTURE SHOWING THEIR DISTINCTIVE DOCTRINES AND THEIR INTER-RELATION

		Key Words*
A	EPHESIANS Seated together	The dispensation (3:2 and 9 R.V.). Mystery (3:3). The church which is His body (1:22,23). The fulness (1:23; 4:10). Christ the Head (1:22). Principalities and powers (1:21).
		Key Words
B	PHILIPPIANS The Prize	Try the things that differ (1:10 margin). Strive (1:27). Press toward the mark (3:14). Prize (3:14). *Depart*# (1:23). *Offered*# (2:17).
C	PHILEMON	The Truth in practice.
		Key Words*
A	COLOSSIANS Complete in Him	Dispensation (1:25). Mystery (1:26). The church which is His body (1:24). Fulness (1:19). Christ the Head (2:19). Principalities and powers (1:16; 2:10).
		Key Words
B	2 TIMOTHY The Crown	Rightly dividing the Word (2:15). Strive (2:5). Course finished (4:7). Crown (4:8). *Depart*# (4:6). *Offered*# (4:6).

PENTECOST

The relationship of Pentecost to the Acts as a whole, and the relationship of Pentecostal Gifts to dispensational teaching, are considered in articles entitled ACTS OF THE APOSTLES[1]; ANOINTING[1]; BODY[1]; CONFIRMATION[1]; CORNELIUS[1]; HEALING[2]; and MIRACLES (p. 46). In this article we deal with:

(1) The typical place of Pentecost (Acts 2:14 to 8:1).

(2) Pentecost Explained — 'this is that' (Acts 2:14-40).

(3) Millennial Foreshadowings (Acts 2:41-47).

---

* None of these expressions occur in Philippians or 2 Timothy.

\# Only occurrences in Paul's epistles.

With Peter's address (Acts 2:14) we commence a new section of the Acts, the structure of which is shown as follows:

Ministry of PETER and others to nation of Israel in Jerusalem and in the land (2:14 to 8:1)

A_1 2:14-47.	PENTECOST EXPLAINED	Wonders and signs in heaven and earth. David's testimony. Christ the King. All things common. Possessions sold. The Lord added those that were being saved (R.V.).
B_1 3:1 to 4:22.	PENTECOST SYMBOLIZED	The miracle of healing. The gate called 'Beautiful'. Moses a type of Christ. Prison for Peter. We cannot but speak. Threatened: let go.
A_2 4:23 to 5:11.	PENTECOST REPEATED	Signs and wonders. David's testimony. The kings of the earth rebel. Place shaken. Filled with holy spirit. All things common. Possessions sold 'part of price kept back'. Great fear on the church.
B_2 5:12-42.	PENTECOST WITHSTOOD	Miracles of healing. Solomon's Porch. Prison for Peter. We ought to obey God rather than men. Beaten: Let go.
A_3 6:1-7.	PENTECOST EXTENDED	The ministry of the deacons; 'Full of Holy Spirit'.
B_3 6:8 to 8:1.	PENTECOST REJECTED	Moses a type of Christ. Stephen stoned. The introduction of Saul strikes the first note in Israel's rejection.

Let us now return to Peter's explanation of what the happenings on the day of Pentecost really meant. Here we are at a disadvantage, for most of us who know anything at all about Pentecost have received that knowledge through tradition. We were sure that it was a feast of the Church; we were convinced that on the day of Pentecost the Church was brought into being; we were positive that there were gathered together on that day a multitude of both Jews and Gentiles who, by having all things in common, gave expression to the truth of the One Body and its fellowship. Yet all these fondly held views vanish in the light of actual truth, for Acts 2 knows nothing of a feast of the Church; it knows nothing of the unity in which there is neither Greek nor Jew; it gives no countenance to the idea that a single Gentile, other than a proselyte, listened to Peter on that momentous day:

> 'But Peter, standing up with the eleven, lifted up his voice, and said...' (Acts 2:14).

We draw attention to the peculiar word used here for 'said' (*apophtheggomai*), which also occurs in Acts 2:4 in the phrase, 'as the Spirit gave them *utterance*'. We are to understand by this that Peter's explanation of the meaning of Pentecost was that it was an exercise of that recently conferred power from on high. We have elsewhere referred to the fact that nearly every important act and word both of Peter and of Paul is echoed later in the Acts. The word *apophtheggomai* occurs but once more, namely in Acts 26:25, this time in the record of Paul's defence before Agrippa. It is suggestive that Peter rebuts a charge of 'drunkenness' in Acts 2:14,15, and Paul rebuts a charge of having become 'mad' through much learning in Acts 26.

Pentecost was a season of rejoicing:

> 'Seven weeks shalt thou number unto thee: begin to number the seven weeks from such time as thou beginnest to put the sickle to the corn. And thou shalt keep the feast of weeks unto the LORD thy God with a tribute of a freewill offering of thine hand, which thou shalt give unto the LORD thy God, according as the LORD thy God hath blessed thee: and thou shalt rejoice before the LORD thy God, thou, and thy son, and thy daughter, and thy manservant, and thy

maidservant, and the Levite that is within thy gates, and the stranger, and the fatherless, and the widow, that are among you, in the place which the LORD thy God hath chosen to place His name there' (Deut. 16:9-11).

The reader may remember that the first epistle to the Corinthians keeps count of several of Israel's feasts:

PASSOVER — 'For even Christ our Passover is sacrificed for us' (1 Cor. 5:7).
'The cup of blessing' (1 Cor. 10:16).

UNLEAVENED BREAD — 'Therefore let us keep the feast, not with old leaven, neither with the leaven of malice and wickedness; but with the unleavened bread of sincerity and truth' (1 Cor. 5:8).

FIRSTFRUITS — 'But now is Christ risen from the dead, and become the firstfruits of them that slept' (1 Cor. 15:20).

PENTECOST — 'I will tarry at Ephesus until Pentecost' (1 Cor. 16:8).

The passage in the Law that best sets out the feasts of the Lord and the place of Pentecost is Leviticus 23. The passage is too long for quotation here, but the following outline will help to keep the whole festal year before the reader. While the length of Israel's year was the same as our own, there are only seven months noted in the calendar of their feasts. These feasts are prophetic, and set forth in type and shadow the whole course of Israel's history from the day that they became a nation (Exod. 12:2) until the great future day of ingathering at the time of the end. The fact that the Lord has used seven months only in which to show this typical unfolding is but further evidence that the number seven is intimately associated with the purpose of the ages. The fact that creation occupied six days, followed by a Sabbath of rest, indicates that at the very beginning, God had this 'rest' in view (Heb. 4:9).

To save space we will, without comment or detail, briefly indicate this close association of seven with Israel's typical history:

Seven DAYS — 'The seventh day is the sabbath of rest' (Lev. 23:3).
Seven WEEKS — 'Seven sabbaths shall be complete' (Lev. 23:15).
Seven MONTHS — 'In the seventh month' (Lev. 23:24).
Seven YEARS — 'The seventh year shall be a sabbath of rest' (Lev. 25:4).
Seven times seven YEARS — 'It shall be a jubilee unto you' (Lev. 25:8-10).
Seventy times seven YEARS — 'Seventy weeks are determined' (Dan. 9:24).

At once we realize that Pentecost cannot be understood if it be taken out of its place in this series of typical periods. To attempt to fit Pentecost into the 'Church' of the Mystery destroys both the typical character of the feast, and the distinctive character of that 'Church'.

The feasts of the Lord, then, in Leviticus 23 are as follows:

A REDEMPTION BY BLOOD **a** 5. PASSOVER.
b 6-8. UNLEAVENED BREAD. Seven days. Egypt.

B REAPING **c** 9-14. FIRSTFRUITS.
d 15-21. PENTECOST. } anticipatory.
c 22. HARVEST.
d 22-25. *TRUMPETS.* } final.

A ATONEMENT BY BLOOD *a* 27-32. DAY OF ATONEMENT.
b 34-44. TABERNACLES. Seven days. Egypt.

The Lord knew that Israel would not repent and be gathered the first time, and that the purpose of the ages would reach out to the trumpets of the Apocalypse and the harvest at the end of the age. Nevertheless the feast of Pentecost was an *anticipation* of harvest, just as firstfruits was, and the gathering of Israel to Jerusalem at this period was an *anticipation* of that great gathering at the time of the end.

A peculiar feature of Pentecost is that a *new* meal offering was commanded:

> 'Ye shall bring out of your habitations two wave loaves of two tenth deals: they shall be of fine flour; they shall be baken with leaven; they are the firstfruits unto the LORD' (Lev. 23:17).

It had already been commanded that 'no meal offering, which ye shall bring unto the LORD, shall be made *with leaven;* for ye shall burn no leaven, nor any honey, in any offering of the LORD made by fire' (Lev. 2:11). The two leavened loaves of Pentecost cannot therefore typify Christ: they are a firstfruits, and typify His people. The reason why two loaves were specified appears to be that the Lord knew that the kingdom would be divided, and that at the restoration the ten tribes and the two tribes (commonly spoken of as Israel and Judah) would come together again as one before Him. Ezekiel 37:15-28 sets this forth under the figure of the two sticks: 'I will make them one nation ... they shall be no more two' (Ezek. 37:22).

The appointment of Matthias to complete the number of *the twelve*, and the gathering of Jews from *twelve* of the nations round about, are therefore features that are living and harmonious when Pentecost is seen in the light of God's purpose to gather Israel again and restore the kingdom. But their import is lost when Pentecost is misinterpreted as of the inception of the 'Church', and, indeed, those who most strongly advocate the doctrine that the 'Church' began at Pentecost have among them those who do not hesitate to call the appointment of Matthias an 'apostolic mistake!'

What digressions have been necessary before reaching Peter's explanation of Pentecost! Had every reader as much knowledge of the teaching of the Old Testament as Peter and the gathered multitudes, we could have gone straight on to his inspired explanation, but, as it is, we should not have appreciated his reference to Joel if we were not in possession of facts which to that assembled multitude were a matter of everyday knowledge. These we have now considered and have therefore done what we could to bring back the atmosphere of the original

Pentecost. This accomplished we will proceed in our exposition.

Pentecost explained: 'This is that' (Acts 2:14-40)

Peter, when he stood up to explain the meaning of Pentecost to the assembled multitude, lifted up his voice and said:

> 'Ye men of *Judæa*, and all ye that dwell at Jerusalem' (Acts 2:14).
>
> 'Ye men of *Israel* ... among you ... in the midst of you' (Acts 2:22).
>
> 'Therefore let all the house of *Israel* know assuredly' (Acts 2:36).
>
> 'The promise is unto *you*, and to your children, and to all that are afar off, even as many as the Lord our God shall call' (Acts 2:39).

'Men of Judæa', 'the Jews who dwelt at Jerusalem' (Acts 2:5), 'Israel', and then, together, 'the whole house of Israel', are those to whom Peter addressed his words. Peter's own recorded act and word given in Acts 10:28, and the attitude of the apostles and brethren that were in Judaea (Acts 11:18), together with the exclusiveness of Acts 11:19 are sufficient to prove that the presence of a Gentile at this feast of Israel would have been intolerable, while the attitude of the Jews as recorded in Acts 21:26-36 shows what is likely to have happened had Gentiles been present at this feast of Pentecost. The nations of the earth shall, one day, go up to Jerusalem to keep the Feast of Tabernacles as Zechariah 14:16-19 reveals, but that event awaits the time when the Lord descends and His feet once more touch the Mount of Olives.

If, as most will admit, the 'Church' cannot be imported into Joel, then that alone should, if we still hold it, shake our faith in the tradition that the Church began at Pentecost. We trust the reader will honour the Holy Spirit at this point, and, leaving these comments of men, turn to the short prophecy of Joel and read it through. Seven minutes is all the time it will occupy. Upon reading the book through, two verses stand out, namely Joel 1:4 and 2:25:

> 'That which the palmerworm hath left hath the locust eaten; and that which the locust hath left hath the cankerworm eaten; and that which the cankerworm hath left hath the caterpillar eaten'.
>
> 'I will restore to you the years that the locust hath eaten, the cankerworm, and the caterpillar, and the palmerworm, my great army which I sent among you'.

'I will restore' are words that find their echo in the question of the apostles: 'Wilt thou restore?' (Acts 1:6), and in the testimony of Peter as to 'the times of restoration' (Acts 3:21 R.V.). Repentance is essential. 'Rend your heart and not your garments and turn unto the LORD your God' (Joel 2:13), and the resulting blessing is not only likened to the restoration of the land from plague and famine, but to the restoring of Israel's access and acceptable worship under the figure of new wine, and drink offering (Joel 1:13; 2:14; 3:18). Prominent also is the 'great and terrible day of the Lord', a prophetic period of no uncertain value, the object of much Old Testament prophecy, and certainly having no connection with the 'Church'. The following outline may help the reader:

Joel

A **a**	1:7.	New wine cut off.
b	1:8-13.	Israel 's harvest spoiled.
B	1:14 to 2:14.	Israel a desolation.
C	2:15-20.	The gathering of Israel.
D	2:21 to 3:1.	I will restore.
C	3:2.	The gathering of the nations.
D	3:2-8.	I will plead.
A *b*	3:9-17.	Gentile harvest.
a	3:18.	New wine restored.
B	3:19-21.	Egypt and Edom a desolation.

The whole prophecy deals with *the* nation and the *nations*. It looks to the Day of the Lord, and has no room for, or reference to, a church in which there is neither Greek nor Jew.

The quotation from Joel made by Peter is divided into two parts. The first was actually fulfilled on the day of Pentecost; the second would have followed had Israel repented. They did not repent, and consequently the signs in heaven await the day of the Lord, with which the book of the Revelation is prophetically concerned. What should intervene between the two parts of Joel's prophecy it was not part of Peter's ministry to explain. He confessed later, when writing to the same dispersion, that they would find help regarding this interval in the writings of Paul (2 Pet. 3:15,16).

We must now indicate the relation of the two parts of Joel's prophecy, quoted by Peter, showing the present interval. This, of course, was not mentioned by Peter, for the times and the seasons which the Father had put in His own power had not been revealed to him. We, too, only know that a new dispensation fills the gap, because Paul, the prisoner of Jesus Christ, has made known the dispensation of the Mystery.

A I will POUR out of My Spirit:

(1) Upon all flesh (2) Sons (3) Daughters (4) Old Men (5) Young Men (6) Servants (7) Handmaids.	The last days. Seven-fold beginning at Pentecost. 'The powers of the age to come'.

B Present interval — Israel not repentant.

B Future Day — Israel repent and look upon Him Whom they pierced.

A I will SHOW wonders:

(1) Heavens (2) Earth (3) Blood (4) Fire (5) Pillars of smoke (6) Sun (7) Moon.	Seven-fold conclusion. Wonders, as spoken of in the Apocalypse, and Isaiah 13:9,10.

It is essential also to the theme that we notice the statement of verse 30:

> 'Therefore being a prophet, and knowing that God had sworn with an oath to him, that of the fruit of his loins, according to the flesh, He would raise up Christ to sit on his throne ...'.

Although to stay here breaks the statement of the apostle, we pause to draw attention to the pertinent fact that Pentecost, instead of speaking of Christ as the Head of the Church, focuses attention upon His right to the throne of David. What possible meaning, other than a literal one, can be given to this passage or to the Psalm that is quoted? If Pentecost sets forth Christ as King in connection with the throne of David, in what way can it be connected with the Church?

Continuing our quotation at verse 33 we read:

> 'Therefore being by the right hand of God exalted, and having received of the Father the promise of the Holy Spirit, He hath shed forth this, which ye now see and hear'.

'*He hath shed forth* THIS': 'THIS *is that*'. Peter is still maintaining his theme. He is still explaining Pentecost; it is the evidence that Christ is King and that the kingdom will one day be restored. Further proof is given by quoting from Psalm 110. David's son is David's Lord (Matt. 22:41-46). The Lord is now there at the right hand of God 'from henceforth expecting' (Heb. 10:13). The heaven must receive Him until the restoration (Acts 3:21). The first thing that Peter commanded his awakened hearers to do was to 'repent'. In this he was continuing the ministry of John the Baptist (Matt. 3:2) and of the Lord (Matt. 4:17). As shown above, the interval between the two prophecies of Joel is a consequence of Israel's non-repentance. (See also LAST DAYS[8]).

Baptism for the remission of sins is not 'church' truth. Not a single passage in any one of Paul's epistles can be found to countenance such teaching. How can we therefore speak of 'continuing stedfastly in the apostles' doctrine' when the very first principles of that doctrine are set aside? The 'untoward generation' (Acts 2:40) is but another description given to 'that wicked and adulterous generation' (Matt. 16:4) to which no sign, but the sign of the prophet Jonah, was to be given. Here that sign is evident. The apostles were witnesses of His resurrection; the signs and wonders were witnesses of His resurrection;

Pentecost was a witness that 'Jesus of Nazareth, a Man approved of God', 'This Jesus', 'That same Jesus', This Son, yet Lord, of David, was 'Lord and Christ'. The day of the Lord was His day. The name of the Lord upon which they called, was His name, the miracle of the next chapter enforcing the fact that 'there is none other name under heaven given among men, whereby we must be saved' (Acts 4:12).

What were the immediate results of Peter's ministry on that day of Pentecost? Three thousand souls were added to the company of believers, and they that believed were together and had all things in common. Gladness and singleness of heart characterized this favoured company, who were not only pleasing to God, but in 'favour with all the people'. It will not do to pass over this section without examination, for in it, in germ, is the goal of Pentecost, and here we shall find a forecast of that future day when not 3,000 only, but all Israel shall be saved.

Acts 2:41-47

A 41. **a** Glad reception of Word, baptism.
  b 3,000 souls added.
  B 42. **c** Stedfast continuance in apostles' doctrine.
    d Fellowship, breaking of bread, prayers.
    C 43. **e** Fear, wonders, signs.
    C 44,45. ***e*** All things common.
  B 46. ***c*** Continuing daily in the temple.
    d Breaking bread from house to house.
A 46,47. ***a*** Gladness, singleness, praise.
  b Saved ones added.

What was the apostles' doctrine in which the believers continued stedfastly? It could not have been that marvellous system of truth with which we associate the epistle to the Romans, written by the, as yet, unconverted Saul. Justification by faith is unrecorded in the testimony of Peter. The term, reconciliation, finds no place in the Ministry of the Circumcision. When we reflect that Peter and the other apostles had only just received power from on high, it is foolish to imagine that there existed some great system of doctrine that could be subscribed to, as though it were a creed. All that could be meant by the 'apostles' doctrine', or teaching, is the witness that had been given concerning the resurrection of Christ, His Lordship, His Kingship, His Coming and the need on the part of the believer to be ready. The breaking of bread has been interpreted as of the Lord's Supper, but this is pure assumption:

> 'Breaking bread from house to house, did eat their meat with gladness' (Acts 2:46),

shows that the term simply meant taking a meal. The same expression is used in the following passage relating to the shipwreck, where Paul exhorts those on board to take food for their 'health':

> 'And when he had thus spoken, he took bread, and gave thanks to God in presence of them all: and when he had broken it, he began to eat' (Acts 27:35).

Without their contexts, we might believe that Acts 20:7 and Luke 24:35 related to the partaking of the Lord's Supper, yet the contexts preclude such a belief. The development known later as 'the breaking of bread' is but one of the traditions of the elders.

> 'And fear came upon every soul: and many wonders and signs were done by the apostles. And all that believed ... had all things common; and sold their possessions and goods, and parted them to all men, as every man had need' (Acts 2:43-45).

In these few lines we have compressed that which is expanded in Acts 3,4 and 5. In those chapters is recorded the prophetically significant miracle of healing, and the equally significant miracle of judgment that caused 'great fear' to come upon all the Church. There is also a fuller statement concerning the having of things in common in Acts 4:32-37, which compels us to ask whether the selling of possessions and community of goods was not a real part of the meaning and purpose of Pentecost. There have been companies of believers, who, taking Pentecost as their basis, have sought consistently to follow out its practice, but the having of all things in common does not seem to have captured their minds in the same way as has the gift of tongues. Yet how can one speak of 'continuing in the apostles' doctrine *and* fellowship', without realizing that this *koinonia* (fellowship) refers to and is expressed by the having of all things in common (*eichon hapanta koina*)?

Turning to Acts 4:32-37, we observe that there is a re-statement of this 'fellowship' and as in Acts 2:24-46, so here, the account of this new state of affairs is punctuated by reference to the witness of the apostles to the resurrection of the Lord. The reader will see that verse 33 of Acts 4 is, as it were, slipped in and breaks the flow of the narrative. This, however, is as intentional as the equally strange insertion found in Acts 1:15. The resurrection of the Lord, as testified by the apostles, was intimately associated with the restoration of the kingdom to Israel, and to the time of the restoration of all things which had been spoken by the prophets. No Jew would need to be told, that just as the feast of Pentecost with its emphasis upon the word 'fifty' was a recurring, annual reminder of the day of Jubilee, so the final prophetic fulfilment of all that Pentecost stood for would be the real, great Jubilee toward which all prophecy pointed. Believing, therefore, the 'apostles' doctrine', these believers put their faith into practice. If the Jubilee was near, all would receive their own inheritance, all forfeitures would be cancelled, all buying and selling of land and possessions would come to nought; consequently, although no one could sell or buy his inheritance, he could sell whatever else he had purchased, and use the proceeds for the common good, while awaiting the Lord from heaven. The case of Barnabas is specially mentioned. He was a Levite, and 'having land, sold it, and brought the money and laid it at the apostles' feet' (Acts 4:37). In Jeremiah 32:6-14 we have the case of Jeremiah (who, like Barnabas, was of the priestly tribe). He *bought* land to demonstrate his faith in the Lord's promised restoration (Jer. 32:15), and Barnabas *sold* land to demonstrate the same conviction.

The law that governed the sale of land is found in Leviticus 25. The voluntary act of Barnabas in selling his acquired land and placing the proceeds at the apostles' feet is in direct contrast with the action of Ananias. He, too, sold a possession; he, too, laid the proceeds at the apostles' feet, but with the difference that he kept back part of the price, while pretending that he had given all. The apostle makes it quite clear that there was no compulsion about the selling of the land when he says, 'while it remained, was it not thine own? and after it was sold, was it not in thine own power?' Ananias sinned in that he lied to the Holy Spirit. The sin of Ananias was the sin of Achan. The reader will find that the very words used of Achan in Joshua 7:1 are used of Ananias. The LXX reads *enosphisanto apo tou anathematos*, 'appropriated for themselves a part of that which was devoted'. Acts 5:2,3, twice applies this particular expression to Ananias and Sapphira: '*kai enosphisato apo tes times*', 'and kept back part of the price'. This is no place to discuss the passage in Joshua, but the interested reader is urged to weigh over the arguments contained in the article on 'Achan, the troubler of Israel' *The Berean Expositor*, Vol. 26, pp. 37-41, which show that the word, 'accursed thing', should be understood as 'a devoted thing', i.e. devoted to the Lord. Peter and the apostles stood somewhat in the same position as did Joshua, and wielded the same awful discipline.

Pentecost anticipates the Millennium; the gifts are called 'the powers of the world to come' (Heb. 6:5), and so the summary judgment of the day of the Lord is seen to be in operation during the early days of the Acts:

> 'He that worketh deceit shall not dwell within My house: he that telleth lies shall not tarry in My sight. Morning by morning will I destroy all the wicked of the land; that I may cut off all wicked doers from the city of the LORD' (Psa. 101:7,8).

Millennial characteristics are also seen in Acts 4:23-26, where the opposition of the rulers to the ministry of the apostles is regarded as a partial fulfilment of the last times:

> 'And being let go, they went to their own company, and reported all that the chief priests and elders had said unto them. And when they heard that, they lifted up their voice to God with one accord, and said, Lord, Thou art God, which hast made heaven, and earth, and the sea, and all that in them is: Who by the mouth of Thy servant David hast said, Why did the heathen rage, and the people imagine vain things? The kings of the earth stood up, and the rulers were gathered together against the Lord, and against His Christ' (Acts 4:23-26).

The language of the passage clearly shows the minds of the apostles fully occupied with millennial expectation.

Such is the setting and dispensational significance of Pentecost.

PEOPLE. Of the thirteen words translated 'people', one Hebrew, and one Greek are of importance in the teaching of Dispensational Truth. *Am* in the Hebrew and *laos* in the Greek. The word *am* occurs in Genesis 11:5,6 and 14:16, but with the third reference, namely in Genesis 17:14, it takes on a distinctive meaning that persists right throughout the Old Testament. Where we read 'people' in Genesis 17:16 it should be translated 'peoples', balancing 'nations', and with one or two notable exceptions the rule holds good that 'people' in the singular refers to Israel, and 'peoples' in the plural to the Gentile nations. The blessing given to Jacob speaks of a multitude of people (Gen. 28:3,4), and this promise is recalled when he blessed Joseph's sons (Gen. 48:3,4). In verse 4 we should note that the word is plural, 'peoples'. In Genesis 49:10 the obedience (not 'gathering', see same word in Proverbs 30:17) of the peoples, refers to 'the obedience of all nations', a 'secret' hushed until the time for its revelation in the days of Paul (Rom. 16:25-27).

Israel do not exist as a 'people' in the book of Genesis, but with the book of Exodus their history as a 'people' begins (Exod. 3:7-10). Over and over again the words, 'My people', are sounded in the ears of Pharaoh. Israel were 'taken to Himself' said God 'for a people', taken by redemption (Exod. 6:7). In Exodus 19:3-7 'peoples' once more refer to the Gentiles. Israel are the 'people' of Exodus 33:3,5,13,16. Balaam speaks of this separated people (Num. 23:9), a people who were to dwell 'alone'. Yet though separated from all other peoples, they had and will have an influence even on the lands that the other nations should inherit (Deut. 32:8). In this book of Deuteronomy, the peculiar blessedness of this people is stressed (Deut. 4:20; 9:29; 32:9). To them had been given the law (Deut. 4:8), they were called 'holy' and 'peculiar' (Deut. 7:6; 14:2,21). They were chosen by sovereign love (Deut. 7:7,8). 'Who is like unto thee,' asked Moses, 'O people saved by the Lord' (Deut. 33:28,29)? What is true in the law, is true also in the Prophets (2 Sam. 7:23,24; Isa. 1:3; 40:1; 42:6; 43:21; Dan. 9:4-21; 12:1 and Hos. 2:21-23). Turning to the New Testament we find that the distinctive character still persists. *Laos* occurs 143 times, and in nine of these occurrences the word is plural. Let us notice these first. Luke 2:31; Acts 4:25,27; Romans 15:11; Revelation 7:9-17; 10:11; 11:9; 17:15 and 21:3. Acts 4:27 presents a difficulty for here the plural refers to Israel. The reason for this departure from the rule is seen when we realize that Israel had *sided with* Herod, Pontius Pilate and the Gentiles. For the rest, every reference to *laos* in the New Testament is a reference to Israel with the following exceptions (Acts 15:14,15). On the assumption that the epistle to Titus was written after Acts 28 when Israel had become *lo-ammi*, 'not My people' the Church is called for *the first time* a 'people' (Tit. 2:14). The earnest student should not rest satisfied with this survey, but should patiently read every reference to 'people' in its context. If this be done, the conviction will grow that the title 'people' in the singular from Genesis 12 and the call of Abraham to Acts 28 upon the rejection temporarily of the Jew, refers to Israel to whom this title strictly applies. This study is not only important for its own sake, but also because it stresses the need for consistency in our use of Scriptural terms.

PERFECTION OR PERDITION

As the epistle to the Hebrews urges its readers to 'go on to perfection', and warns them of the dread alternative of 'drawing back to perdition', so we discover both 'perfection' and the same Greek word that is translated 'perdition' form the alternatives in the third chapter of the epistle to the Philippians.

The words 'perfect', 'perfection' and 'finisher' that occur in Hebrews are the translations of *teleios, teleioo, teleiosis* and *teleiotes*, all derivatives of the root that gives us the word *telos,* 'end'. The idea of the word 'perfect' here, is not so much 'improvement' as the taking anything to its *complete end.* The root TEL enters into a number of words that have been brought over from the Greek, as TELescope, TELephone, TELegram and TELevision. In each case something at a distance is in view. The idea of 'perfection' in Scripture is that of 'running a race', of 'finishing' a course, of reaching an 'end'.

Let us commence with this basic word *telos.*

> 'Whose house are we, if we hold fast the confidence and the rejoicing of the hope firm *unto the end*' (Heb. 3:6).
> 'For we are made partakers of Christ, if we hold the beginning of our confidence stedfast *unto the end*' (Heb. 3:14).
> 'And we desire that every one of you do shew the same diligence to the full assurance of hope *unto the end*' (Heb. 6:11).

In Philippians the word *telos* occurs but once, and echoes the usage of the word in Hebrews 6:8 :

> 'But that which beareth thorns and briars is rejected, and is nigh unto cursing; *whose end is to be burned*'.
> 'Whose *end is destruction*, whose god is their belly, and whose glory is in their shame, who mind earthly things' (Phil. 3:19).

We shall have to return to these two references presently, but at the moment only seek to show that the word 'perfect' has in view an end, disregarding, for the present, what that end may be.

In Hebrews 5:14 we read that 'strong meat belongeth to them that are of full age' *(teleios,* 'perfect'), 'even those who by reason of use have their senses exercised to discern both good and evil'. The epistle to the Philippians uses this same word when it says, 'Let us, therefore, as many as be perfect, be thus minded' (Phil. 3:15).

In Philippians 3:12 we have the one occurrence of *teleioo* in that epistle: 'Not as though I had already attained, either were already perfect, but I follow after, if that I may apprehend that for which also I am apprehended of Christ Jesus'. This same word occurs nine times in Hebrews.

(1) *It is used of Christ Himself.* '*To make* the Captain of their salvation *perfect* through sufferings' (Heb. 2:10).
'And being *made perfect,* He became the Author of eternal salvation' (Heb. 5:9).
'The Son, Who *is consecrated* for evermore' (Heb. 7:28).

(2) *It is used of His finished work.* 'For by one offering *He hath perfected for ever* them that are sanctified' (Heb. 10:14).

(3) *It is used of the believer.* 'That they without us should not be *made perfect*' (Heb. 11:40). 'But ye are come unto mount Sion ... to the spirits of just men *made perfect*' (Heb. 12:22-23).

(4) It *is used of the Law* which made no man *perfect* (Heb. 7:19; 9:9; 10:1).

To this list should be added 'The Finisher', *teleiotes* (Heb. 12:2) in connection (a) with running a race and (b) associated with Hebrews 2:10 where the word 'Captain' is the translation of the same Greek word that is rendered 'Author', and so by the use of these two words, 'Author' and 'Finisher', emphasizing the double idea of beginning and end.

Over against the idea of 'going on' (Heb. 6:1) the apostle places the idea of 'drawing back' (Heb. 10:39), the one to 'perfection' the other to 'perdition'. The *Oxford Dictionary* says of 'perdition', that theologically, it means 'the condition of final damnation; the fate of those in hell, eternal death'. Now, those addressed in Hebrews 10 are believers, who had endured much, but were losing patience, and were exhorted to 'cast not away therefore your confidence, which hath great recompense of reward' (Heb. 10:32-37). The loss of possible reward is entirely in line with both the teaching of Hebrews, and the epistle to the Philippians, but the possibility that any redeemed child of God could draw back to 'final damnation' is entirely opposed to the whole teaching of the Scriptures.

Turning to Philippians, where the same word occurs and is translated 'destruction', we again perceive that it is impossible to believe that the Philippians needed a warning not to imitate those who were on the road to 'final damnation'. In Philippians 3 the apostle is not dealing either with salvation or damnation, but with attaining or losing 'the prize of the high calling'. In Matthew 26:8 we find the word which is translated both 'perdition' and 'destruction' employed naturally, without the taint of theological prejudice. It is employed by the disciples when they said 'to what purpose is this *waste*?' The unfruitful field is 'nigh unto' cursing, truly, but not actually cursed. Its end is to be burned, but such burning, while it destroys the crop of weeds, leaves the earth free even as the believer whose 'works' may be burned up in that day, will himself be saved, *yet so as by fire*.

These two words, 'perfection' and 'perdition', are further enforced and illustrated by the figure of a race, a contest and a prize, figures that fit the main purpose of these two epistles, but which are foreign to the message of the Ephesian epistle.

The Race

> 'Wherefore seeing we also are compassed about with so great a cloud of witnesses, let us lay aside every weight, and the sin which doth so easily beset us, and let us run with patience the race that is set before us' (Heb. 12:1).
>
> 'I press toward the mark' (Phil. 3:14).

The Prize

> '... looking unto Jesus the Author and Finisher of our faith; Who for the joy that was set before Him endured the cross, despising the shame, and is set down at the right hand of the throne of God' (Heb. 12:2).
>
> 'Cast not away therefore your confidence, which hath great recompense of reward' (Heb. 10:35).
>
> 'Esteeming the reproach of Christ greater riches than the treasures in Egypt: for he had respect unto the recompense of the reward' (Heb. 11:26).
>
> 'I press toward the mark for the prize of the high calling of God in Christ Jesus' (Phil. 3:14).

The background of this exhortation is provided by the record of Israel in the wilderness. Of the great number that were redeemed out of Egypt, two only of all who were twenty years old and upward, were counted worthy to enter the land of promise, namely Caleb and Joshua. This historical background supplies the material for Hebrews 3 and 4 and no exposition of this epistle can be acceptable that does not take this background into account.

It is recorded in Numbers 14:4 that Israel said, 'Let us make a captain and let us return into Egypt'. The word there translated 'captain' is rendered in the LXX *archegos*, the very word used in Hebrews 2:10, 'Captain', and in 12:2 'Author', the one related to 'leading many sons to glory', the other to 'running with patience the race', and both as we have already seen, associated with 'perfecting'. 'Finisher' in Hebrews 12:2 is literally 'Perfecter'.

We have further parallels to record between Hebrews and Philippians.

> 'We remember', said the Israelites, 'the fish, which we did eat in Egypt freely' (Num. 11:5).
>
> 'Leaving ... let us go on' (Heb. 6:1).
>
> 'Forgetting those things which are behind' (Phil. 3:13).

It is a true conception of the teaching of Scripture that is expressed in the saying, 'no cross, no crown', and it will be discovered that the 'cross' is referred to in Hebrews and

Philippians in connection with the 'perfecting' and the 'prize', while enmity to the cross is also associated with failure to go on to perfection and attain to the prize.

The Cross

> 'Let us run with patience the race that is set before us, looking unto Jesus the Author and Finisher of our faith; Who for the joy that was set before Him *endured the cross*, despising the shame, and is set down at the right hand of the throne of God' (Heb. 12:1,2).
>
> 'He humbled Himself, and became obedient unto death, *even the death of the cross*. Wherefore God also hath highly exalted Him' (Phil. 2:8,9).

Enemies of the Cross

> 'It is impossible ... if they shall fall away, to renew them again unto repentance; seeing they *crucify* to themselves the Son of God afresh, and put Him to an open shame ... *whose end* is to be burned' (Heb. 6:4-8).
>
> 'For many walk, of whom I have told you often, and now tell you even weeping, that they are the *enemies of the cross* of Christ: *whose end is* destruction' (Phil. 3:18,19).

Here in these references to Race and Prize, to pressing on and to drawing back, to the association of the cross with overcoming we have further links between the themes of Hebrews and Philippians. These links are integral, they are not the mere superficial likeness of words robbed of their contexts, they cannot be ignored or denied without loss and damage to both teacher and those taught.

The pressing on to 'perfection' and the warning of the danger of drawing back unto 'perdition', which we have seen is the central theme of both the epistles to the Philippians and the Hebrews (Phil. 3:12-19; Heb. 6:1; 10:39) borrow from the Greek sports their imagery, and speak of the believer running a race, and pressing on toward a prize.

Now in Philippians this prize is associated with a special resurrection, see THE PRIZE (p. 305), and in Hebrews this is balanced by a 'better' resurrection. Moreover, in both epistles, power for this conflict is derived in a marked manner from the risen Christ and is, moreover, linked with the 'working out' of salvation, which is also a characteristic of both epistles.

The Better Resurrection

> 'Women received their dead raised to life again: and others were tortured, not accepting deliverance; that they might obtain a better resurrection' (Heb. 11:35).

The word 'better' is an irregular comparative of *agathos*, 'good', and cannot be used without comparison. This 'resurrection' which involved 'torture' was even 'better' than that which restored those who had died to their loved ones. It is said of these that they would not accept 'deliverance', the reason given being, 'in order that a better resurrection they might obtain'.

The idea of 'obtaining' does not fit the doctrine of grace in its simple and initial meaning. There is an element of 'chance' (1 Cor. 15:37) or 'may be' (1 Cor. 14:10) in the word, and the five passages that do translate *tugchano* 'obtain', speak of something over and beyond that salvation which is 'the gift' of God.

Let us see for ourselves:

> 'But they which shall be accounted worthy to obtain that world, and the resurrection from the dead ... are equal unto the angels' (Luke 20:35,36).
>
> 'Having therefore obtained help of God, I continue unto this day' (Acts 26:22).
>
> 'But now hath He obtained a more excellent ministry, by how much also He is the Mediator of a better covenant, which was established upon better promises' (Heb. 8:6).
>
> 'That they might obtain a better resurrection' (Heb. 11:35).
>
> 'Therefore I endure all things for the elect's sakes, that they may also obtain *the salvation* which is in Christ Jesus *with eternal glory* ... If we suffer, we shall also reign with Him' (2 Tim. 2:10-12).

In Philippians this 'better resurrection' finds its parallel in what we must call 'the out-resurrection'.

> 'If by any means I may attain unto the out-resurrection, out from among the dead' (Phil. 3:11).

The Greek word employed here is *exanastasis*, not merely *anastasis*. A Pharisee believed in *anastasis nekron*, 'the resurrection of the dead' (Acts 23:6). So did Martha for she said, 'I know that he shall rise again in the resurrection at *the last day*' (John 11:24).

It seems strange, therefore, to read of the very disciples that they questioned with one another 'what the rising from the dead should mean' (Mark 9:10), for it is not reasonable to suppose that what was common to the faith of a Pharisee and even to Martha, was inexplicable to Peter, James and John. The solution of the problem of course lies in the recognition of a new factor, the introduction of the preposition *ek*, *ek nekron anaste.*

We have before us a booklet that analyses the different forms in which resurrection is presented in Scripture. The Out-Resurrection is, however, given short shrift. The presence of the preposition *ek*, instead of leading to the necessary comparison of spiritual things with spiritual and the words which the Holy Ghost uses, is dismissed as of little or no consequence, one solitary example of its use, namely Matthew 7:5, being all that the reader will know unless Berean-like he searches to see.

We are told that:

'No special significance can be attached to this double occurrence of *out* (in Matt. 7:5) except that it makes the statement doubly emphatic. In view of this it is evident that we will be reading too much into Philippians 3:11 if we make it teach a special resurrection of a special company'.

We are amazed to read 'in view of this', namely the doubtful effect of *ek* in Matthew 7:5, when all the time the presence of *ek* in Mark 9:10 is *completely ignored.*

When the apostle used the words, 'if by any means I might attain', *he* certainly would not forget their dread significance, for identical words are found in Acts 27:12, and on that occasion he knew only too well that the attempt ended in ship-wreck. How could he use such a term of the blessed *hope*? How exactly it fitted the added *prize*.

He was not speaking of that resurrection which none can avoid, but a 'better resurrection', one associated with 'perfecting', with 'attaining', with 'apprehending', with salutary diffidence, with the 'prize of the high calling', not the high calling itself. See the close of article, PHILIPPIANS (p. 187) for usage of '*ek*' with resurrection.

The Power of His Resurrection

> 'Now the God of peace, that brought again from the dead our Lord Jesus, that great Shepherd of the sheep, through the blood of the everlasting covenant, make you perfect in every good work to do His will, working in you that which is well-pleasing in His sight, through Jesus Christ' (Heb. 13:20,21).

Here we have two features combined. The resurrection, and the doing of His will. These are found in Philippians:

> 'That I may know Him, and the power of His resurrection, and the fellowship of His sufferings, being made conformable unto His death; if by any means I might attain unto the out-resurrection, that which is out from among the dead' (Phil. 3:10,11).
>
> 'Work out your own salvation with fear and trembling. For it is God which worketh in you both to will and to do of His good pleasure' (Phil. 2:12,13).
>
> 'Bearing His reproach' (Heb. 13:13).

This is in line with the apostle's desire to have 'fellowship with His sufferings', being 'made conformable unto His death'. Not salvation, but those 'better things' that accompany salvation (Heb. 6:9); working out, as God works in; a 'better resurrection' in the shape of a 'prize'; overcoming as did Caleb and Joshua; it is these things that characterize these epistles and unite them together.

The figure of race and prize which both Philippians and Hebrews associate with going on unto perfection, is further emphasized by the 'athletic' terms that are found in both epistles. The 'race' which was set before the Saviour is, in the Greek, *agona* and the word is used by Paul in 2 Timothy 4:7, where he says, 'I have fought a good fight'. So, in Hebrews 10:32, 'great fight of afflictions', which the Hebrew believers had endured, is the translation of the Greek *athlesis*. So, too, the argument that is derived from Hebrews 12:1,2 uses the word *antagonizomai*, 'striving against' sin (Heb. 12:4). Even those who 'subdued' kingdoms (Heb. 11:33) did so in this same spirit of contest, the word translated 'subdue' being *antagonizomai*. When the apostle opened his appeal to the Philippians in chapter 1:27 the word translated 'striving together' which he used is *sunathleo*, a word repeated in Philippians 4:3, 'laboured with'. At the close of this section the apostle refers to the 'conflict', as being the same which they had seen in him, and now heard to be in him, and here he goes back to the word *agona* (Phil. 1:30). None of these words has any place in the epistle to the Ephesians.

This conflict is epitomized and carried to its extreme in the cross of Christ — 'Even the death of the cross' (Phil. 2:8), He 'endured the cross' (Heb. 12:2), and in both epistles the cross is brought in, not to speak of redemption from sin, but as an example in association with conflict and crown.

Closely linked with this theme is the majestic revelation of the Person of Christ, Who was originally in 'the *form* of God' (Phil. 2:6), which is but another aspect of the truth set forth in Hebrews 1:3, where He is shown to be 'the *express* image of His person'. Where Philippians says that, at last, 'every knee shall bow' (Phil. 2:10), Hebrews says, 'Let all the angels of God worship Him' (Heb. 1:6). Where Philippians says 'that Jesus Christ is Lord' (Phil. 2:11), referring to the end, Hebrews says, 'Thou, Lord, in the beginning hast laid the foundation of the earth' (Heb. 1:10). Where, with holy awe, Philippians tells us that 'He made Himself of no reputation' (2:7), Hebrews says, 'He was made a little lower than the angels' (2:7).

The reader will have noticed in these comparisons, that there is a greater height and depth in Philippians than in Hebrews. Where Hebrews is content to say of His humiliation, 'a little lower than the angels', and of His exaltation to the right hand of God, 'being made so much better than the angels' (Heb. 2:9; 1:4), the theme of the Philippian epistle demands a greater sweep. There, He not only was made a little lower than the angels, but He 'took upon Him the form of a slave' (Phil. 2:7). He was not subsequently made 'better than the angels', but will yet be 'highly exalted' so that every knee shall bow and every tongue confess, of things in heaven, in earth and under the earth (Phil. 2:10,11).

Hebrews indeed speaks of the Saviour's 'exaltation', 'made higher than the heavens' (Heb. 7:26 *hupselos*) but Philippians uses the superlative term, *huperupsoo*, 'highly exalted' (Phil. 2:9). All this is in conformity with the higher glory of the calling administered in the Philippian epistle. Hebrews ministers to the heavenly calling of those whose sphere of blessing is the heavenly Jerusalem, whereas Philippians holds out the offer of an added prize to those already 'blessed with all spiritual blessings in heavenly places in Christ' (Eph. 1:3).

When speaking of the heavenly glory that awaited the overcomer, Hebrews says:

> 'For ye had compassion on them that were in bonds, and took joyfully the spoiling of your goods, knowing in yourselves that ye have in heaven a better and an enduring substance' (Heb. 10:34).

Now the word translated 'goods' is *huparxis*, and the word translated 'substance' is *huparcho. So*, when we read of the condescension and self-renunciation of Christ, the word 'being' in the phrase, 'Who being in the form of God' (Phil. 2:6), is *huparcho*. It was something that was His real property, a substance, something of value, that He willingly laid aside. Also, when we read at the close of Philippians 3 (after its references to 'loss' willingly suffered by Paul), of the fellowship of His sufferings in the prospect of the out-resurrection as the prize, we find that the same word *huparcho* is employed when it speaks of 'our citizenship *existing as a fact* in heaven'. In addition to this, we remember that 'perdition' or 'destruction' are alternatives in both chapters, which in view of the 'loss' or 'gain' that is intimated, can be summed up in the language of Matthew 16:

> 'If any man will come after Me, let him deny himself, and take up his cross, and follow Me ... for what is man profited, if he shall gain the whole world, and lose his own soul? ... He shall reward every man according to his works' (Matt. 16:24-27).
>
> 'Let no man beguile you of your reward' (Col. 2:18).

For further items of importance, see BIRTHRIGHT[1]; CROWN[1]; HEBREWS[2]; PHILIPPIANS (p. 187).

PHILEMON. This epistle, written from prison, is part of the group made up of Ephesians, Philippians, Colossians and 2 Timothy, and takes its place in the structure of these epistles as follows:

A Ephesians — Basic truth setting forth the Mystery
    B Philippians — Exhortations to run, the Prize in view
        C Philemon — A letter from Paul, requesting hospitality, etc.
A Colossians — Basic truth, complement to Ephesians
    B 2 Timothy — Exhortations, complement to Philippians.

Philemon is as much a part of all Scripture as Ephesians, but the reason we speak of 'four' Prison Epistles, and not 'five' is because the four contain definite teaching concerning the dispensation of the Mystery and form the basis of our hope and calling, whereas Philemon, precious as it is, does not contribute anything specific that is not set out in fuller measure in the other four epistles.

As this analysis is primarily concerned with Dispensational Truth, we refrain from further or fuller comment, except that every believer should seek grace to emulate the love that breathes through this brief epistle.

PHILIPPIANS

The essential teaching of Philippians can be summarized under the following heads:

(1) Pattern (1:27 to 4:2). In which the examples of Christ Himself (2:6-11) of Paul, Timothy and Epaphroditus (2:12-30; 3:1-14) are exhibited.

(2) Prize (3:14).

(3) Perfecting (3:12).

(4) Prior-Resurrection (3:11).

(5) Pursuit (3:13).

Let us first of all set out the literary structure:

The Structure of the Book as a Whole
(Introversion)

A 1:1,2. *Epistolary* Salutation. Bishops and deacons.
 B 1:3-26. Fellowship in gospel from first day.
  C 1:27 to 2:5. Conversation here. Stand fast. Mind of Christ. Now.
   D 2:6-11. The sevenfold humiliation of Christ. *Example.*
    E 2:12-17. *Exhortation* to work out.
     F 2:17-30. *Example* of Paul, Timothy and Epaphroditus.
    E 3:1-3. *Exhortation* to beware.
   D 3:4-19. The sevenfold loss of Paul. *Example.*
  C 3:20 to 4:10. Conversation there. Stand fast. Body of glory. Then.
 B 4:11-20. Fellowship in beginning of gospel.
A 4:21-23. *Epistolary* Salutation. Cæsar's household.

Fellowship in the Gospel opens and closes the epistle proper (1:3-26; 4:11-20).

The epistle opens very differently from that to the Ephesians, which commences as follows:

> 'Blessed be the God and Father of our Lord Jesus Christ, Who hath blessed us … before the overthrow of the world' (Eph. 1:3,4).

In Philippians the opening words are:

'I thank my God ... for your fellowship in the gospel from the first day until now' (Phil. 1:3-5).

With this thought of active co-operation with the gospel the epistle opens and closes. It is an indication of the trend of the teaching before us; not so much what is ours in Christ, but what we are doing with it. Not so much to look backward, 'before the overthrow of the world', or upward, to the 'spiritual blessings in heavenly places', or forward, 'that in the ages to come He might shew the exceeding riches of His grace in kindness towards us', but a survey of present activities in view of 'the day of Jesus Christ'. There is no trusting to self, however, but confidence that He Who had begun the good work would perfect it until the day of Jesus Christ. While 'fear and trembling' must ever accompany our endeavours to 'work out our own salvation', such a state of mind is not incompatible with a settled confidence in the Lord, or with a peace that passeth all understanding.

The opening theme of the epistle is threefold:

(1) Fellowship and defence of the gospel.
(2) Furtherance of the gospel.
(3) Furtherance of faith.

Each of these three phases is marked with either thanksgiving or prayer, and in each case with 'confidence':

'*Being confident*, that He which hath begun ... will finish' (Phil. 1:6).
'*Waxing confident* by my bonds' (Phil. 1:14).
'*Having this confidence*, I know that I shall abide' (Phil. 1:25).

We now approach a section of the epistle that demands great care in its exposition, and patient examination of the words used so that we do not miss the Spirit's teaching:

> 'For I know that this shall turn to my salvation through your prayer, and the supply of the Spirit of Jesus Christ, according to my earnest expectation and my hope, that in nothing I shall be ashamed, but that with all boldness, as always, so now also Christ shall be magnified in my body, whether it be by life, or by death. For to me to live is Christ, and to die is gain' (Phil. 1:19-21).

The 'salvation' here is not, of course, salvation from sin, but deliverance from prison. The apostle, however, makes it clear that he would not pray for 'deliverance' for its own sake; in fact in the structure his 'departure' is the corresponding member. The one concern of the apostle was the glory of Christ and the blessing of His people; whether that should be accomplished by continuance in this life, or by dying and departing, did not greatly trouble him. One interpretation which is very attractive is that we have here a *chiasmos* (a figure of speech indicating a cross over, in verse 21), which we indicate as follows:

> 'For to me to live is Christ's (gain) and to die is (Christ's) gain'.

In this view the apostle is not thinking of his own gain, but of the furtherance of the gospel, the furtherance and joy of faith, and that whether by life or by death. This interpretation is the one set out in *The Companion Bible* and appeals very much to the renewed heart. To us with our modern depreciation of the doctrine of reward, such an interpretation sounds very satisfying. And yet, if we rule out personal gain from Philippians 1:21, we must face it in chapter 3:8 where the verbal form of the word translated 'gain' is there used in the phrase, 'that I might win Christ', a passage in close connection with the 'prize' of the high calling (Phil. 3:14).

The parallel epistle, Hebrews, certainly does not exhibit any sensitiveness in speaking of reward. Not only is Moses seen acting in faith because he had respect to the recompense of the reward, but the very title of God is there said to be 'The Rewarder' of them that diligently seek Him.

Kerdos, the word translated 'gain' is not so much 'hire' for service as 'gain' acquired by trading (Matt. 16:26; Jas. 4:13; Tit. 1:11). It is impossible to make the words, 'that I may win Christ' mean that Christ may gain something by the apostle's effort. The Greek of Philippians 3:8 reads *hina Christon kerdeso*, and the Greek of 1 Corinthians 9:20 'that I might gain the Jews' reads *hina Ioudaious kerdeso*, the person 'Christ' being exchanged for the person the 'Jews', but otherwise identical.

Writing to another company of believers Paul said:

> 'For what is our hope, or joy, or crown of rejoicing? Are not even ye in the presence of our Lord Jesus Christ at His coming. For ye are our glory and joy' (1 Thess. 2:19,20).

Paul's 'Gain' and the 'Prize' of the high calling run in parallel lines and belong to parallel truths. The statement that Christ shall be 'magnified in my body' has a bearing upon 'the body of humiliation' (vile body) of Philippians 3:21, which we shall observe in its place.

> 'But if I live in the flesh, this is the fruit of my labour: yet what I shall choose I wot not. For I am in a strait betwixt two, having a desire to depart, and to be with Christ; which is far better: nevertheless to abide in the flesh is more needful for you. And having this confidence, I know that I shall abide and continue with you all for your furtherance and joy of faith; that your rejoicing may be more abundant in Jesus Christ for me by my coming to you again' (Phil. 1:22-26).

As the passage stands, it seems that Paul was in some sort of perplexity, not knowing what to choose, 'what I shall choose I wot not'. The word translated 'I wot' is *gnorizo,* and is used by Paul eleven times in the prison epistles. Let us examine the other ten occurrences before we go further.

Gnorizo in the Prison Epistles

'Let your requests *be made known* unto God' (Phil. 4:6).

'*Having made known* unto us the mystery of His will' (Eph. 1:9).

'By revelation He *made known* unto me the mystery' (Eph. 3:3).

'Was not *made known* unto the sons of men' (Eph. 3:5).

'Unto the principalities ... *might be known* (made known, R.V.) by the church' (Eph. 3:10).

'That I may open my mouth boldly, to *make known* the mystery' (Eph. 6:19).

'Tychicus ... shall *make known* to you all things' (Eph. 6:21).

'To whom God would *make known* what is the riches' (Col. 1:27).

'All my state shall Tychicus *declare* unto you' (Col. 4:7).

'They shall *make known* unto you all things' (Col. 4:9).

These are eleven out of twenty-four occurrences. We give a summary of the Authorized Version usage of the word: sixteen times, 'to make known'; four times, 'declare'; once each, 'do to wit', 'certify', 'give to understand' and 'wot'. There is but one meaning for *gnorizo*, and that is 'to make known'. The idea that Paul did not know what to choose is inaccurate; he knew, but he *would not tell.* The sequel shows that, while his own personal desires were in one direction, he had chosen against his wishes for the benefit of others. True modesty, not perplexity, is the cause of his reticence to make known his choice.

What does Paul mean by being 'in a strait'? Was he 'pressed out' of the two possibilities, those of living or dying, by a third, the second coming of Christ, to which the word 'depart' is sometimes made to refer? There is only one thing to do, to make sure of the meaning of the words employed. 'I am in a strait' is a translation of *sunecho,* a word occurring twelve times. Let us see its usage:

'The love of Christ *constraineth us*' (2 Cor. 5:14).

'*Keep* thee *in* on every side' (Luke 19:43).

'Paul was *pressed* in spirit' (Acts 18:5).

'Cried out ... and *stopped* their ears' (Acts 7:57).

'The multitude *throng* Thee' (Luke 8:45).

'The men that *held* Jesus' (Luke 22:63).

'How am I *straitened* till it be accomplished' (Luke 12:50).

'*To be taken with*' (sickness or fever) (Matt. 4:24; Luke 4:38; 8:37).

'*To lie sick* of a fever' (Acts 28:8).

The word does not mean to press *out*, but rather to hold *in*. Following the verb *sunecho* is the preposition 'out', and some have been led astray as to the meaning of the preposition by the ambiguity of the English word 'press'. While *ek* primarily denotes *out*, the translation of the word needs care. Here are some examples, in which 'out' loses all sense of direction — 'out of' — and is correctly translated 'with'.

'They ... bought *with* them the potter's field' (Matt. 27:7).

'Thou shalt love the Lord thy God *with* all thy heart' (Mark 12:30).

'Wearied *with* His journey' (John 4:6).

'Drunk *with* the wine ... *with* the blood of the saints' (Rev. 17:2,6).

Again, *ek* is correctly translated 'by' fifty times, e.g.:

'The tree is known *by* his fruit' (Matt. 12:33).

'*By* the fire ... which issued *out of* their mouths' (Rev. 9:18).

(Here *ek* is rightly translated 'by' and 'out of' in the one verse).

Revelation 8:13 renders *ek*, 'by reason of'; we could not very well translate it: '*Woe* to the inhabitants of the earth *out of* the other voices'. In Philippians 1:23 also, 'by reason of' is the best rendering.

'For I am held in constraint by reason of the two (here follow "the two"), (1) having a desire to depart and be with Christ, which is very far better, but (2) to remain in the flesh is more necessary for you'.

Something very far better for himself is weighed over against something necessary 'for you', and, with the thoughts of verses 12-20 in mind, we know what was the choice. 'Departing' is balanced by 'remaining', and 'with Christ' is answered by 'with you'.

We must now examine the word 'depart', which is the translation of *analuo*. We have two important factors to consider: (1) the usage of the word, and (2) the etymology. The words of Philippians 1:23, 'having a desire to depart', are echoed in 2 Timothy 4:6, where we have the substantive form *analusis*, 'the time of my departure is at hand'. It is beyond argument that in 2 Timothy 4 the apostle refers to his approaching death, and this settles for us the parallel passage in Philippians 1.

Dr. E.W. Bullinger's *Critical Lexicon and Concordance* reads:

> 'ANALUO — To loosen again, set free; *then* to loosen, dissolve or resolve, as matter into its elements (hence Eng. analysis); *then*, to unfasten as *the fastening of a ship*, and thus prepare for departure *(and with the force of ana*, back) to return'.

Schrevelius's Lexicon defines the word thus:

> 'ANALUO — To unloose, free, release, relax, untie, undo; dissolve, destroy; abolish; solve, explain, analyse; weigh anchor, depart, die, return from a feast'.

There is no doubt that the word *analuo* means exactly the same as does our English word *analyse*, to break up a thing into its elements, and so return. The fact that the English word 'return' has a double meaning, has misled some into speaking here of the Second Coming of Christ, but how can the Second Coming of the Lord be His 'analysis'? At this point Luke 12:36 is brought forward, for a hasty reading of this passage has given colour to the idea that *analuo* can refer to the return of Christ. What we must notice is that there are *two* statements, not *one*, in this verse.

> 'When He will return from the wedding;
> That when He cometh and knocketh' (Luke 12:36).

Rotherham has the somewhat strange rendering: 'He may *break up* out of the marriage feast'. This is exactly the same idiomatic use of the word that is with us today, as every schoolboy knows when he 'breaks up' for the holidays.

'I am "in a fix" by reason of the two, namely:

(1) Having a strong desire to the return (dissolution), and to be with Christ, for it were very far better, but

(2) The abiding in the flesh is more needful for you, and having this confidence, I perceive that I shall abide and continue beside you all for your progress and joy of faith' (Phil. 1:23-25).

Among the essential features which are of dispensational importance in this epistle, are 'the Prize of the High Calling' and 'the out-resurrection', these are given a careful examination in articles bearing these titles. The article PERFECTION OR PERDITION (p. 179) also has a great bearing on the theme of Philippians. The parallel between Philippians and Hebrews, exhibited at the close of the article entitled HEBREWS[2] should also be consulted.

When we read of Christ as an 'Example' we can be sure that *salvation is* not in view, but either service or manner of life. Here in Philippians, example is connected with prize.

Patterns in Philippians (1:27 to 4:2).

A 1:27 to 2:4. Stand fast; same love; same soul.

  B 2:5. The MIND OF CHRIST *Now*.

    C 2:6-11. Sevenfold humiliation and consequent exaltation of Christ given as an EXAMPLE.

      D 2:12-30. Philippians 'Wherefore ... work out'.
      Paul 'If I be offered ... I rejoice'.
      Timothy 'He did not seek his own'.
      Epaphroditus 'Nigh unto death in service'.

    C 3:1-14. Sevenfold loss and gain of Paul. Suffering in view of the Prize. Paul bids us note his walk as an EXAMPLE.

  B 3:21. The BODY of His glory *Then*.

A 4:1,2. Stand fast; same mind.

The 'mind' of Christ, exhibited pre-eminently in His wonderful *kenosis* ('He emptied Himself'), and partially seen in the lives of Timothy, Epaphroditus and Paul, is essential to the attaining of the prize, 'The body of His glory'.

Paul's Desire (Phil. 1:21-26)

A 1:21. To me (*emoi*); to live is Christ.
  B 1:22,23. **a** Live in flesh. Fruit.
    b Paul's desire. Not made known (I wot not).
      c Paul's desire. To be with Christ.
  B 1:24,25. *a* Alive in the flesh. Needful for you.
    b Paul's confidence. I know.
      c Paul's continuance. With you all.
A 1:26. By me (*moi*); my presence; glorying in Christ.

To summarize what we have learned concerning certain keywords used here. '*I wot not*'. The word *gnorizo* occurs in the New Testament twenty-four times. Paul uses it eighteen times, and of these eleven are found in the Prison Epistles (Phil. 1:22; 4:6; Eph. 1:9; 3:3,5,10; 6:19,21; Col. 1:27; 4:7,9). One meaning only fits all cases, i.e. 'to make known'. This disposes of the idea that Paul did not know which to choose.

'In a strait' (*sunecho*), Luke 8:45; 12:50; 19:43; 22:63; Acts 7:57. Every passage demands the meaning 'to hold fast', 'to keep in', 'to stop'.

'*Betwixt two*' (*ek*). Sometimes means 'with' (Matt. 27:7; Mark 12:30; John 12:3). Sometimes means 'by' (Matt. 12:33; Titus 3:5; Rev. 9:18). Sometimes means 'by reason of' (Rev. 8:13; 9:2; 18:19).

'*The two*'. They are:

(1) The desire to depart and be with Christ.
(2) The necessity to remain in the flesh.

One would be the apostle's own gain; but the other would benefit the Philippians. He chose the latter, while desiring the former.

'*To depart*' (*analuo*) — gives us 'to analyse' (Luke 12:36).

Rotherham translates, 'break up at the marriage feast' (the schoolboy's 'breaking up' for the holidays). Paul settles his own meaning by repeating himself in 2 Timothy:

Phil. 2:17.	Ready to be *offered.*	2 Tim. 4:6.	About to be *offered.*
Phil. 1:23.	Desiring to *depart.*		Time of my *departure* has come.

The Perfecting (Phil. 3:12)

The Analogy of 'Hebrews'

(1) The Law made nothing perfect (7:19; 9:9; 10:1).
(2) 'Perfect' in contrast with 'babes' (5:13,14).
(3) The Perfecter (10:14; 12:1,2).
(4) The perfecting of Christ (2:10; 5:8,9).
(5) The spirits of perfected righteous ones (12:23; 11:40). (The parallel with Phil. 1 and 3).
(6) Marks of perfection (6:1).
(7) Factors in perfection (2:10; 5:8; 7:28; 10:1,14; 11:40).

The Prior, or Out-Resurrection (Phil. 3:11)

This cannot be the general resurrection of all believers, for Paul says, 'if by any means I might attain' unto it.

The words of the original, in the Critical Texts, are *ten exanastasin ten ek nekron*, 'the OUT resurrection, that which is OUT from the dead'.

Anastaseos nekron the simplest expression of all. Believed by Pharisees (Acts 23:6).

To ek nekron anastenai 'the rising out from the dead' (Mark 9:10). This was something new to the disciples. This new expression gives us such passages as Romans 1:4.

Tes anastaseos tes ek nekron 'the resurrection, that which is out from the dead' (Luke 20:35). This is connected with being 'worthy to attain', and approaches to Philippians 3:11.

Ten exanastasin ten ek nekron 'the out-resurrection, that which is out from dead ones' (Phil. 3:11).

See also PRIZE (The Out-Resurrection, p. 305); HEBREWS[2]; and RESURRECTION[4,7].

PLEROMA

Of all the terms used in dispensational truth, the *Pleroma* by its very nature and meaning is surely one of the most comprehensive. Accordingly, we are setting ourselves *no restrictions on space* in this Analysis, and have introduced into this volume a full-paged illustration. We commend this theme to every lover of the Word, and particularly to those who have the responsibility of teaching others.

The Chart is so mounted that it can be left open for reference while the article is read. (See back of book).

THE PLEROMA

(1) INTRODUCTION AND CHART

THE problem of the ages is the problem of the presence of evil, of the apparent necessity for suffering, yet with a baffled feeling of frustration. Men like Job and Asaph and books like Ecclesiastes, ventilate this feeling, but the consciousness of redeeming love, enables the believer to trust where he cannot trace. The present study is set forth with an intense desire, to borrow the words of Milton 'to justify the ways of God with men', to show that there is a most gracious purpose in process, and that there are indications of that purpose in sufficient clearness to enable the tried believer to say with Job 'when He hath tried me, I shall come forth as gold'.

In the present study, we commence with the primary creation of Genesis 1:1 which is followed by the 'rent' or gap of Genesis 1:2, and conclude with the creation of the new heavens and new earth of Revelation 21, which, according to Peter, is ushered in by a convulsion of nature similar to the condition described as 'without form and void' at the beginning.

By observing the parallel between the word of Ephesians 1:4 and 2 Timothy 1:9 we are able to show that 'the ages' commence with the reconstruction of the earth in Genesis 1:3. What follows is a series of 'fillings' in the persons of men like Adam, Noah, Abraham, and Nebuchadnezzar, with the economies associated with them, but all such are provisional, failing and typical only, and they carry the unfolding purpose on to 'the fulness of time' when 'the Seed should come to Whom the promises were made'. Adam was but a 'filling', he was not 'the fulness', that title belongs only to the Lord Jesus Christ Himself. The only company of the redeemed who are themselves called 'the fulness' is the Church of the Mystery, the church of 'heavenly places', the church which is most closely associated with the seated Christ.

Two words found in Matthew 9:16 must ever be kept together in the course of this study, they are the words 'fulness', and 'fuller'. We shall see presently that God is preparing during the ages, as it were a piece of 'fulled' cloth, so that at last there may be a perfected universe, the 'rent' of Genesis 1:2 healed, and 'God all in all'. Fulling involves several processes, most of them drastic and rigourous.

> 'Clooth that cometh fro the wevying is nought comely to were til it be fulled under foot' (Piers Plowman).

Nitre, soap, the teasel, scouring and bleaching processes at length make the shrunken cloth 'as white as snow' (Mark 9:3). We can say, therefore, concerning the problem of the purpose of the ages 'no fulness without fulling'. We do most earnestly desire that consummation, when the Son of God shall deliver up to the Father a perfected Kingdom with every vestige of the 'rent' of Genesis 1:2 entirely gone. We do most ardently desire to be found in that day, as part of that blessed *pleroma* or fulness, but we must remember that every thread that goes to make the 'filling' will have passed through the 'fuller's' hands, 'fulled under foot' must precede being 'far above all'.

At the end of this volume the reader will find a chart, which endeavours to set forth the way in which the Divine purpose of the Fulness is accomplished. At either end of the chart stand 'the beginning' and 'the end', the black division that immediately follows the former representing the catastrophe of Genesis 1:2, 'without form or void'; the black division that immediately precedes the consummation represents the corresponding state of dissolution indicated in Isaiah 34:4 and 2 Peter 3 leading up to 1 Corinthians 15:24-28. Running along the bottom of the chart is 'the deep' that was the vehicle of judgment in Genesis 1:2 and that which is to pass away at the end, for John says, 'and there was no more sea' (Rev. 21:1). By comparing Ephesians 1:4, 'before the foundation of the world' with 2 Timothy 1:8-9, 'before the world began (literally, before age times)' we have the start and the finish of the ages indicated.

What follows is a series of 'fillings' rather than a fulness. Adam, Noah, Abraham, Nebuchadnezzar are but 'stop-gaps', types and shadows, pointing on. The fulness of time (Gal. 4:4) did not come until 4,000 years after Adam and the fulness of the times (seasons) will not come until the day which is about to dawn ushers in the glory that will be revealed, when all things in heaven and on earth will be gathered together under the Headship of Christ.

Not until we reach the dispensation of the Mystery do we come to any company of the redeemed which constitute a 'fulness', and we read of this 'Church which is His Body, the FULNESS of Him that filleth all in all' in Ephesians 1:23. The fulness of the Godhead dwells bodily in Christ, and the heavenly places, far above all, with which both the seated Christ, and His Church are associated, is a sphere untouched by the catastrophe of Genesis 1:2. Those heavenly places are where Christ sits far above all heavens (Eph. 4:10), that is, far above the temporary heaven called 'the firmament' which is likened to a spread-out curtain. This 'tabernacle', characteristic of the Adamic earth, is of extreme importance; it places the whole purpose of the ages under a redeeming aegis, and the reader is advised to give the article which deals with this aspect: FIRMAMENT[2], careful attention.

As these studies proceed, we shall turn aside to consider various themes that bear upon the main subject, but unless that main subject is already held before the mind, we may sometimes 'not see the wood for the trees'. A reference back to the chart at the commencement of each section might be wise, and to enable the reader to see at the beginning the course we follow, we conclude this introduction with a conspectus of the articles that follow:

(2) Some lessons taught by the parable of the 'patch' with an answer to the question 'are there gaps in the outworking of the divine purpose?'
(3) Creation, its place in 'the purpose', in which the purport of the words 'in (the) beginning' are considered.
(4) The first 'gap'. 'Without form and void'.
(5) The present creation, a tabernacle.
(6) The testimony of Peter to the days of Noah. This is a new approach to a matter of importance involving the true intention of 2 Peter 3.
(7) Paradise lost and restored.
(8) The filling up of the nations (Genesis 48:19. Rotherham).
(9) The fulness of the Gentiles (Romans 11:25).
(10) The title 'Head', and its relation to the 'Fulness'.
(11) The fulness of the seasons.
(12) All the fulness of God.
(13) All the fulness of the Godhead. Bodily-wise.

(2) SOME LESSONS TAUGHT BY THE PARABLE OF THE 'PATCH'

To the reader who has travelled so far, we trust the principle of Right Division needs neither introduction nor commendation. Its recognition underlies every article that has been printed in these pages, and determines both the Gospel we preach, the Church to which we belong, and the hope that is before us. Dispensational Truth is not confined to one aspect or phase of the Divine purpose, for every dealing of God with man, whether under law or grace, whether with saint or sinner, has its own dispensational colouring which is inherent to its teaching and is in no wise accidental. Much has yet to be written and presented along these suggestive and attractive lines of study, but the particular application of this principle, now before us, focuses the reader's attention upon one thing, namely, that while in the mind of God the whole purpose of the ages is seen as one and its end assured, in the *outworking* of that purpose, the fact that moral creatures are involved, creatures that can and alas do exercise their liberty to disobey as well as to obey the revealed will of God, has had an effect upon the manifest unfolding of the purpose of the ages.

This is seen as a series of 'gaps' and 'postponements' which are filled by new phases and aspects of the purpose until at length He Who was once 'All' in a universe that mechanically and unconsciously obeyed, will at length be 'All in all' in a universe of willing and intelligent creatures, whose standing will not be that of Creation and Nature, but in Redemption and Grace.

In this section we can do little else than indicate the presence of these 'gaps' and consider the terms that are employed in the Hebrew of the Old Testament and the Greek of the New Testament and of the LXX. The well-known example of the Saviour's recognition of a 'gap' in the prophecy of Isaiah 61 must be repeated for the sake of completeness and for the value of its endorsement.

We learn from the fourth chapter of Luke's Gospel, that the Lord attended the service at the Synagogue at Nazareth, and apparently, after the reading of the law by the official reader of the Synagogue, He (Christ) stood up 'for to read' the *Haphthorah*, or the recognized portion from 'the Prophets' that was appointed for the day. He found the place, and commenced to read from Isaiah 61. Now it is laid down by Maimonides that:

> 'He that reads in the prophets, was to read at least one — and — twenty verses',

but he allowed that if 'the sense' be finished in less, the reader was under no necessity to read so many. Even so, it must have caused a deal of surprise to the congregation then gathered, for Christ to read but one verse and one sentence of the second verse, shut the book, and sit down. He did so because 'the sense' was indeed finished in less than twenty-one verses. He was about to focus attention upon one aspect of His work, and said:

> '*This* day is *this* Scripture fulfilled in your ears' (Luke 4:21).

The sentence with which the Saviour closed His reading of Isaiah 61 was 'to proclaim the acceptable year of the Lord'. The next sentence, separated in the A.V. by but a comma reads 'and the day of vengeance of our God' yet that comma represents a 'gap' of at least nineteen hundred years, for the days of vengeance are not referred to until in Luke 21:22 when the Second Coming and the end of the age is at hand. This passage we have examined in the article RIGHT DIVISION[4].

The recognition of some such gap is important when reading passages like 1 Peter 1:11, or the quotation of Joel 2:28-32 in Acts 2. Peter, who was a minister of the circumcision, refers to the testimony of the prophets, as though 'the sufferings of Christ and the glories that should follow' had no interval of centuries between them. The outpouring of the Spirit on the day of Pentecost is linked with the blood and fire and vapour of smoke that usher in the great and notable day of the Lord, even though Pentecost took place nineteen hundred years ago and the day of the Lord has not yet come (see PENTECOST, p. 160).

We shall discover that the whole purpose of the ages is a series of 'gaps' each filled by a succeeding dispensation, which in its turn lapses, until the central dispensation, that of the Mystery, is reached, which, though it has had a central period of darkness and ignorance yet is not succeeded by any other, as the other dispensations have been. All that follow the Mystery are *resumptions* of the dispensations which had come to a temporary halt.

This peculiar and central dispensation is occupied by the Church, which alone of all companies of the redeemed is called 'the fulness of Him that filleth all in all' (Eph. 1:23).

The word translated fulness is the Greek *pleroma*, and its first occurrence in the New Testament places it in contrast with a 'rent' or a 'gap'. The two references are:

> 'No man putteth a piece of new cloth unto an old garment, for that which is put in to fill it up taketh from the garment, and the rent is made worse' (Matt. 9:16).
>
> 'No man also seweth a piece of new cloth on an old garment: else the new piece that filled it up taketh away from the old, and the rent is made worse' (Mark 2:21).

The parallel passage in Luke is Luke 5:36 which must be added, though it does not use the word *pleroma.*

> 'No man putteth a piece of a new garment upon an old; if otherwise, then both the new maketh a rent, and the piece that was taken out of the new agreeth not with the old' (Luke 5:36).

The words that call for attention are:

'That which is put in to fill up'. This is the translation of the Greek *pleroma* a word of extreme importance in the epistles, and there translated 'fulness'. In contrast with this 'fulness' is the word 'rent' which in the Greek is *schisma.* The word translated 'new' in Matthew 9:16, and in Mark 2:21 is *agnaphos*, not yet fulled, or dressed, from *gnapheus*, a fuller. (See NEW, p. 105).

In place of 'put into' or 'put upon' used in Matthew 9:16 and Luke 5:36, we find the word 'to sew on', *epirrhapto* employed in Mark 2:21. One other word is suggestive, the word translated 'agree' in Luke 5:36. It is the Greek *sumphoneo.*

Now as these terms will be referred to in the course of the following exposition, we will take the present opportunity of enlarging a little on their meaning and relationship here, and so prepare the way.

Pleroma. This word which is derived from *pleroo* 'to fill' occurs seventeen times in the New Testament. Three of these occurrences occur in Matthew and Mark, the remaining fourteen occurrences are found in John's Gospel and in Paul's epistles. It is noteworthy that the word *pleroma* 'fulness' is never used in the epistles of the Circumcision. When Peter spoke of the problem of the 'gap' suggested by the words, 'where is the promise of His coming?' *he referred* his readers to the epistles of Paul, who, said he, deals with this matter of longsuffering and apparent postponement and speaks of these things (2 Pet. 3:15,16).

The word *pleroma* is used in the Septuagint some fifteen times. These we will record for the benefit of the reader who may not have access to that ancient translation. 1 Chronicles 16:32, 'Let the sea roar and the fulness thereof'. So, Psalm 96:11; 98:7. 'The earth is the Lord's and the fulness thereof' Psalm 24:1, so with slight variations, Psalm 50:12; 89:11. In several passages, the fulness, or 'all that is therein' is set over against flood or famine, as Jeremiah 8:16; 47:2; Ezekiel 12:19; 19:7, and 30:12.

Some of the words used in the context of these Septuagint references are too suggestive to be passed over without comment.

Instead of a 'time of healing' we find 'anxiety', the land 'quaking', 'deadly serpents' and a 'distressed heart' (Jer. 8:15-18).

Again, in Jeremiah 47:2 (29:2 in the LXX), we have such words of prophetic and age-time significance as 'an overflowing flood' Greek *katakluzomai, kataklusmos* and variants, a word used with dispensational significance in 2 Peter 2:5 and 3:6, and preserved in the English 'cataclysm', a word of similar import to that which we have translated 'the overthrow' of the world. The bearing of 2 Peter 2 on this 'gap' in the outworking of the purpose of the ages, will be given an examination here.

In the context of the word 'fulness' found in Ezekiel 12:19, we have such words as 'scatter' *diaspeiro*, a word used in James 1:1 and in 1 Peter 1:1 of the 'dispersed' or 'scattered' tribes of Israel, also the word 'waste', which calls up such passages of prophetic import as Isaiah 34:10,11, and Jeremiah 4:23-27 where the actual words employed in Genesis 1:2 are repeated.

The *pleroma* or 'fulness' is placed in direct contrast with desolation, waste, flood, fire, scattering, and a condition that is without form and void. *Schisma*, the word translated 'rent' in Matthew 9:16, is from *schizo* which is used of the veil of the temple and of the rocks that were 'rent' at the time of the Saviour's death and resurrection. *Agnaphos*, translated 'new', refers to the work of a 'fuller', who smooths a cloth by carding. The work of a fuller also includes the washing and scouring process in which fuller's earth or fuller's soap (Mal. 3:2; Mark 9:3) is employed. A piece of cloth thus treated loses its original harshness, and more readily 'agrees with' the cloth that has been more often washed.

The whole process of the ages is set forth under the symbol of the work of a fuller, who by beating and by bleaching at length produces a material which is the acme of human attainment, for when the Scriptures would describe the excellent glory of the Lord, His garments are said to have been 'exceeding white as snow, so as no fuller on earth can white them' (Mark 9:3). So too, the effect upon Israel of the Second Coming is likened to 'a refiner's fire and like fuller's soap' (Mal. 3:2). It is this 'fulled' cloth that makes the 'fulness', although there is no etymological connection between these like-sounding words.

There is another word translated 'new', *kainos*, which has the meaning of 'fresh, as opposed to old', 'new, different from the former', and as a compound, the meaning 'to renew'.

It is this word that is used when speaking of the new covenant, the new creation, the new man, and the new heaven and earth. We shall have to take this into account when we are developing the meaning and purpose of the 'fulness'. The Septuagint version of Job 14:12 reads in place of, 'till the heavens be no more', 'till the heavens are unsewn'! The bearing of this upon the argument of 2 Peter 3, the present firmament, and the fulness, will appear more clearly as we proceed.

Finally, we have the word *sumphoneo* 'to agree'. *Sumphonia* is translated 'music' in Luke 15:25, and of course is the Greek original of our word Symphony. In Ecclesiastes 7:14, the word is used with a rather different meaning than 'agreement'. 'In the day of prosperity be joyful, but in the day of adversity consider: God also *hath set the one over against the other*, to the end that man should find nothing after him'. This God will do when at the end of the ages He sets His Peace over against the present conflict, and symphony takes the place of discord.

The presence of so many terms of age-importance in the homely parable of the patching of a torn garment is wonderful in itself, but the wonder grows when we remember that He, in Whom dwells all the *pleroma* of the Godhead bodily, used this profound and significant term in such a homely and lowly connection. However vast the purpose of the ages may be, and however difficult it is for mortal minds to follow, the first use of *pleroma* in the New Testament encourages the reader in his search, for does not the purpose of the ages at length lead to a sphere where all things are new, where that which caused the rent or overthrow is entirely removed, and the Father is at length at home with His redeemed family?

(3) CREATION AND ITS PLACE IN THE PURPOSE

In the vision of Ezekiel, recorded in the opening chapters of his prophecy, the prophet saw the living creature which he afterward identified with the cherubim (Ezek. 10:20). These not only had four faces, namely that of a man, a lion, an ox and an eagle (Ezek. 1:10), but were associated with dreadful rings and wheels, 'as it were a wheel in the middle of a wheel' (Ezek. 1:16). This element of complication, one wheel within another, seems to be a reflection of the way in which one dispensation encloses another, so that between the annunciation of the opening phase of the purpose, and the attainment of its purpose and goal, a great gap intervenes, which is filled by another and yet another succeeding dispensation until in the 'fulness' of time Christ came (Gal. 4:4) born of a woman, with a view to the fulness of the seasons (Eph. 1:10), when He in Whom all the fulness dwells (Col. 1:19) shall bring this purpose of the ages to its blessed consummation.

In harmony with the fact that this purpose is redemptive in character, various companies of the redeemed during the ages, have been associated with this word 'fulness', even the earth itself and its fulness being linked with the glory of the Lord (Isa. 6:3 *margin*). The outworking of the purpose of the ages, therefore, can be represented, very crudely it is true, thus:

(((((((————————————————————)))))))

The purpose of the ages opens with Genesis 1:1 in the creation of the heavens and the earth, but between the attainment of the purpose for which heaven and earth were created 'in the beginning', and the day when God shall be 'all in all' lies a great gulf, a gulf caused by a moral catastrophe and not merely by a physical land-slide, a gap that is 'filled' by a series of wheels within wheels, Adam and his world, Noah and his world, Israel and their inheritance, and at last that church which is itself 'the fulness of Him that filleth all in all'.

The two extremes, therefore, of the purpose are found in the following passages which are themselves separated in the sacred volume by the rest of the Scriptures and by the Age-Times.

> 'In the beginning God created the heaven and the earth' (Gen. 1:1).
> 'Then cometh the End' (1 Cor. 15:24-28).

The 'gap' in the outworking of the purpose is expressed in Genesis 1:2, 'The earth was without form and void and darkness was upon the face of the deep', and in Revelation 21:1 by the added words:

'For the first heaven and the first earth were passed away; and there was no more sea'.

Let us consider in fuller detail some of the terms that are here employed to set before us this opening and closing feature of the purpose of the ages.

'In the beginning'. Hebrew *b're-shith*, Septuagint Greek *en arche*. While the fact must not be unduly stressed, it should be observed that neither in the Hebrew nor in the Greek is the article 'the' actually used. Moreover, it is certain that *b're-shith* denotes the commencement at a point of time as Jeremiah 26:1; 27:1 and 28:1 will show. But it is also very certain that the selfsame word denotes something more than a point of departure in time, for it is used by Jeremiah in 2:3 for 'the firstfruits', even as it is used in Leviticus 2:12 and 23:10 which are 'beginnings' in that they anticipate the harvest at the end, 'the fulness of seasons' (Eph. 1:10). The 'beginning' of Genesis 1:1 purposely looks to the end; it is more than a note of time.

The same can be said of the Greek *arche*. While it most certainly means 'beginning', it is noteworthy that in Genesis 1:16 where the next occurrences are found (in the LXX) it means 'rule' even as in Ephesians 1:21; 3:10 and 6:12 *arche* in the plural is translated 'principalities' while in Philippians 4:15 it is used once again in its ordinary time sense.

While God knows the end from the beginning, and nothing which He has caused to be written for our learning can ever be anything but the truth, we must nevertheless be prepared to find that much truth is veiled in the Old Testament until in the wisdom of God, the time was ripe for fuller teaching. If we leave Genesis 1:1 and go straight over to the last book of Scripture, namely the book of the Revelation, we shall see that the words 'in the beginning' acquire a fuller sense than was possible at the time when they were first written by Moses.

Arche occurs in Revelation four times, as follows:

> 'I am the Alpha and Omega, the *beginning* and the ending, saith the Lord, which is, and which was, and which is to come, the Almighty'.
>
> 'These things saith the Amen, the faithful and true witness, *the beginning of the creation of* God'.
>
> 'And He said unto me, It is done. I am Alpha and Omega, *the beginning* and the end. I will give unto him that is athirst of the fountain of the water of life freely'.
>
> 'I am Alpha and Omega, *the beginning* and the end, the first and the last' (Rev. 1:8; 3:14; 21:6; 22:13).

Here, in the last book of the Bible *arche* ceases to bear a *time* significance, it is the *title of a Person*, a Person in Whom Creation and the purpose of the ages find their meaning and their goal.

Paul uses *arche* eighteen times, the word having the time sense 'beginning' in five occurrences (Phil. 4:15, the only occurrence with this meaning in the Prison Epistles), once in the earlier epistles (2 Thess. 2:13) and three times in Hebrews (1:10; 2:3; 7:3). The remaining references have the meaning 'principalities', 'rule' and 'principles' (Rom. 8:38; 1 Cor. 15:24; Eph. 1:21; 3:10; 6:12; Col. 1:16,18; 2:10,15; Tit. 3:1; Heb. 6:1). The Hebrew word *rosh*, which gives us the word for 'beginning', is translated 'head' in Genesis 3:15 and both 'beginning' and 'head' in Exodus 12:2 and 9 respectively.

In Colossians 1:18, Paul uses *arche* of Christ in a somewhat similar sense to the usage of the word in the Revelation:

> 'Who is the Image of the Invisible God, the firstborn of every creature: for by Him were all things created ... and He is the head of the body, the church: Who IS THE BEGINNING, the firstborn from the dead ... in Him should ALL FULNESS dwell' (Col. 1:15-19).

The two phrases 'by Him' all things were created, and 'in Him' all fulness dwells, are obviously complementary. It is a fact, that the preposition *en* is translated many times 'by', but it is difficult to understand how it is that in

Colossians 1:16 *en auto* should be translated 'BY Him' while in Colossians 1:19 *en auto* should be translated 'IN Him'. Moreover the preposition *en* occurs in the phrases 'in heaven', 'in all things'. Again, the A.V. reads in verse 17, 'By Him all things consist' where the preposition is *dia*, which only makes the need more felt that *en* should not be translated 'by' in the same context.

There does not appear any grammatical necessity to depart from the primary meaning of *en* 'in' in Colossians 1:16, and this is the considered opinion of such exegetes as Bishop Lightfoot and Dean Alford, and the translators of the R.V.

'In Him' therefore, all things were created (Col. 1:16); He Himself is 'the beginning' in the New Creation (Col. 1:18) even as He is 'the beginning of the Creation of God' (Rev. 3:14). We therefore return to Genesis 1:1 and read with fuller insight and meaning 'IN THE BEGINNING God created the heaven and the earth'. When dealing with the word *pleroma*, this passage in Colossians will naturally come up for a more detailed examination.

Christ is 'the Beginning' of Genesis 1:1, although at the time of Moses such a truth was not clearly perceived, just as the significance of the name Jehovah was not realized before the revelation given in the days of Moses. What was known as the Creation of the Almighty, is subsequently revealed to have been the work of Jehovah, the God of Redemption. In Genesis 1:1 we learn that *Elohim* 'God' created the heaven and the earth, and subsequently we learn in John 1, Colossians 1 and Hebrews 1 that all was the work of Him Who is 'The Word', 'The Image', the 'One Mediator'. From the beginning, creation had in view the redemptive purpose of the ages, but just as it would have been impolitic to have answered the question of the apostles in Acts 1:6 before the time, so the true purpose of Creation was not revealed until man had sinned and Christ had died for his redemption.

Bara, the word translated create, must now be given a consideration. Metaphysics, 'the science of things transcending what is physical or natural', attempts to deal with the question of 'being' and in that department of thought the question of creating 'something out of nothing' naturally arises. Scripture, however, never discusses this metaphysical problem. Even in Genesis 1:1 it does NOT say, 'in the beginning God created the basic matter of the Universe', it commences with a highly organized and differentiated universe 'heaven and earth'. The Hebrew word *bara* in its primary meaning of 'create' is reserved only for the work of God, not being used of man, except in a secondary sense, and that in five passages only, out of fifty-four occurrences. (Josh. 17:15,18; 1 Sam. 2:29; Ezek. 21:19 and 23:47).

Adam is said to be 'created', although the 'dust of the ground' from which he was made was in existence long before. God is said to be the Creator of Israel (Isa. 43:1,7,15), yet Israel descended from Abraham. *Bara* gives us the Chaldaic word *bar* 'son', which but perpetuates the idea already recognized in *bara*. The Septuagint translates Joshua 17:15 and 18, 'thou shalt clear it', which the A.V. renders 'cut down', thereby revealing, as the lexicographers point out, that *bara* primarily means 'to cut, to carve out, to form by cutting'. When we remember that the word 'the world' *kosmos* is derived from the word *kosmeo* 'to adorn', as with 'goodly stones', with 'gold' and 'to garnish' as with all manner of precious stones (Luke 21:5; 1 Tim. 2:9; Rev. 21:2,19) we perceive a richer reason for the choice of *bara*.

The words with which revelation opens, 'in the beginning God created the heavens and the earth' begin to bear deeper significance.

> 'In Him Who is the beginning of the Creation of God, Elohim, Who was subsequently known as Jehovah, the God of Redemption, fashioned as one would a precious stone, the heavens and the earth'.

Creation was dual, from the start. Not heaven only, but heaven and earth. Man was created male and female, and before we read of the generations of Adam, namely of his descendants, we read of the 'generations of the heavens and the earth' (Gen. 2:4). Heaven is intimately concerned with the earth; in the heavens God is 'ALL' ('the Heavens do rule', 'as it is in heaven') and when at last the Will of God is done on earth as it is in heaven, the goal of the ages will be attained, and God will not only be 'All' but 'All in all'.

Such are faint shadows of His ways. By searching we shall never find out God unto perfection, but to stand as we have in a cleft of the Rock while His glory passes before us, and be permitted to behold even the 'back part' of His ways is joy unspeakable:

> 'Lo, these are but the outlines of His ways;
> A whisper only, that we hear of Him;
> His wondrous pow'r, who then, can comprehend?'
>
> (Job 26:14, Dr. Bullinger's Metrical Version).

(4) THE FIRST 'GAP'. 'WITHOUT FORM AND VOID'

Whatever the ultimate purpose of creation may prove to be, it is certain that it will not be attained without much sorrow and great sacrifice; 'the Fuller' will be at work, and between the opening announcement of Creation in Genesis 1:1 and the bringing in of the New Heaven and New Earth (Rev. 21:1; 2 Pet. 3:13) will roll the *eons* or the ages with their burden of sin and of redeeming love. When the new heaven and earth was seen by John in the Apocalypse, he adds the words 'and there was no more sea'. That is a most evident reference back to Genesis 1:2, where darkness and the deep are there revealed.

> 'And the earth was without form, and void; and darkness was upon the face of the deep' (Gen. 1:2).

Thus the condition that is described in Genesis 1:2 is included with the other 'no mores' of Revelation 21:1,4 and 22:3.

When we read in Genesis that man 'became' a living soul, we immediately gather that he was not a living soul *before* he breathed the breath of life. When we read that Lot's wife 'became' a pillar of salt (Gen. 19:26), we understand that this was consequent upon her looking back. When Cain said, 'And it shall come to pass' (Gen. 4:14) we understand his fears concerning what would happen *after* others had heard of his deed. So, when we read, 'the earth *was* without form and void', and realize that the same verb that is here translated 'was', is translated 'became' or 'come to pass' in these other passages in Genesis, we realize that here in Genesis 1:2, we are looking at the record of the first great gap in the outworking of the Divine purpose, and must read:

> 'And the earth BECAME without form and void'.

The translation 'was' in Genesis 1:2, however, is perfectly good, for in our usage we often mean 'became' when 'was' is written. A speaker at a meeting of the Victoria Institute used the following illustration. If writing on two occasions concerning a friend we should say (1) 'He *was* a man', and (2) 'He *was* very ill', everyone would understand that in the second case, this friend had 'become' ill, and so 'was' ill at the time spoken of, but it would be impossible to think that anyone would understand by the word 'he was ill' that he had been created, or born in that state. Darkness both in the Old Testament and in the New Testament is associated with death, judgment and evil, and Paul's use of Genesis 1:2,3 in the words, 'God, Who commanded the light to shine out of darkness' (2 Cor. 4:6) most surely indicates that in his estimation, the darkness of Genesis 1:2 is a fit symbol of the spiritual darkness of the unregenerate mind.

Two words, however, are found in Genesis 1:2, which are so used in subsequent Scriptures as to compel every one that realizes what a great place 'usage' has in interpretation, to acknowledge that nothing but catastrophic judgment can be intended by this verse. The two words that describe the condition of the earth, in verse two are the Hebrew words *tohu* and *bohu*, 'without form and void'. *Tohu* occurs twenty times in the Old Testament and *bohu* twice elsewhere. The only occurrence of *tohu* by itself in the writings of Moses is Deuteronomy 32:10, where it refers to 'the *waste* howling wilderness'. The use which Isaiah makes of this word is highly suggestive and full of instruction.

Isaiah 24. This chapter opens with a judgment that is reminiscent of Genesis 1:2. 'Behold, the LORD maketh the earth *empty*, and maketh it *waste*, and turneth it *upside down*, and scattereth abroad the inhabitants thereof ... the land shall be *utterly emptied*, and utterly spoiled' (Isa. 24:1,3).

When Isaiah would once again refer to this state of affairs, he sums it up in the epithet, 'the city of confusion (*tohu*)' Isaiah 24:10, and there can be no doubt but that the desolation here spoken of is the result of judgment. Another example of its usage is found in Isaiah 45:18, 'For thus saith the LORD that created the heavens; God Himself that formed the earth and made it; He hath established it, He created it not in vain, He formed it to be inhabited'. Here the A.V. treats the word *tohu* as an adverb 'in vain' which the R.V. corrects, reading 'a waste'. Whatever rendering we may adopt, one thing is certain. Isaiah 45:18 declares in the name of Him Who created the heavens, who formed the earth and made it, that He did not create it TOHU, it therefore must have become so. Even more convincing are the two passages other than Genesis 1:2, where *bohu* is employed, for in both instances the word is combined with *tohu*. The first passage is Isaiah 34:11. The context is one of catastrophic judgment and upheaval. The presence of such terms as 'indignation', 'fury', 'utterly destroy', 'sword' and 'vengeance' in the first eight verses are sufficient to prove this, and one verse is so definitely prophetic of the upheaval at the time of the end, as to leave no option in the mind:

> 'And all the host of heaven shall be dissolved, and the heavens shall be rolled together as a scroll: and all their host shall fall down, as the leaf falleth off from the vine, and as a falling fig from the fig tree' (Isa. 34:4).

This passage is almost identical with the language employed by Peter when he speaks of the signs that shall precede the coming of the day of God and the setting up of the new heavens and the new earth, wherein dwelleth righteousness (2 Pet. 3:13).

The words *tohu* and *bohu* occur in Isaiah 34:11, to which all these symbols of judgment point:

> 'He shall stretch out upon it the line of confusion (*tohu*), and the stones of emptiness (*bohu*)',

nor is it without significance that unclean birds like the cormorant and the bittern possess this devoted land, that nettles and brambles appear in the fortresses, and that dragons, wild beasts, screech owls and satyrs gather there. The whole is a picture in miniature of what the earth became in Genesis 1:2.

Isaiah's usage of tohu and *bohu is* convincing, but 'in the mouth of two or three witnesses every word shall be established', and accordingly we find the prophet Jeremiah using *tohu* and *bohu* in a similar context.

In the structure of Jeremiah 4, verses 5-7 are in correspondence with verses 19-31:

> 'The lion is come up from his thicket, and the destroyer of the Gentiles is on his way; he is gone forth from his place to make thy land *desolate*; and thy cities shall be *laid waste*, without an inhabitant' (Jer. 4:7).
>
> 'Destruction upon destruction is cried'.
>
> 'I beheld the earth, and, lo, it was *without form, and void*; and the heavens, and they had no light ... lo, there was no man ... lo, the fruitful place was a wilderness ... '.
>
> '... broken down ... by His fierce anger' (Jer. 4:20-26).

Here then are the three inspired occurrences of the two words *tohu* and *bohu*, Genesis 1:2, Isaiah 34:11 and Jeremiah 4:23. If Genesis 1:2 does not refer to a day of 'vengeance' or 'fierce anger' should we not have to acknowledge that both Isaiah and Jeremiah by the use of these peculiar words, have misled us? And if once that be our conclusion, inspiration is invalidated, and it does not matter much what Genesis 1:2 means, for our trust is shaken, and Moses is evidently wrong: this, however, cannot be. All Scripture is given by Inspiration of God, and Moses, Isaiah and Jeremiah speak with one voice, because inspired by one Spirit.

Nothing is said in Genesis 1:2, concerning the cause of this primeval judgment, any more than any statement is offered to explain the presence of the serpent in the Garden of Eden, but there are evidences that can be gathered from various parts of Scripture to make it clear that there was a fall among the angels, that Satan is a fallen being, and that the catastrophe of Genesis 1:2 is associated with that fall.

Into the 'gap' thus formed, the present six-day creation is placed as a temporary 'fulness' ('replenish the earth' Genesis 1:28), carrying the Redemptive purpose on to the threshold of Eternity. It is here also that 'age-times' begin.

See ANGELS, FALLEN[1]; CHERUBIM[1]; SATAN[4].

(5) THE PRESENT CREATION, A TABERNACLE

'The things which are seen are temporal' (2 Cor. 4:18).

'For by Him were all things created, that are in heaven, and that are in earth, visible and invisible' (Col. 1:16).

'And the Spirit of God moved upon the face of the waters. And God said, Let there be light: and there was light' (Gen. 1:2,3).

With these words of Genesis the first movement toward the goal of the ages is recorded. That it indicates a regenerative, redemptive movement, is made clear by the allegorical use that Paul makes of it when writing to the Corinthians:

'For God, Who commanded the light to shine out of darkness, hath shined in our hearts, to give the light of the knowledge of the glory of God in the face of Jesus Christ' (2 Cor. 4:6).

When we come to consider the place that Israel occupies in the outworking of the purpose of the ages, we shall find that there will be repeated in their case these allegorical fulfilments of Genesis 1:2,3.

> 'And He will destroy in this mountain the face of the covering cast over all people, and the vail that is spread over all nations' (Isa. 25:7).

The 'veil' plays a big part in the imagery of 2 Corinthians 3 and 4. Like the rising of light in Genesis 1:3, Israel's light shall dispel the gross darkness that has engulfed the nations (Isa. 60:1,2), and both in this passage, in 2 Corinthians 4:6 and from such prophetic passages as Isaiah 11:9, 'the earth shall be full of the knowledge of the LORD, as the waters cover the sea', we perceive that 'light' symbolizes 'knowledge' and prepares us to find in the midst of the garden not only the tree of life, but the tree of the knowledge of good and evil. These matters, however, are anticipatory of future studies, and the parallel of Israel with the six days creation will be better seen when we reach the Scriptures that speak of their call and destiny. At present we must confine ourselves to the consideration of the fact that here, in the calling into existence of the creation of the six days, we meet the first of a series of 'fulnesses' that carry the purpose of the ages on to their glorious goal.

When we traverse the gap formed by the entry of sin and death, and reach the other extreme of this present creation, we find that instead of natural light as in Genesis 1:3, 'The Lamb is the light thereof', 'The Lord God giveth them light', and we read further that the city 'had no need of the sun neither of the moon'. Instead of the stars which are spoken of in Genesis 1:16, we have the Lord holding 'the seven stars in His right hand', and He Himself set forth as 'the bright and morning star'. These are indications that 'the former things' are about to pass away. Perhaps the most suggestive item in the six days' creation, apart from man who was made in the Image of God, is the provision of the 'Firmaments'.

> 'And God said, Let there be a firmament in the midst of the waters, and let it divide the waters from the waters ... and God called the firmament Heaven' (Gen. 1:6-8).

The first fact that emerges from this passage, whatever for the moment the word 'firmament' may prove to mean, is that this firmament which was 'called' heaven must be distinguished from that which was created 'in the beginning'. Here is something peculiar to the *present temporary creation*, and as we shall discover, destined to pass away at the time of the end.

The margin of the A.V. draws attention to the fact that the Hebrew word *raqia* translated 'firmament' means, literally, an 'expansion', and so indicates the Scriptural anticipation by many thousand years, of the modern scientists' 'expanding universe'. *Raqah* the verb is used by Jeremiah to speak of 'silver spread into plates' (Jer. 10:9). Job speaks of Him 'which alone *spreadeth out* the heavens' (Job 9:8), and who *'stretcheth out* the north over the *empty* place' *(tohu*, 'without form' of Genesis 1:2), (Job 26:7). The stretched-out heavens are likened to a tent or tabernacle:

> 'That stretcheth out the heavens as a curtain, and spreadeth them out as a tent to dwell in' (Isa. 40:22).
>
> 'He that created the heavens, and stretched them out' (Isa 42:5).
>
> '... stretched forth the heavens ...' (Isa. 44:24; 51:13; Zech. 12:1).

Not only is the firmament spoken of in language that reminds of the Tabernacle, there is a reference in Job, that suggests that the earth too, is looked upon as the ground upon which this tabernacle of the sky rests:

> 'Whereupon are the foundations thereof fastened?' (Job 38:6).

At first sight there may not appear much in this passage to link it with the tabernacle, but when it is known that this same word which is translated 'foundation' is translated 'socket' fifty-three times, and that fifty-two of the occurrences refer to the sockets on which the Tabernacle rested in the wilderness, then the reference in Job 38, takes on a richer and deeper meaning.

The firmament of Genesis 1:6 is a lesser and temporary 'heaven', destined like a tent to be folded up and to pass away when the ages come to an end.

The 'firmament' is not merely the distant 'heaven' of the sun, the moon and stars, it is also the place where birds can fly (Gen. 1:20) consequently we can understand that when Christ ascended, He is said to have 'passed through the heavens', *dierchomai* not 'passed into' (Heb. 4:14).* In Hebrews 7:26 Christ is said to have been 'made higher' than the heavens, while Ephesians declares that He ascended up 'far above all heavens' with the object that He might 'fill' all things (Eph. 4:10). Christ is said to have passed through the heavens, to have been made higher than the heavens, and to have ascended up far above all heavens, consequently it is impossible for Him to be far above all heavens, and yet be at the same time seated in those very heavens, for even though knowledge of heaven and heavenly things may be very limited, we can understand the simple import of the language used. Consequently we discover that two words are employed for 'heaven', one *ouranos*, which includes the highest sphere of all, but nevertheless can be used of that 'heaven' which is to pass away (Matt. 5:18), of the 'air' where birds fly (Matt. 6:26), the heaven of the 'stars' (Matt. 24:29) and of the 'angels' (Mark 13:32), and the other *epouranios*.

We perceive that in many passages *ouranos* refers to the 'firmament' of Genesis 1:6, while *epouranios* refers to the heaven of Genesis 1:1 which was unaffected by the overthrow of verse 2, will not be dissolved and pass away, and is where Christ now sits at the right hand of God 'far above all of the heavens'. Hebrews 9:24 speaks of this sphere as 'heaven itself'. In two passages, the heavens are said to be rolled together or to depart 'as a scroll' (Isa. 34:4; Rev. 6:14). The present heaven and earth is a

---

* The student should note that this reference is omitted in Young's *Analytical Concordance to the Bible.*

temporary 'tabernacle' (Psa. 19:4) in which the God of Creation can dwell as the God of Redemption. This creation is to be folded up as a garment (Heb. 1:11,12), the firmament is likened to the curtains of a tabernacle, which will be 'unstitched' at the time of the end (Job 14:12 LXX *margin*, see also p. 206), and pass away as a scroll.

The figure is one that appeals to the imagination. A scroll of parchment stretched out and suddenly released, is a figure employed to indicate the sudden departure of the 'firmament', 'the stretched out heavens'. The word used in Revelation 6:14 is *apochorizo*, which occurs but once elsewhere, and that of a departure that followed a violent 'paroxysm' or 'contention' (Acts 15:39). *Chorizo* which forms part of this word means 'to put asunder' (Matt. 19:6); and 'separate' (Rom. 8:35).

Isaiah 34:4 which speaks of the heavens being rolled together as a scroll, and so speaks of the 'firmament' of Genesis 1:6, leads on to the repetition of the condition of Genesis 1:2, for in Isaiah 34:11, as we have seen, 'confusion' is *tohu* and 'emptiness' is *bohu*, the two words translated 'without form and void'.

The position at which the record of the ages has now reached is as follows:

←————'Heaven Itself' which does not pass away————→
'Above the heavens'

Gen. 1:1 Heaven and Earth	Gap	← The Firmament → Stretched out	Gap	Rev. 21:1 New Heaven and Earth
	Tohu *Bohu*	←— The Ages —→	*Tohu* *Bohu*	
	Gen. 1:2	← *The Pleroma* —→	Isa. 34:11	

Into the gap caused by the overthrow of Genesis 1:2, is placed the present creation which together with its temporary heaven is to pass away. This present creation, headed by Adam, constitutes the first of a series of 'fulnesses' that follow a series of 'gaps' until we at length arrive at Him, in Whom 'All fulness dwells'. We read in Genesis 1:28, 'be fruitful and multiply and replenish the earth' where the word 'replenish' is the verb *male*, a word which as a noun is translated 'fulness' in such passages as 'the earth is the Lord's and the fulness thereof' (Psa. 24:1). The Septuagint uses the verb *pleroo* to translate *male* in Genesis 1:28. We are, therefore, fully Scriptural when we speak of the six days Creation as a part of the 'Pleroma' or 'Fulness'.

(6) The Testimony of Peter to the Days of Noah

After the great gap formed by the loss of Paradise, the record divides into two according as the false or the true seed are spoken of, until we come to the next great crisis, the Deluge. Here history seems to repeat itself. The deep (Heb. *tehom*) of Genesis 1:2, is not referred to again until we read the record of the flood (Gen. 7:11; 8:2). The 'dry land' (Heb. *yabbashah*, Gen. 1:9,10), which appeared on the third day from beneath the waters, finds an echo in the 'drying up' of the earth after the flood (Heb. *yabesh*, Gen. 8:7,14). There are a number of interesting parallel features between Adam and Noah which establish that the relationship is intentional.

For example, both Adam and Noah are commanded to replenish the earth, both have three sons, one of whom becomes involved in a curse and is either 'of that wicked one' or the father of Canaan, who in his turn is seen to be of the evil seed. These parallels are so close that most commentators have accepted without question that Peter, in 2 Peter 3, refers to Genesis 1:1 and 2, whereas a careful study of his epistles will show that he had, primarily, the days of Noah before his mind. This testimony is important, and the examination of it will necessitate a fairly intensive study, but the subject matter is of the deepest solemnity and fully justifies all the time and space which we can devote to its elucidation.

Just as the Primal Creation is balanced across the gap of the ages, by the new heavens and new earth, and just as

Paradise lost is balanced by Paradise restored, so the structure persists and another pair of corresponding members appears.

C The days of Noah. The nations just before the call of Abraham.

a The irruption of the sons of God (Gen. 6).

b Preservation in the Ark. Noah uncontaminated (Gen. 6:9).

c Punishment by flood (Gen. 7,8).

d Spirits in prison (1 Pet. 3:19-22; Jude 6).

C As it was in the days of Noah. The nations just before Israel are saved and blessed.

a Antichrist, and the Son of Perdition (2 Thess. 2).

b Preservation, the Lamb's book of life. Uncontaminated (Rev. 21).

c Punishment by fire (Rev. 14:9,10).

d Spirits liberated for a season (Rev. 9:14).

Let us now attend to the teaching of Scripture with regard to this great epoch.

A very superficial reading of Scripture will convince the student that there are revealed three great creative movements — one past, one present and one future.

(1). 'In the beginning' (Gen. 1:1). Primal Creation.

(2). 'In six days' (Gen. 1:3 to 2:3). Present Creation.

(3). 'In the day of God' (2 Pet. 3:12,13). New Heavens and Earth.

The Primal Creation of Genesis 1:1 is separated by the chaos of Genesis 1:2 from the Present Creation — while the Present Creation is again separated from the New Heavens and Earth by the dissolution of 2 Peter 3:10, and the following diagram visualizes this great purpose of the ages.

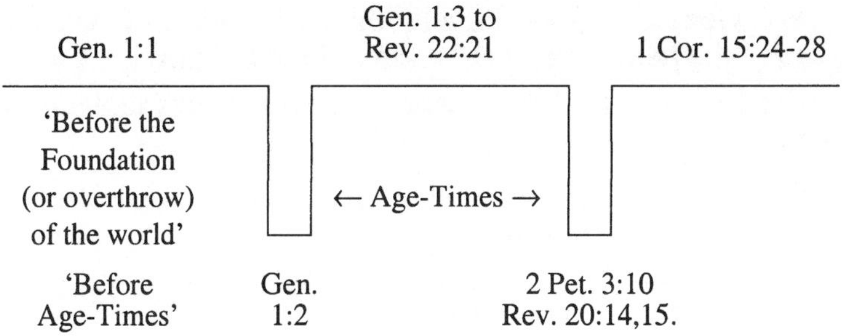

The 'first' heaven and earth of Revelation 21:1 is strictly 'the former' of two (see Rev. 21:4 where the same Greek word is translated 'former'). This is the sequel to the six days' creation, not to Genesis 1:1. A reference to Isaiah 65:17-20, and to 66:22-24 will show that in the new heaven and earth (outside the Holy Mountain), death will still be possible. Not until the end of the ages, long past the end of the Revelation will the last enemy be destroyed and God be all in all (1 Cor. 15:24-28).

Peter as a minister of the Circumcision, is particularly concerned with that portion of the purpose of the ages that impinges upon the hope of Israel. There is, however, in the history of Israel much that is typical of vaster things, and we are not surprised, therefore, to discover much that adumbrates the larger issues dealt with by Paul alone. This vast sweep of the ages which we have suggested in the diagram given above, finds an echo in the words of Peter, when he speaks of past, present and future heavens and earth, as they appear in the prophetic view of Israel and its hope.

We may use Peter's language as a guide to the wider purpose of the ages thus:

For Genesis 1:1 we may use the words, 'the world that then was'.*

---

* Although Mr. Welch is using *the words* of 2 Peter 3:6 to describe Genesis 1:1, he is *not* suggesting that Peter was referring to Genesis 1:1 in 2 Peter 3:6. See p. 212, line 25 and p. 232, line 25.

For Genesis 1:3 — Revelation 20:13 we may use the words, 'the heavens and the earth, which are now'.

For Revelation 21:1 the words, 'new heavens and a new earth'.

Peter was 'a minister of the circumcision' (Gal. 2:7-9), and wrote his epistles to:

> '... the strangers scattered throughout Pontus, Galatia, Cappadocia, Asia, and Bithynia' (1 Pet. 1:1).

As 2 Peter 3 opens with the words, 'This second epistle, I now write unto you', it is evident that the chapter before us was equally addressed to the 'circumcision'. The term *diaspora*, 'scattered' became a name to designate 'the twelve tribes scattered abroad' (Jas. 1:1), or the 'dispersed among the Gentiles' (John 7:35, R.V. *margin*). This term had become fixed during the two hundred years before Christ that the Septuagint had been in use, for in such passages as Deuteronomy 30:4; Nehemiah 1:9; Psalm 147:2; *diaspora* is used of the 'outcasts of Israel'. As we shall have occasion to compare some of the language of Peter with the Gospel according to Mark, it will be well to make sure that the reader is aware of the close association of these two servants of the Lord.

From Acts 12:12 we learn that Peter was friendly with Mark's mother and in 1 Peter 5:13 he speaks of 'Marcus my son'. Jerome speaks of both Paul and Peter with their assistants thus:

> 'Therefore he (Paul) had Titus for a Secretary, as the blessed Peter had Mark, whose Gospel was composed by him after the dictation of Peter'.

To this may be added the testimony of Eusebius:

> 'After the departure of Peter and Paul, Mark the disciple and secretary (*hermeneutes* or "interpreter") of Peter, transmitted to us in writing what Peter had preached'.

The four Gospels, therefore, stand related to one another as follows:

Relationship of the Gospels to one another

A		Matthew	Independent.
	B	Mark	Interpreter of Peter.
	B	Luke	Fellow worker with Paul.
A		John	Independent.

We are now free to examine 2 Peter 3, and we shall remember as we do it, that Peter, the minister of the circumcision, admits in that same chapter that the apostle Paul has many things to say, which were hard to be understood both by himself and his hearers, and we shall not expect to find the sweep backward beyond Gen. 1:2 in Peter's most far-flung statement, that we find in Paul's great epistles of the Mystery. We must now make a preliminary inquiry into the testimony of 2 Peter 3:1-14 and discover the scope of Peter's Ministry and epistle.

We note that chapters 1 and 2 must be considered as introductory, for it is chapter 3 that opens with the words, 'this second epistle, beloved, I now write to you', and the burden of the chapter is the denial by 'scoffers' of the possibility of the Lord's return by an appeal to a supposed 'Uniformity of Natural Law', and the exposure of the weakness of this objection by the apostle. An examination of the first chapter will show that this was prominently in the apostle's mind all the time. 2 Peter 1:16-21 is an anticipation of 2 Peter 3:2,3 and 2 Peter 2:1-22 is an anticipation of 2 Peter 3:3-13 and correspond in the structure which will be given later.

These selfsame scoffers, or their predecessors, had evidently charged the believer who expected the personal return of the Lord, with following 'cunningly devised fables' (2 Pet. 1:16), and from this the apostle proceeds to the nature and trustworthiness of prophecy, recalling in passing the conviction he himself had received of its truth when upon the Mount of Transfiguration.

The structure of the passage is as follows:

A 2 Pet. 1:16. What the apostle's witness was NOT 'Cunningly devised fables'.
  B 2 Pet. 1:16,17. What it WAS 'Honour and glory'.
    C 2 Pet. 1:17,18. How it CAME 'The voice from heaven'.
  B 2 Pet. 1:19. What the Prophetic Word IS 'A light, till the day dawn'.
A 2 Pet. 1:20. What it is NOT 'Not of its own unfolding'.
    C 2 Pet. 1:21. How it CAME 'Moved by the Holy Ghost'.

In this opening argument we have similar features that are restated or amplified in chapter 3.

Chapter 1

The Second Coming of Christ.
The charge made 'cunningly devised fables'.
The testimony of apostle and Prophet.
The introductory phrase 'knowing this first'.

Chapter 3

The Second Coming of Christ.
The scoffers' charge 'where is the promise of His coming?'
The testimony of the Prophets and apostles.
The introductory phrase 'knowing this first'.

To piece together the complete structure in all its details would take us too long, and is not necessary for our present purpose. The following abridged outline will be all that is required to demonstrate the scope of the epistle and particularly the correspondence that exists between 2 Peter 1:16-21 and 2 Peter 3:2,3, and 2 Peter 2:1-22 with 2 Peter 3:3-13. If this be realized, we shall have reached the first step in our inquiry.

We draw special attention to the two words 'overthrow' *katastrophe* and 'overflow' *katakluzo*, and the correspondence established between the destruction of Sodom and Gomorrah, with the dissolution of the elements.

The Second Epistle of Peter

A 1:1-4. Opening Benediction. Grace, peace, through the knowledge of God. Called to His own glory.

B 1:5-11. Give all diligence — never fall (*ptaio*). Give diligence — make sure.

C **a** 1:12-15. 'Stir up', 'remembrance'.

b 1:16-21. The apostles and Prophets (details given above). 'Knowing this first'.

c 2:1-22. False prophets and False teachers. Reference to fall of angels, the Flood and the destruction of Sodom and Gomorrha. An overthrow (*katastrophe*). Lusts of flesh and uncleanness.

C a 3:1. This second epistle beloved, I now write unto you: in both which I *stir up* your pure minds by way of *remembrance.*

b 3:2,3. The Prophets and the apostles 'Knowing this first'.

c 3:3-13. Scoffers. Reference to Creation and Flood. Dissolution of elements. Overflow (*katakluzo*). Walking after their own lusts.

B 3:14-17. Be diligent — fall (*ekpipto*) stedfastness.

A 3:18. Closing Benediction. Grow in grace and knowledge of our Lord and Saviour. To Him be glory.

In the second chapter, which corresponds with the section dealing with the scoffers and their condemnation, Peter speaks of the following recorded interventions of the Lord, showing how untrue the scoffers were when they attempted to rule out the future Divine intervention of the Lord's return by saying, 'since the fathers fell asleep all things continue as they *were*'. Four instances are given by the apostle of judgments that could not be the mere working of natural law.

The casting down of the angels that sinned (2 Pet. 2:4).
The bringing in a flood in the days of Noah (2:5).
The turning of the cities of Sodom and Gomorrha into ashes, condemning them by an 'overthrow' *katastrophe* (2:6).
The rebuking of Balaam by the speaking of a dumb ass (2:15,16).

From these examples the apostle draws the conclusion:

'The Lord knoweth how to deliver the godly out of temptations, and to reserve the unjust unto the day of judgment to be punished' (2 Pet. 2:9).

We have now advanced a step in our pursuit of the truth. The fact has been established, that there were three Creative Movements recorded in Scripture, and that Peter whose reference to Creation is occupying our attention, was a minister of the circumcision, when he wrote his second epistle. To this we have now added some idea of the general scope of this epistle, and of 2 Peter 3:3-14 in particular. We are, therefore, now ready to give 2 Peter 3:3-14 a fuller and more detailed examination.

Before we can come to any definite conclusion about the intention of the apostle in 2 Peter 3:3-14, we must arrive at some certain understanding of the terms he uses. There are few students of Scripture who, when they read the words of 2 Peter 3:4, 'the BEGINNING of creation', but will go back in mind immediately to Genesis 1:1 and John 1:1, where the same word *arche* 'beginning' is found either in the Septuagint or in the original Greek New Testament. Yet upon examination, such a reference back is proved to be untrue. We have already spoken of Mark the 'interpreter' of Peter and the present is an opportunity to test his words. Mark uses the word *arche* 'beginning' four times thus:

'Beginning' in the Gospel of Mark

A 'The *beginning* of the gospel of Jesus Christ, the Son of God' (1:1).
  B '*From the beginning of the creation*' (10:6).
A 'The *beginnings* of sorrows' (13:8).
  B '*The beginning of the creation which God created*' (13:19).

The two references to creation challenge our attention, and we are sure that the established meaning of these two passages in Mark's Gospel must influence most profoundly our interpretation of the same words in 2 Peter 3. Here, therefore, is the second passage in full:

> 'But from the beginning of the creation God made them male and female' (Mark 10:6).

It is not a matter of debate, therefore, that Mark uses the expression, 'the beginning of the creation', to refer exclusively to the creation of Genesis 1:3 to 2:3, and so by logical necessity *cannot* include Genesis 1:1.

Let us read the second reference:

> 'For in those days shall be affliction, such as was not from the beginning of the creation which God created unto this time, neither shall be' (Mark 13:19).

All we need to do to show that the same limitation must be observed is to place beside this reference, two parallel passages:

> 'For then shall be great tribulation, such as was not since the beginning of the world to this time, no, nor ever shall be' (Matt. 24:21).
>
> 'There shall be a time of trouble, such as never was since there was a nation even to that same time' (Dan. 12:1).

We cannot conceive that any reader with these passages before him, would wish to read into Mark 13:19 a reference back to Genesis 1:1. The words 'since there was a nation' being the earliest statement, out of which the others have grown.

We are, therefore, certain that the words quoted by Peter 'from the beginning of the creation' are limited to the Adamic earth. The context moreover of any expression has a part to play in deciding its meaning, so we must now observe the way in which it is introduced and with what other terms it is associated.

> 'Since the fathers fell asleep, all things continue as they were from the beginning of the creation' (2 Pet. 3:4).

It is strange enough to think of linking up the death of Abraham, Isaac and Jacob ('the fathers') with the six days' creation; it is unthinkable when we attempt to link such events with the remote period of Genesis 1:1. The argument appears to be that just as the 'fathers' died one after the other, and no interference with 'nature' has yet broken the hold of death, so, from the beginning of the world all things have continued without a break, and ever will, so rendering either the hope of resurrection, the Second Coming or the Day of Judgment unreasonable.

Peter, however, has already met this argument. Did all things continue as they were, in the days of Noah? Was there no Divine intervention in the days of Sodom? Is there no import in the use of the two distinctive words *katastrophe* and *katakluzo*?

Further, we must not forget that the words in question were spoken by the 'scoffers'. What did these scoffers know about the primal creation? What did they know of the 'overthrow of the world'? Not one of them so far as there is any record had ever seen the skeleton of a brontosaurus or a fossilized ichthyosaurus. The science of their day made creation originate from chaos (see Hislop's *Two Babylons*), and these scoffers most certainly did not know more of ancient history than the inspired apostle.

In his opening rejoinder the apostle says, 'For this they willingly are ignorant of', a sentence that does not do justice to either the English language or the inspired original. The R.V. reads, 'for this they wilfully forget' and Dr. Weymouth renders the passage, 'for they are wilfully blind to the fact'. No person can be charged with 'wilful forgetfulness' if the matter lies beyond his ken. The heathen world was without excuse in their idolatry because of the witness of creation around them, but not even the scoffers could 'wilfully neglect' the evidences of the primal creation because they were unrevealed and were unattainable by human search at that time. These scoffers, however, could be charged with wilful neglect of the Divine record of Genesis which shows how the selfsame water that played so prominent a part in the six days' creation, was actually used to bring about the flood in the days of Noah. This they could have known, and with its neglect they could be charged.

Lanthano, the word translated 'be ignorant' in 2 Peter 3:5 A.V. occurs again in verse 8, 'be not ignorant of this one thing'. This fact must not be 'ignored' by ourselves, as it is evident that such a recurrence indicates a structural feature, and is of consequence to true interpretation. The word *lanthano* seems to demand an English equivalent that lies somewhere between the 'ignorance' of the A.V. and the 'forgetting' of the R.V., and Moffatt seems to have chosen wisely here, for he renders the word in both passages 'ignore'. Ignorance of any fact modifies the culpability of a person, forgetfulness while serious, nevertheless modifies the guilt of an act, but to 'wilfully ignore' leaves no such margin of excuse, and that is the thought here. Without making too great a diversion by dealing with the structure of 2 Peter 3:1-13 as a whole, it will be sufficient for our present purpose to confine ourselves to verses 4-9.

A 2 Pet. 3:4. *The Promise.* Where is this promised Advent? False argument derived from misconception as to time.

B 2 Pet. 3:5-7. *They wilfully ignore.*

a Heavens of old and Earth.		
b The Word.		
c The World.	Water	
d Perished.		
a Present Heaven and Earth.		
b Same Word.		
c Ungodly Men.	Fire	
d Destruction.		

B 2 Pet. 3:8. *Do you not ignore.* The argument concerning relative time.

A 2 Pet. 3:9. *The Promise.* The apparent 'slowness' of the Lord must not be misconstrued as 'slackness'. The day of the Lord will come.

God does not hold man accountable where knowledge is unattainable. Knowledge concerning things that happened during the Primal Creation of Genesis 1:1 could not be 'ignored' by anyone, because no details are given in the Revealed Word. These men, however, could, and evidently did, wilfully ignore the testimony of Genesis 1:3 to 8:22, and so were without excuse. The reference to 'the world that then was being overflowed with water perished' must either refer to the chaos of Genesis 1:2 and must exclude the flood in the days of Noah, or it must refer to the flood of the days of Noah and exclude Genesis 1:2, *it cannot refer primarily to both.* We have positive evidence that Peter makes reference to the Deluge of Noah's day as part of his teaching and while this does not prove anything so far as 2 Peter 3:6 is concerned, it is a weight in the scale. We must continue our study of the terms used by Peter.

'The heavens were of old'. Do these words refer to the primal creation of Genesis 1:1? or do they refer to the creation of the world for Adam and his race? *Ekpalai* occurs in but one other passage in the New Testament, namely in 2 Peter 2:3 :

> 'Whose judgment now *of a long time* lingereth not'.

There is no need for any argument here. These false prophets must belong to the Adamic creation, and consequently there is added reason to believe that Peter's second use of the term will be but an expansion of the first, and that 2 Peter 3:6 refers back as far as Genesis 1:3 but no farther.

Palai simply means 'old', *palaios, palaiotes* and *palaioo* also occur and should be examined. We give just two examples.

> 'But he that lacketh these things is blind, and cannot see afar off, and hath forgotten that he was purged from his *old sins*' (2 Pet. 1:9).
>
> 'God, Who at sundry times and in divers manners, spake in *time past*' (Heb. 1:1).

The expression, 'the heavens were of old', therefore refers quite legitimately to Genesis 1:6. This 'firmament' was temporary and is to pass away, as many passages of Scripture testify. There is no passage, however, that teaches that *Heaven Itself*, the dwelling place of the Most High, will ever pass away, and this is an added reason for limiting Peter's words to the present creation.

The earth 'standing' out of the water, appears to refer to the way in which the present system was brought into being. *Sunistemi* is translated 'consist' in Colossians 1:17, and while it would take a scientist to explain the meaning of 2 Peter 3:5, the reference is so evidently back to Genesis 1:3 onwards that scientific proof is not necessary to our argument.

The association of the 'water' and creation, with the 'water' that caused the 'overflow' of 2 Peter 3:6, is emphasized when one observes that after the many references to water in Genesis 1, no further mention is made until the ominous words of Genesis 6:17 are reached, 'I do bring a flood of waters upon the earth'.

These things the scoffers 'wilfully ignored'. The future dissolution will involve the heavens as well as the earth (2 Peter 3:10) whereas it was 'the world' not the heaven and the earth that 'perished' in the days of Noah. The heavens and the earth remained, and so could be called by Peter 'the heavens and the earth which are now'. In the second chapter of his epistle, Peter refers to the Flood and speaks of 'the old world' and 'the world of the ungodly' (2 Peter 2:5), similarly in both 2 Peter 2:4 and 2 Peter 3:7 he uses the word 'reserved' in reference to judgment.

Again in 2 Peter 3:6 the Greek word *katakluzo* is used where the translation reads *'being overflowed* with water'. In 2 Peter 2:5 he uses the word *kataklusmos* (which becomes in English 'cataclysm') 'bringing in the flood upon the world of the ungodly', which makes the parallel between these two chapters even more obvious. The result of our examination leaves us with the conviction that Peter refers to the creation that came into being for the habitation of man, and that we are not justified in using his words to cover the whole of the record of Scripture, except as a type and shadow of the greater event.

(7) Paradise Lost and Restored

If 'before the overthrow of the world' and 'before the age times' refer to the same datum line, and, if the 'overthrow' be Genesis 1:2, then this must have taken place before the ages began, and consequently we have an indication that the ages are coincident with the present temporary creation, which together with its 'firmament' will pass away when the purpose of the ages shall be accomplished.

The opening and closing members of the Purpose of the Ages may be set out as follows:

A	The beginning. 'Before Age times'.	**a**	Christ Firstborn of all Creation. Image of Invisible God.
		b	Satan Cherub (Ezek. 28:12-19).
		c	The overthrow (Gen. 1:2).

* * *

A	The end. Ages finish.	***a***	Christ Head. Every knee shall bow.
		b	Church in the heavenlies. Satan destroyed.
		c	Reconciliation achieved.

The space indicated by the * * * is spanned by the ages. The first of the series of fulnesses that fill this gap is, as we have seen, the 'six-day creation' of Genesis 1:3 to 2:3.

The opening 'generation' is NOT that of Adam, as recorded in Genesis 5:1, but of 'the heavens and the earth' which occupies Genesis 2:4 to 4:26. This is followed by twelve generations, which open with 'the book of the generations of Adam' (Gen. 5:1), and closes with 'the book of the generation of Jesus Christ'.

The relationship of these generations may be set out as follows:

A The generations of the heavens and the earth (Gen. 2:4 to 4:26).

A **a** The BOOK of the generations (plural), of Adam (Gen. 5:1 to 6:8).

b The generations of Noah (Gen. 6:9 to 9:29).

c The generations of the Sons of Noah (Gen. 10:1 to 11:9).

d The generations of Shem (Gen. 11:10-26), The line of the Seed.

e The generations of Terah (Gen. 11:27 to 25:11), In Mesopotamia and Canaan.

f The generations of Ishmael (Gen. 25:12-18), Bondwoman.

f The generations of Isaac, (Gen. 25:19 to 35:29), Free woman.

e The generations of Esau (Gen. 36:1-43), In Canaan and Mount Seir.

d The generations of Jacob (Gen. 37:2 to 50:26), The line of the Seed.

c The generations of Aaron and Moses (Num. 3:1-4).

b The generations of Pharez (Ruth 4:18-22). The line of the Seed.

a The BOOK of the generation (singular), of Jesus Christ (Matt. 1:1-17).

It will be observed that the word 'generation' is used in the plural of each except the last. The generations refer to the descendants, as may be seen by an isolated generation like that of Ruth 4:18-22, the generation of Jesus Christ however, refers to His human ancestry not to His descendants, for He had none.

In the generations of the heaven and the earth, are recorded the following features:

(1) The forming of man from the dust, and his becoming a living soul.

(2) The planting of the garden eastward in Eden.

(3) The prohibition concerning the tree of the knowledge of good and evil.

(4) The naming of the animals and Adam's conscious loneliness.
(5) The formation of the woman as a help meet for him.
(6) The temptation and the fall, the curse and sorrow.
(7) The promise of the seed of the woman and ultimate victory.
(8) The return of man to the dust from whence he had been taken.
(9) The expulsion from Eden and the placing of the Sword and Cherubim.
(10) The two seeds as manifested in Abel and Cain.
(11) The appointment of Seth 'instead' of Abel.

Fuller details could, of course, be included, and the reader must remember that there is no significance in the number that we have indicated. In view of the balancing feature in the book of the Revelation we can write over this period the words 'Paradise Lost', without borrowing any ideas from Milton, even as we can write over the closing chapter of the Revelation 'Paradise Restored'.

Two main themes commence in Genesis 3, that continue to the end of time, and which constitute the conflict of the ages. These are (1) the promise of the woman's seed, (2) the continuous enmity between the two seeds until ultimate victory is achieved. (See *The Book of Job*). The loss sustained as a consequence of the fall is symbolized in the expulsion from the garden, with the consequent loss of access to the tree of life, but restoration is pledged by the placing of the Cherubim together with a flaming sword 'to keep' the way of the tree of life. (See CHERUBIM[1]). In the sequel, when the intervening gap is filled by the fruits of redemption, we are taken by a series of steps back to Eden and its blessedness, as is made manifest by the following extract from the close of Revelation:

> 'And God shall wipe away all tears from their eyes; and there shall be no more death, neither sorrow, nor crying, neither shall there be any more pain: for the former things are passed away ... and he shewed me a pure river of water of life, clear as crystal, proceeding out of the throne of God and of the Lamb. In the midst of the street of it, and on either side of the river, was there the tree of life ... and there shall be no more curse ... that they may have right to the tree of life, and may enter in through the gates into the city' (Rev. 21:4; 22:1-3,14).

Here is the complete reversal of the consequence of the fall of man in Eden, and we have surveyed yet another 'fulness', the fulness of Redemption that spans the ages and their burden of sin and death. The creation of the universe, being the act of the infinitely wise God, brought into being a definite purpose, and that purpose can be perceived at least in some measure by reading what the Scriptures indicate will be the condition of things at the end. The Tabernacle of God will then be with men and He will dwell with them, God will be all in all. Two things are linked with the Cherubim in the Scriptures, 'dwelling' (1 Sam. 4:4), and 'speaking' (Num. 7:89). Where the word is used in the singular, we read, 'He rode upon a Cherub and did fly', but this has to do with deliverance from enemies. While we read both in Exodus and Ezekiel of a 'Cherub' in the singular, it always has reference to 'one' of the Cherubim, but in Ezekiel 28:14 and 16 'the anointed Cherub' seems to be associated with 'the overthrow of the world'. The change from the singular to the plural takes place after the fall of man, and the Cherubim with their four faces, the lion, the ox, the man and the eagle, symbolize Adam and the dominion put in subjection under his feet, who in turn is the figure of Him that was to come. While the purpose of God to dwell with His creatures was temporarily checked by the failure of the first creation, it was reintroduced at the creation of man, for we have the homely words of Genesis 3, that speaks of the 'voice of God in the garden at the cool of the day' and the call, 'Adam, where art thou?' Once again the fall of the creature hindered the attainment of the Divine purpose, yet Love found a way; the purpose was not abandoned but the whole purpose was placed upon a redemptive basis, consequently the Cherubim are seen to be an integral part of the Mercy Seat. Some idea of the way the purpose is pursued through the ages may be visualized by the following graph:

ORIGINAL PURPOSE	THE 'GAP' FILLED	THE GOAL REACHED
Purpose to dwell. The Cherub. 'Cover' (Exod. 28:14,16 Exod. 26:14).	Cherubim. Man and his dominion enters and Cherubim now part of the Mercy seat.	'The Tabernacle of God is with men and He will dwell with them'.
THE OVERTHROW OF THE WORLD		DISSOLUTION OF HEAVEN

From the 'Anointed' that failed, on via the cross to the glory of the 'Anointed' Who gloriously succeeded, the purpose of love is carried to its goal on the wings of the Cherubim, or rather on the grace that these strange creatures set forth. Thus the outstretched firmament coincides with the outstretched wing of the Cherubim, the whole span of the ages being *Under the Redeeming Aegis.*

> 'The term "aegis", really a Latin word, means "a goat skin", and later a shield ... This redeeming conception took on a primeval form in the cherubim set up, together with the sword of flame, at the gate of the lost Eden ... the idea of atonement, therefore is as old as the Bible, nay as redemption itself ... This "day of Atonement" itself was called "Yom Kippur", i.e. the "Day of Covering" ... Ours is at bottom an evangelical universe, no other form was ever conceived for it in the mind of God'. (*Under the Redeeming Aegis*, by H.C. Mabie, D.D., LL.D.).

We can, therefore, set out the steps of the goal of the ages, thus:

B	The Ages begin.	*Earth*	Remade and blessed (Gen. 1:2 to 2:4).
	Paradise lost.		Subjected to curse. Thorns and thistles (Gen. 3).
		Man	For a little lower than angels (Psa. 8).
			The First Adam. Living Soul. The image of God. Dominion over the earth.
		Usurper	The Serpent. The Shining one. Nachash (Gen. 3). Ye shall not surely die. Ye shall be as God.
		Hope	The seed of the woman.

* * * * * * *

B	The Consummation of the ages.	*Earth*	Restored and blessed (Hos. 2:18-23).
			Curse removed (Rev. 22:3; Isa. 55:13).
	Paradise restored.	*Man*	Christ, made much better than angels (Heb. 1:4).
			Last Adam. Quickening Spirit. Image.
		Heir	Lamb is the light, brightness of glory.
			Immortality conferred (1 Cor. 15).
			Every knee shall bow.
		Hope	Creation's groan hushed (Rom. 8:21; 16:20).

(8) THE FILLING UP OF THE NATIONS (Gen. 48:19, Rotherham)

The family of Noah after the flood were told to 'replenish' the earth, which would have consisted a fulness, had this replenishing been accompanied by grace and righteousness. Alas, by the time we reach the eleventh chapter of Genesis, the evil character of the world was made manifest, and Babel, and the scattering of the people, brought another movement in the purpose of the ages to a close. Babel in Genesis 11, will yet find its corresponding member when great Babylon comes up for judgment, but the gap formed by the rebellion of Nimrod and the introduction of idolatry which is so closely associated with this mighty hunter before the Lord, was filled by the calling of Abraham and the promises made to him concerning the great nation Israel.

In Genesis 48:19 we read, 'his seed shall become a multitude of nations'. It so happens that the word 'multitude' occurs earlier in this same chapter, namely in verse 4, where we read:

> 'Behold, I will make thee fruitful, and multiply thee, and I will make of thee a multitude of people' (Gen. 48:4).

Two words are found in the Hebrew original which are here translated 'multitude' and these must be distinguished.

The word translated 'multitude' in verse 4 is the Hebrew word *qahal* 'to call' or 'to assemble', but the word translated 'multitude' in verse 19 is entirely different, it is the Hebrew word *melo* 'fulness'.*

Let us bring together all three passages which make the promise that Israel shall be a multitude or company of (*qahal*) people or nations.

> 'And GOD ALMIGHTY bless thee, and make thee fruitful, and multiply thee, that thou mayest be a multitude of (*qahal*) people' (Gen. 28:3).
>
> 'And God said unto him, I am GOD ALMIGHTY: be fruitful and multiply; a nation and a company of (*qahal*) nations shall be of thee' (Gen. 35:11).
>
> 'Behold, I will make thee fruitful, and multiply thee, and I will make of thee a multitude of (*qahal*) people' (Gen. 48:4).

In these passages 'multitude' or 'company' translate the Hebrew word *qahal*. When Jacob blessed Joseph's younger son Ephraim, putting his right hand upon his head, instead of upon the head of Manasseh his elder brother, Joseph said:

---

* Readers who use *The Companion Bible* (early editions) should observe that the note against `multitude' in verse 19 should be transferred to the margin of verse 4 in the same chapter.

> 'Not so, my father ...' Jacob answered, 'I know it, my son, I know it: he also shall become a people, and he also shall be great: but truly his younger brother shall be greater than he, and his seed shall become a multitude of (*melo*) nations' (Gen. 48:19).

Here, as we have already observed, the Hebrew word translated 'multitude' is *melo*, 'fulness'.

We must, therefore, become acquainted with the usage and meaning of these two words which are translated 'multitude' before we can proceed with our study. *Qahal*, means 'to call together', 'to assemble', and the noun form is translated 'congregation', 'assembly' and 'company'. In seventy passages, the Septuagint renders the Hebrew *qahal* by *ekklesia*, and Stephen speaks of 'the church in the wilderness' (Acts 7:38). In the three passages quoted from Genesis, 'multitude' and 'company' are represented by 'synagogue' in the Septuagint. In Genesis 48:19 *melo* which is translated 'multitude' is rendered in the Septuagint *plethos*, which in the New Testament is rendered by the A.V. 'multitude' thirty times, 'company' once and 'bundle' once. Unfortunately the English word 'multitude' has to stand for two very different conceptions. *Plethos*, is from the same root as *pleroma* and retains the idea of fulness or filling, but there is another Greek word translated multitude, namely *ochlos* which means rather 'a crowd' or 'a mob', the unruly nature of which is reflected in the verbal forms which mean 'to vex' or 'to trouble' (Acts 5:16; 15:19; 17:5; Heb. 12:15). While, therefore, we are compelled to use the English word multitude in these passages of Genesis, we must dismiss the thought of a 'mob' or of an unruly 'crowd', and retain the idea of a properly assembled gathering and a filling.

Returning to the usage of the word *qahal*, we observe that from Exodus 12:6 where we read '*the* whole *assembly*', the word is used of Israel as a nation, but in Genesis, before Israel as a nation existed, it is used prophetically, looking down the ages to the day when the seed of Abraham shall indeed become 'a filling of the nations' (Rotherham). The four occurrences of *qahal* fall into their place in the structure, which can be seen set out in full in *The Companion Bible.*

The following extract will be sufficient to demonstrate this fitness here.

Gen. 27:42 to 28:5. Departure. Jacob to Padan-aram.
'*that thou mayest be a multitude of people*'.

* * *

Gen. 35:1-15. Return. Jacob from Padan-aram.
'*a nation and a company of nations*'.
Gen. 48:1-20. Blessing of Joseph and his sons.
'*I will make of thee a multitude of people*'.

* * *

Gen. 49:1-28. Blessing of all his sons.
'*unto their assembly, mine honour, be not thou united*'.

It will be remembered that in the endeavour to obtain the birthright and the Abrahamic blessing, Jacob, at the instigation of his mother who knew that 'the elder shall serve the younger' (Gen. 25:23), attempted by fraud to make the prophecy sure, but failed. When Jacob as a consequence was obliged to leave home, the coveted blessing for which both he and his mother had schemed was given to him freely:

> 'And GOD ALMIGHTY bless thee, and make thee fruitful, and multiply thee, that thou mayest be a multitude of people; and give thee the blessing of Abraham, to thee, and to thy seed with thee; that thou mayest inherit the land wherein thou art a stranger, which God gave unto Abraham' (Gen. 28:3,4).

Not only is 'the land' a definite feature of this promise, but a peculiar character attaches to it, it is called 'the land wherein thou art a stranger'. This is repeated in Genesis 37:1, and in 47:9 Jacob uses the same word where it is translated 'pilgrimage'. The margin of Genesis 28:4, reads, 'the land of thy sojournings'. This term is used seven times in the law and is repeated in Hebrews 11:9,13. After the formation of Israel and the giving of the law, the nation is not again reminded that they were strangers and sojourners except in one passage, namely in Leviticus

25:23, where the laws governing the sale of land showed that the Lord Himself was the true Owner, Israel only holding the land as it were on a lease. One further note is necessary before we attempt a conclusion, and that concerns the word translated 'nation'. An attempt has been made, in order that a certain popular theory might be supported, to show that Ephraim was to become 'Gentilized'. The Hebrew word translated 'nations' is *goyim*, the plural of *goi*. This word is translated in the A.V. as follows: 'Gentile' thirty times, 'heathen' 142 times, 'nation' 373 times, 'people' eleven times. It is easy, when we are reading the passages where 'Gentile' and 'heathen' occur, to jump to the conclusion that the word means, 'all nations of the world, excepting the Jews', but this is an error.

The first six occurrences of *goyim* occur in Genesis 10, and as Israel was not in existence at the time, it is evident that the word can only mean 'nations'; the inclusion of the word 'Gentiles' in the A.V. of Genesis 10:5, being an anticipation and having no immediate meaning until placed over against the word 'Jew'. The R.V. has recognized this, and inserted 'nations' instead. In Genesis 12:2 we read the words of the great prophetic promise to Abraham concerning his seed, Israel, 'I will make of thee a great nation', while in Genesis 17:4,5,6 this promise is expanded to include 'many nations', returning in 18:18 once more to the 'great nation'. So in Genesis 35:11 we read, 'a nation and a company of nations', the only distinction between Jew and Gentile being, not in the use of a different word, but in the use of the singular for the Jew, and the plural for the Gentile. So again in Deuteronomy 4, we have interchangeably 'this great nation', 'what nation is so great', 'the heathen', 'a nation from the midst of another nation' and 'the nations', that were to be driven out of Canaan, all being translations of the one Hebrew word. Even in the Greek New Testament when the distinction between Jew and Gentile is acute, we still find *ethnos* used both of the Gentiles and of Israel (Acts 22:21; 26:4,17; 28:19,28). (See GENTILE[2]).

While, therefore, *goyim* means at times Gentile or heathen, it always means 'nation' whether the nations outside the covenant, or the great nation of promise. The promise that Israel should be 'great' must not be misunderstood. With us, 'greatness' is associated with nobility of mind, but originally the word *gadol* translated 'great' means 'growth' or 'augmentation'. So we read of 'great lights', 'great whales', a 'great city' in Genesis. The word, moreover, is used to indicate 'the elder' son (Gen. 10:21; 27:1; 29:16) who may not necessarily have been 'greater'.

Israel are indeed at the present day 'minished and brought low through oppression' (Psa. 107:39), but it is an integral part of the promise to Abraham, that Israel should not only be great in spiritual qualities, but great in numbers. The promise reads, 'I will make thy seed as the dust of the earth: so that if a man can number the dust of the earth, then shall thy seed also be numbered' (Gen. 13:16).

The figure is changed in Genesis 15:5 to the innumerable stars of heaven, with the added words, 'so shall thy seed be'. Yet once again the figure is changed to 'the sand upon the sea shore' (Gen. 22:17).

> 'Sir Arthur Eddington is of the opinion that one hundred thousand million stars make one galaxy, and one hundred thousand million galaxies, make one universe. The number of stars in a universe therefore would be ten thousand trillion, or expressed in figures,
>
> 10,000,000,000,000,000,000,000,
>
> that is equal to the number of drops of water in all the oceans of the world, or grains of fine sand sufficient to cover the whole of England and Wales, to a depth of a foot, and each one of them comparable in size to our sun'. (*The Endless Quest*, Westaway).

While it is not intended that Israel are ever to reach such astronomical figures, the contemplation of the possible number of the stars, compels us to admit that an extraordinary increase in number constitutes an essential feature of the Divine purpose for this 'great nation'. According to Deuteronomy 1:10 these promises were on the way to fulfilment even when Israel stood upon the borders of the promised land, and the present drop in their numbers is coincident with their being in disfavour. 'If ye walk contrary to Me, I will make you *few in number*' (Lev. 26:21,22).

When at length the Lord causes the captivity of both Judah and of Israel to return 'as at the first', when He performs that good thing which He has promised unto the house of Israel and of Judah, then 'as the host of heaven cannot be numbered, neither the sand of the sea measured: so will I multiply the seed of David My servant, and the Levites that minister unto Me saith the LORD' (Jer. 33:7,14,22).

At the time of the end of this age the world will be so ravaged and desolated by the destructive method of atomic or other superscientific weapons that the prophet Zechariah speaks of 'every one that *is left* of all the nations which came against Jerusalem' (Zech. 14:16), words that suggest a terrible depletion in the number of the inhabitants of the earth at that day. In Zechariah 13:8 the prophet's meaning is made very clear, when he says, 'and it shall come to pass, that in all the land, saith the LORD, two parts therein shall be cut off and die; but the third shall be left therein'. Something of what may be expected when atomic warfare breaks out over this devoted earth can be sensed by the words of the Apocalypse:

> '*The third part of* trees was burnt up'.
> '*The third part of* the sea became blood'.
> '*The third part of* the ships were destroyed'.
> '*The third part of* men', slain (Rev. 8:7,8,9; 9:15).

The day is passed when these catastrophic times could be brushed aside as mere figures of speech, we have lived through days when 'a third part of the ships' were well nigh literally destroyed. We have seen that following the desolation of Genesis 1:2 came the creation of man and the command, '*replenish* the earth'. We have seen that the same command was given to Noah after the cataclysm of the flood. This same command will be fulfilled in Israel when they, too, shall 'blossom and bud, and fill the face of the world with fruit' (Isa. 27:6). Ephraim, as the 'firstborn' will indeed be great, and his seed 'shall become a FILLING UP of the nations' (Gen. 48:19).

Once again we see the principle of the *pleroma* at work, with its promise of a better day, when sorrow and sighing shall have fled away, when the true seed shall flourish, and the seed of the serpent be no more.

(9) THE FULNESS OF THE GENTILES (Rom. 11:25)

We have seen that the promise to Abraham concerning his seed, has followed the same pattern that has characterized the earlier moves in the outworking of the purpose. Their failure came to a head just before the Babylonian captivity and, with Nebuchadnezzar, 'the times of the Gentiles' began:

> 'In the third year of the reign of Jehoiakim king of Judah came Nebuchadnezzar king of Babylon unto Jerusalem, and besieged it. And the Lord gave Jehoiakim king of Judah into his hand, with part of the vessels of the house of God: which he carried into the land of Shinar to the house of his god' (Dan. 1:1,2).

With these words the book of Daniel opens, and it may not be too much to say that they are only paralleled by the words of Acts 28 in their burden of crisis and dispensational change. With such vast issues hanging upon these momentous words, vast because they cover the whole sweep of Gentile dominion, and vaster still because they lead steadily on to that kingdom of Christ which is to last for ever; with such issues and such a burden, no pains should be spared in acquainting ourselves with all that God has written for our learning in relation to this crisis in the history of man. Space will not permit of the full quotation of Jeremiah 25:1-26. We can but point out one or two features that connect this passage with the opening words of Daniel.

The reader will be struck by the fact that whereas Daniel 1:1 speaks of the 'third' year of Jehoiakim, Jeremiah 25:1 speaks of the 'fourth' year of that same king in connection with the coming of Nebuchadnezzar against Jerusalem. This apparent discrepancy has not passed unnoticed by the critic, being one of his many 'proofs' of the untrustworthiness of the book of Daniel.

The Hebrew word translated 'came' in Daniel 1:1 is *bo*, and it frequently has the sense of 'went' or 'marched'. This, however, has been denied. Dr. Samuel Davidson says, 'the verb *bo* does not mean *to set out* ... but to *arrive at*' ... (*Introduction to the Old Testament*, Vol. III, p. 181), and, when men of such standing and authority speak thus, who are we to oppose them? Humility is indeed a grace to seek and preserve, but while Galatians 2 remains for our encouragement, we may still dare to bring all statements to the touchstone of the Word. Dr. Davidson's statement but illustrates the uncritical character of so-called 'higher criticism' for it has been computed that the Hebrew word *bo* is used in the sense of 'to set out' in each of the five books of Moses, in Joshua, Judges, Ruth, Samuel, Kings, Chronicles, Ezra, Nehemiah, Esther, Job, Psalms, Proverbs, Isaiah, Jeremiah, Ezekiel, and in six out of the twelve minor prophets!

Let us look at Jonah 1:3 and translate it as Dr. Davidson would have it: 'And Jonah ... went down to Joppa, and he found a ship *arriving* at Tarshish'! If this could be sense, then in some miraculous way Jonah would have no sooner set foot on board at Joppa than he would have 'arrived' at Tarshish.

Doubtless this would have made the journey far more pleasant than it actually was, but the simple fact is that the Hebrew word *bo* does mean that the ship was 'going' or 'setting out' for Tarshish. The plain fact of Daniel 1 and Jeremiah 25 is that the former writer tells us the year in which Nebuchadnezzar 'set out' from Babylon, while the latter tells us when he 'arrived'. Moreover, Jeremiah tells us what occupied Nebuchadnezzar on his journey from one capital to the other:

> 'Against Egypt, against the army of Pharaoh-necho king of Egypt, which was by the river Euphrates in Carchemish, which Nebuchadnezzar king of Babylon smote *in the fourth year of Jehoiakim* the son of Josiah king of Judah' (Jer. 46:2).

Instead therefore of discovering a discrepancy in the narrative of Scripture, we have the obvious fact that Nebuchadnezzar took time to accomplish this march from Babylon to Jerusalem, and was obliged to meet and overcome Pharaoh at Carchemish by the Euphrates before he could arrive.

In Jeremiah 25:3 the prophet reminded Israel that since the thirteenth year of Josiah (see Jeremiah 1:1,2), the word of the Lord had come urging them to turn from their evil, and because they had not turned He said:

> 'Behold, I will send and take all the families of the north, saith the LORD, and Nebuchadnezzar the king of Babylon, my servant, and will bring them against this land ... And this whole land shall be a desolation, and an astonishment; and these nations shall serve the king of Babylon seventy years' (Jer. 25:9-11).

What God therefore had threatened, He brought to pass in the fourth year of Jehoiakim, and the historic record of the captivity of Jehoiakim is found in 2 Chronicles 36, *the last chapter of the Hebrew Bible!*

Yet with all this apparent on the surface of Scripture, and needing no more scholarship than ability to read in one's mother tongue, Kuenen in his historic *Critique de l'Ancien Testament* has the audacity to say:

> 'We know by the book of Jeremiah that no such event (as the siege of Jerusalem, (Dan. 1:1) took place in the reign of Jehoiakim'.

'We know'! We also know that it is written, 'professing themselves to be wise they became fools', and by such statements they demonstrate that they are but 'blind leaders of the blind'.

Jehoiakim was appointed king of Judah by Pharaoh-nechoh in the place of Jehoahaz (2 Kings 23:34). He did evil in the sight of the Lord, and filled Jerusalem with innocent blood. He was succeeded by Jehoiachin. In the reign of the latter, Nebuchadnezzar carried out thence *all* the treasures of the house of the Lord, whereas Daniel 1:1,2 tells us that at the first he only carried away *a part*.

Jehoiachin or Jeconiah is deprived of the Jehovah element in his name, and under the name Coniah is utterly rejected by the Lord:

> 'Thus saith the LORD, Write ye this man childless, a man that shall not prosper in his days: for no man of his seed shall prosper, sitting upon the throne of David, and ruling any more in Judah' (Jer. 22:30).

It is evident that Israel is passing; dominion is leaving them and is being transferred for the time being to the Gentiles. This is emphasized by such statements as Daniel 1:2, 'And the Lord gave ... into his hand', or Jeremiah 25:1, 'The fourth year of Jehoiakim ... that was the *first* year of Nebuchadnezzar'. The times of the Gentiles had therefore begun. And so with Zedekiah the glory departs, and Ezekiel 21 reveals the condition of things that will obtain 'until He come':

> 'And thou, profane wicked prince of Israel, whose day is come, when iniquity shall have an end, thus saith the LORD God; Remove the diadem, and take off the crown: this shall not be the same: exalt him that is low, and abase him that is high. I will overturn, overturn, overturn it: and it shall be no more, until He come Whose right it is; and I will give it Him' (21:25-27).

'Until He come'; Gentile dominion obtains on the earth until the coming of the Son of Man. No interim 'Kingdom' is to be found here. Daniel's prophecies are occupied with this period of overturning, of the exalting of the base and abasing of the high. 'This shall not be the same', saith the Lord, 'this shall not be this', as the Hebrew reads, i.e. Nebuchadnezzar's dominion and dynasty would not be a real continuance of the throne of David. It would be in character rather a rule and dominion of wild beasts. The words, 'it shall be no more, until He come', leave us in no doubt that the throne thus vacated shall be occupied by none other than the Lord Jesus Christ Himself.

The times of the Gentiles are characterized by one great feature, marked by the Lord in Luke 21:24, 'and Jerusalem shall be trodden down of the Gentiles, until the times of the Gentiles be fulfilled'. The kingdoms that succeeded Babylon may have been larger or smaller, more powerful or weaker, more autocratic or less so, but the one essential characteristic of Babylon, Persia, Greece, Rome, Turkey and any succeeding mandatory power is the Gentile domination of Jerusalem. *That* is the great distinguishing feature, and will only be removed when 'He comes Whose right it is'.

We have, therefore, a period of time which fills the 'gap' caused by Israel's failure, which gap is filled by the dynasty started with Nebuchadnezzar and *which will persist* until, in the Day of the Lord, 'the stone cut out without hands' strikes this colossus, and 'the kingdoms of this world become the kingdom of our Lord and of His Christ'.

It is characteristic of the times of the Gentiles that this Jerusalem should be 'trodden down'. Those times will not end until Jerusalem is free from the yoke of Gentile dominion, surveillance or protection. Each succeeding ruler of the Gentiles has dominated Jerusalem — Babylon, Medo-Persia, Greece, Rome, Turkey, the League of Nations, the British Mandate, the United Nations, and so on to the last great Dictator and his ten subsequent kings at the time of the end.

When Jerusalem is at length free, the times of the Gentiles will be 'fulfilled' (*pleroo*), and 'the fulness (*pleroma*) of the Gentiles' will have come (Luke 21:24; Rom. 11:25). Immediately following this statement concerning the times of the Gentiles, the epistle to the Romans goes on to say 'and so' or 'thus' 'all Israel shall be saved' (Rom. 11:26). The 'gap' in the outworking of the Divine purpose in Israel is stressed in Romans 9 to 11, because of their failure, but a 'remnant' shall be saved at the beginning, for had the Lord not left them a 'seed' they would have been like Sodom and Gomorrah. Throughout the period covered by the Acts, 'all day long' the Lord stretched out his hands 'to a disobedient and gainsaying people' (Rom. 10:21). However low Israel may have fallen during this period, the answer of God to Elijah has a parallel, 'I have reserved to Myself seven thousand men, who have not bowed the knee to the image of Baal' (Rom. 11:4). Yet such is the grace of God, the very diminishing of them led to the enriching of the Gentiles, and leads the apostle to ask, 'how much more their fulness?'

The figure of the olive tree, with its broken branches but emphasizes the 'gap' that is in view, and the fulness of the Gentiles occupies the interval occasioned by Israel's blindness (Rom. 11:25). Israel's failure, in the days of Nebuchadnezzar led to the times of the Gentiles, speaking nationally, but Israel's spiritual failure registered in Acts 28 led to the present dispensation of Gentile blessing, the Church which is called by the wondrous title, 'the fulness of Him that filleth all in all'. This, however, is so great a theme that it must be considered in a separate study.

(10) THE TITLE HEAD AND ITS RELATION TO 'THE FULNESS'

The highest title ascribed to Christ in any dispensation other than that of the Mystery is that of 'a Priest for ever after the order of Melchisedec'. This priesthood is superior to that of Aaron, it functions at the right hand of God, its sphere is the true tabernacle which God pitched and not man, namely 'heaven itself', and it combines the two offices of King and Priest. Just as water cannot rise above its own level, so no calling can rise above the position set by Christ, and the calling that recognizes Him as King-Priest is itself 'a Kingdom of Priests', 'a holy nation and a royal priesthood'. It is significant that throughout the Prison Epistles, Christ is never called either 'King' or 'Priest', even as it is equally true that the church of that calling is never called a kingdom or a priesthood, but is called 'the Body' of Christ. Argument from the absence of terms, like arguing from a negative is in most cases suspect, but in this particular instance it cannot be said that a 'kingdom' is never mentioned in the Prison Epistles. We read in Ephesians 5:5 of 'the Kingdom of Christ and of God'; in Colossians 1:13 and 4:11 of 'the kingdom of His dear Son' and of 'the kingdom of God', and in 2 Timothy 4:1 and 18, 'His appearing and His kingdom', and 'His heavenly kingdom'. In the epistles of Paul other than the four great Prison Epistles, a 'kingdom' is mentioned nine times, but the only passage where Christ can be said to have the title King is in 1 Timothy 6:15, where however the exhibition of the title is spoken of as a future event 'which in His times He shall shew, Who is the blessed and only Potentate, the King of kings, and Lord of lords'.

The epistles to the Ephesians and the Colossians contain terms that seem to demand the work of a priest, such as 'acceptance', 'access', 'made nigh', 'offer', yet there is not a single reference outside of Hebrews to Christ as a priest. In epistles before and after Acts 28, Christ is represented as 'seated at the right hand of God', yet never, outside of Hebrews, is the office of priest mentioned. If a 'dominion' and a 'coronation' are indications of the presence of a king, then Adam was a king. The 'dominion' given to him is the translation of the Hebrew *radah*, a word translated elsewhere 'reign' and 'rule' and used of Christ 'the King's Son' in Psalm 72:8. The word translated 'crowned' in Psalm 8:5 is the Hebrew *atar*, which is the verb form of *atarah* 'the king's crown' (2 Sam. 12:30). Adam, however, is never once spoken of as a king. He was a figure of Him that was to come, and can be spoken of with propriety as HEAD of the human race, and as such he embraced all that kingship can mean, but *much more*.

Noah not only had dominion in his degree (Gen. 9:2) but he offered sacrifices with acceptance (Gen. 8:20,21). The word 'sweet' which is used of the savour of the sacrifice offered is employed throughout the Old Testament to indicate the 'savour' or 'odour' of sacrifice. We should, therefore, not be surprised to find that Noah was a 'priest'. Yet he is never so called. He can be, however, designated as Adam was before him HEAD of the race of which those delivered from the flood were the progenitors.

Abraham was the father of 'kings' (Gen. 17:6), and even of THE KING, the Lord Himself, Who was according to the flesh both son of Abraham and son of David, yet Abraham himself is never called a king. Abraham not only built an altar, at the beginning of his pilgrimage upon which the only sacrifices permitted would have been those taken from the herd and the flock, he came nearer to the heart of all true sacrifice when he was called upon to offer his only begotten son Isaac, yet Abraham is never called a priest. Like Adam and Noah, Abraham is more than king, more than priest, he is the father of Israel, to which he stands without contradiction as HEAD. Even when we leave the chosen people, and turn our attention to the first great king whose reign commenced the times of the Gentiles — Nebuchadnezzar, he too is spoken of by Daniel as 'This HEAD of gold' (Dan. 2:38). Each one of the great outstanding figures that have foreshadowed the *pleroma*, or fulness, were 'Heads' and in this they foreshadowed all that the office of King, Priest and Prophet alone could set forth. Even though Christ be never called either Prophet, Priest or King in the epistles of the Mystery, the Church of the One Body loses nothing if Christ is its Head; He is more than King and Priest and Prophet to the Church, for headship covers all.

With this preparation, let us turn to the epistles of the Fulness, the Prison Epistles of Paul, and observe the way in which this title 'head' is employed. The Greek word *kephale* is used of Christ in the Prison Epistles seven times, and the verb *anakephalaioomai* once. Let us look at the usage of this verb, which means 'to head up'. It occurs in Ephesians 1:10 where it is translated 'to gather together in one' in the A.V., 'to sum up' in the R.V. and in Weymouth's translation 'of restoring the whole creation to find its one Head in Christ', and by J.N. Darby 'to head up all things in Christ'. It is in connection with the 'pleroma' of the seasons that this figure of 'heading up' is used, no other term being so appropriate or so complete. When the 'fulness' arrives, Christ will be infinitely more than King, or Priest, He will be 'Head'. The references to Christ as 'Head' in the Prison Epistles are limited to the epistles to the Ephesians and to the Colossians (Eph. 1:22; 4:15; 5:23; Col. 1:18; 2:10; 2:19).

These six references to *kephale*, expand the promise of Ephesians 1:10, the Church of the present dispensation being the most complete foreshadowing of the goal of the ages that the Scriptures contain. To turn back to the types and shadows employed in earlier Scriptures is to turn by comparison from substance to shadow, although the 'substance' here in its turn must necessarily be but a 'shadow' of the reality yet to come. The first passage brings us back from the day when all things in heaven and earth shall be headed up in Christ, to the present period when in a day of rejection, confusion and darkness, an elect company find that Christ is to them what He will be universally in the future.

Kephale 'Head' in Ephesians and Colossians

A Eph. 1:22. Head over all things to the Church which is His Body. In the context Christ is seen raised and seated 'far above all principality and power'. The word *pleroma* being used as a title of the Church.

B **a** Eph. 4:15. Grow up ... which is the Head, even Christ. In the context is seen the body 'fitly joined' together, every 'joint' working toward the 'increase' of the Body. The word *pleroma* being used in verse 13 as the goal of the Church 'the measure of the stature of the fulness of Christ'.

b Eph. 5:23. Christ is the Head of the Church.

A Col. 1:18. He is the head of the Body the Church. In the context principalities and powers are seen to be His creation, and the word *pleroma is* used in verse 19, 'It pleased the Father that in Him should all fulness dwell'.

B *b* Col. 2:10. Christ is the head of all principality and power. The word *pleroma* being found In verse 9.

a Col. 2:19. Holding the head, from which all the Body by 'joints and bands' being 'knit together' 'increaseth with the increase of God'.

'And gave Him to be Head over all things TO THE CHURCH' (Eph. 1:22). Christ is not yet recognized as 'Head over all things', the day is future when 'every knee shall bow and every tongue confess' but what will be true then, in its widest sense, is true now of 'the Church which is His Body'. In the glorious future 'God' will be all in all (1 Cor. 15:28), but that day has not yet come. In the Church which is His Body 'Christ is all, and in all' (Col. 3:11). In the glorious future 'all things are put under His feet' (1 Cor. 15:27), but as in Hebrews, we say today, 'we see not yet all things put under Him' (Heb. 2:8); we can see His Ascension 'far above all principality and power, and might, and dominion, and every name that is named, not only in this world, but also in that which is to come' and the fact that He is already Head over all things *to the church*, is a most glorious anticipation of this universal subjection of all to Him, and this Ephesians 1:22 indicates, by joining together the two themes:

(1) 'And hath put all things under His feet'.

(2) 'And gave Him to be Head over all things to the Church'.

This Church then is in a unique position. It anticipates as no other calling and company has or can, the goal of the ages. It is meet, therefore, that this should be set forth, and the apostle follows the passage already quoted by revealing that this Church, which is His Body, is something more, it is 'the fulness' of Him, Who in His turn is the One that 'filleth all in all' (Eph. 1:23). All the fulness of the Godhead dwells in Him 'bodily', the Church which is His 'Body' and in whom He dwells (Eph. 2:22; 3:17) is His fulness. What Christ is to the invisible God, the Church is to Christ. What Christ is to the whole purpose of the ages, the Church of the One Body is in the heavenly realm.

Ephesians 1:10 is here illustrated, foreshadowed, and anticipated and this of itself is a glorious position to occupy, quite apart from all the other wonders of grace and glory that are associated with this high calling.

Rotherham translates Ephesians 1:23:

> 'Which indeed is His Body. The fulness of Him Who the all things in all is for Himself filling up'.

Moffatt reads: 'Filled by Him Who fills the universe entirely'. Possibly the rendering given by Cunnington is nearest the truth:

> 'The fulness of Him Who all in all is receiving His fulness',

to which he appends a footnote, 'Cf. Philippians 2:7, process of cancelling the Emptying'.

'Cancelling the Emptying'. What a thought!

A.T. writing in *The Differentiator* of August 1955 comments:

> 'Here we have a most beautiful thought. When Christ Jesus (note the term) emptied Himself, He must have emptied Himself of His fulness. But after His resurrection He got back His fulness — "in Him delights the entire fulness to dwell" (Col. 1:19) — "in Him is dwelling the entire fulness of the Deity bodily"' (Col. 2:9).

Dr. Robinson gives a new thought from Colossians 2:9:

> 'For in Him dwelleth all the fulness of the Deity in a bodily way, and ye are filled (or fulfilled) in Him'. This is usually taken to refer to the Godhead residing in the Lord's body in all its completeness. But Dr. Robinson says this would be to neglect Paul's special use of the terms 'fulness' and 'body' in his epistles. The empty deceit of the philosophical despoiler can only give tradition and world elements in place of the heavenly Christ ... Thus St. Paul looks forward to the ultimate issue of the Divine purpose for the universe ... this is found in Christ 'by way of a body'; that is to say; in Christ as a whole in which the head and the body are inseparably one'.

The Saviour had a glory 'before the world was' (John 17:5); He emptied Himself (Phil. 2:7), and has been subsequently highly exalted. THAT GLORY He can and will share with the redeemed.

> 'And the *glory which Thou gavest Me* I have given them; that they may be one, even as We are one' (John 17:22).

The fulness of Him that filleth all in all is the most blessed anticipation of the day when God shall be all in all (1 Cor. 15:28).

We have seen that the title 'Head' gathers up into itself all that the separate titles 'King', 'Priest' and 'Prophet' imply, with ever so much more than any of these titles taken separately, or all together can ever teach or contain. That Church of which Christ is 'Head' not only lacks nothing, but is infinitely more blessed, is in a closer relationship with Christ, and anticipates the goal of the ages in a way that no other company could ever do. We have seen that Ephesians 1:10 finds its expansion and anticipation in Ephesians 1:22,23, and we now pass on to the other references to Christ as the Head as they occur in the epistles of the Mystery. The next reference to Christ as 'Head' occurs in the practical section of Ephesians:

'But speaking the truth in love, may grow up into Him in all things, which is the head, even Christ' (Eph. 4:15).

Practice grows out of doctrine, and doctrine deals with calling, sphere of blessing, and standing in grace. What is stated as a fact before God in the revelation of the doctrine of Ephesians, awaits experimental realization in the practical section. Let us see this in the large, before concentrating our attention upon the detail.

As a consequence of the Saviour's exaltation, 'far above all', in Ephesians 1:20-22, He is seen as Head over all things to the Church, which church is called 'the fulness of Him that filleth all in all'. Turning to Ephesians 4, we find that the Ascension 'far above all' is restated, and the 'fulness' indicated as a goal.

'He that descended is the same also that ascended up FAR ABOVE ALL heavens, that He might FILL ALL THINGS' (Eph. 4:10). The gift of apostles, etc., from this Ascended One has as its goal 'the perfect man', and its measure the stature of 'the fulness' of Christ (Eph. 4:13). It is evident from this language of Ephesians 4:8-13, that we are here presented with the *outworking* of the truth set out in chapter 1.

Coming now to Ephesians 4:15, we observe that the words of the A.V., 'speaking the truth in love', are somewhat free, there being no equivalent in the Greek, for the word 'speaking'. The A.V. margin puts as an alternative 'being sincere' and the R.V. margin reads 'dealing truly'. The Greek word under consideration is *aletheuein*, of which Alford, in his commentary, says 'it is almost impossible to express it satisfactorily in English', and suggests the translation 'being followers of truth' but says of this 'the objection to "followers of truth" is that it may be mistaken for "searchers after truth", but I can find no expression which does not lie open to equal objection'. The only other occurrence of *aletheuein* is Galatians 4:16, where the A.V. renders it, 'because I tell (you) the truth'.

It is not possible in English to say 'truthing in love', we must say, 'being sincere', 'being true or truthful' or 'speaking the truth'. None of these expressions, however, exactly present to the mind what the verb *aletheuein* does. The LXX of Genesis 42:16 employs this word where we read, 'ye shall be kept in prison, that your words may be proved, whether *there be any* truth in you; or else by the life of Pharaoh surely ye are spies'.

In Isaiah 44:26, the LXX employs *aletheuein* to translate the word *shalam* 'perform', but when the same Hebrew word occurs again in verse 28, it is there translated by the Greek *poiein* 'to make or to do'. If we can imagine a word in English that conjures up to the mind a person whose whole life is truth, whose very breath and atmosphere is truth, whose desires, will, plans and activities are truth, we may perhaps approach the meaning of Ephesians 4:15. This utter regard for 'truth', however, is balanced, for it must be held 'in love'; without that, such zeal in present circumstances would lead to fanaticism and a persecuting spirit.

This utter regard for truth held in love is the great accessory to 'growth', 'may grow up into Him in all things'. Growing up into Christ in all things is the practical echo of the basic doctrinal fact that has already been revealed concerning the constitution of the Church of the One Body in Ephesians 1:22,23. Not only so, but it is the practical and experimental echo of the truth revealed in Ephesians 2:21.

> 'In Whom all the building FITLY FRAMED TOGETHER (*sunarmologeo*) GROWETH (*auxano*) unto an holy temple in the Lord'.

The word *sunarmologeo* is repeated in Ephesians 4:16 where it is translated 'FITLY JOINED TOGETHER', and the words *auxano* and *auxesis* are found in Ephesians 4:15,16, 'may GROW (*auxano*) *UP* unto Him'; 'maketh INCREASE (*auxesis*) of the Body'.

Not only do these words recur, but just as the Church of the One Body is the fulness of Him that filleth ALL (*ta panta* 'all these') in all, so this growth of Ephesians 4:15 is unto Him in ALL (these) THINGS (*ta panta*). Most translators supply the preposition 'in' before 'all things' in order to make easy reading, and this reading may give the intention of the apostle, namely, that the Church should grow up into Christ in every particular, in all ways, in all things. Nevertheless, the mind returns to the fact that what the apostle actually wrote was *auxesomen eis auton ta panta*, which rendered literally reads, 'we may grow into Him the all things'. This rendering, while it does not 'read' and is not good English, leaves in the mind a different conception from that of the A.V. Can it be the apostle intends us to understand him to mean, that by holding the truth inviolate in love, we shall be encouraging that growth into Him, which the New Testament speaks of as *ta panta*, some specific, blessed totality of glory, in which Christ is now the summary *ta panta* Himself, 'the all things' in all? (Col. 3:11), anticipating the goal of God, when God Himself shall be *ta panta en pasin* (1 Cor. 15:28 in the Received Text), 'the all things in all'? Before, however, such words can have their true effect, it becomes necessary that we pause here, in order to place before the reader, the peculiar usage of the phrase *ta panta*, for the phrase 'the all things' sounds strange to our ears.

Pas is an adjective, translated either 'all' or 'every' in the majority of cases. The plural *panta* 'all things' is used with or without the article, and these two forms must be distinguished. We cannot very well translate *ta panta* 'the all things' for that has an un-English sound, but a survey of the usage of these two forms *panta* and *ta panta*, may enable us to reach some agreed rendering that will satisfy every claim, and present a fair translation of the inspired original. The two forms are found in Romans 8 and their fitness is easily recognized by reason of the context of each form.

There is a good deal of suffering in Romans 8, induced both by the failure and frailty of the believer himself, and coming upon him by reason of his fellowship with Christ, his place in a groaning creation, and the attack of enemies. In consequence, he is sometimes at a loss to know 'what to pray for' as he ought, but he does know, in the midst of all life's uncertainty, that 'all things work together for good to them that love God' (Rom. 8:28). Here 'all things' is *panta* without the article 'the' *ta*, all things whether *good or evil*. Later in the chapter the apostle says:

> 'He that spared not His own Son, but delivered Him up for us all, how shall He not with Him also freely give us all things?' (Rom. 8:32).

Here 'all things' is *ta panta*, some specific 'all things' namely those things which come under the heading of Redemption, and which constitute the goal and consummation of the ages. *Panta* without the article is unlimited, *panta* with the article is restricted to the realm of redeeming grace. 'All these' is the translation of *ta panta* in Colossians 3:8 which is a good example of its restricted meaning.

Romans 11 does not teach that 'all things' without limit or restriction owe their origin, persistence and final blessing to the Lord:

'For of Him, and through Him, and to Him are ta *panta*' (11:36), namely that conception of the universe that embraces all in heaven and in earth that come under the grace and power of the Redeemer. The advocates of universal reconciliation, while recognizing the presence of the article in Romans 11:32, use this verse to support their doctrine and omit the articles in their translation. It is not the teaching here that 'God hath concluded ALL in unbelief, that He might have mercy upon ALL', but the whole verse should be rendered:

> 'For God had concluded THEM ALL in unbelief, that He might have mercy on THEM ALL' (11:32).

Where universality is intended in Romans 9:5, the article is omitted, God is over ALL, without limitation or reserve. In the verses that follow, Paul uses ALL without the article with this same discrimination, 'for they are not all Israel (*pantes* without the article) which are of Israel' the 'seed' were called 'in Isaac' (Rom. 9:6,7). We must therefore read the words, 'and so all Israel shall be saved' (Rom. 11:26) in the light of Romans 9:6,7. The 'all' that are to be saved being those who were 'in Isaac', a type and shadow of the greater company of the saved at the end. In case the reader should expect to find the article here we point out that the word 'all' does not here stand alone and without qualification, *pas Israel* 'all Israel' is already limited and does not need the article 'the'.

Let us note the use of *panta* and *ta panta* in Ephesians, and by this we do not intend every single occurrence, for such phrases as 'all spiritual blessings' do not come within the scope of this inquiry.

That which is to be 'gathered together in one' is *ta panta* (Eph. 1:10) not *panta* without the article. That which is 'put in subjection under His feet' is *panta* all things *including* enemies (Eph. 1:22). He is also head over all things, *panta*, good as well as evil, to the Church which is His Body (Eph. 1:22), and He is the One who fills *ta panta*, that special company, without limit or reserve. The second reference to 'all' is without the article, and *en pasin* has been rendered 'everywhere', 'in every way' and 'in every case'. The creation of 'all things' *ta panta* of Ephesians 3:9 is limited, because it is directly associated with the Mystery which had been hid in God.

Where the words 'One God and Father of ALL, Who is above ALL, and through ALL and in (you) ALL' (Eph 4:6) occur, the word used is *panton* and *pasin* without the article. The subject is already limited to 'the Unity of the Spirit', and the insertion of *humin* 'you' in the text followed by the A.V. shows that this sense was clearly understood. J. N. Darby adopts the reading *hemin* 'in us all', which has been rendered by some 'and in all TO YOU', making the passage balance Ephesians 1:22, where Christ is not revealed as Head over all in the fullest sense yet, but as Head over all TO THE CHURCH.

One passage in Colossians must be included. Paul speaks of the new creation 'where there is neither Greek nor Jew ... but (*ta panta kai en pasin Christos*, in the Received Text) the all things and in all Christ' (Col. 3:11). Here 'Christ' is put in apposition to 'the all things', He Himself sums up in Himself the entire new creation. Of this He is the Head, it is in His image that all will be renewed, all other categories of worth and privilege are lost and put aside.

So also in Ephesians 4:15 *ta panta* 'the all things' is in apposition with the 'Head, even Christ'. The 'Fulness' that embraces this 'all things' is Christ and His Church, not Christ alone, and certainly not the Church alone. Of both Christ and His Church is 'Fulness' predicated, but only as Head and Body making one blessed company. True growth presses to 'the measure of the stature of the fulness of Christ', and in this dispensation, the growth of the One Body up into Him Who is the Head is the great example and exhibition of what the day of glory will reveal in its perfection.

Christ as 'Head', that is our theme, and here we see the first unfolding which is in germ in Ephesians 1:22,23.

As we prosecute our studies we shall learn that other phases of this growth and perfecting are associated with Christ the Head until, we hope, when the survey is completed, every reader will concur with our proposition, set out earlier in this exposition, that whatever blessings are to be associated with the great title of King, Priest and Prophet, they are all absorbed, filled and taken to their true end, in the one great title given to Christ in the epistles of the Mystery, 'The Head'.

(11) THE FULNESS OF THE SEASONS

The failure of Israel at the time of Nebuchadnezzar was answered by the times of the Gentiles, which commenced in the third year of Jehoiakim, king of Judah (Dan. 1:1), but, although earthly dominion passed from Israel at that time, they did not become *lo-ammi* in the full sense of the term until a fuller and deeper apostasy opened a deeper gulf, that could only be spanned by a greater and more spiritual fulness among the Gentiles. In the fulness of time, God sent forth His Son, and His birth at Bethlehem and His genealogy constitute the opening chapter of the book of the New Covenant (Matt. 1). The earthly ministry of the Saviour opened with a proclamation concerning the kingdom of heaven (Matt. 4:17), and as 'The King of the Jews' He was crucified (Matt. 27:37). The earlier stages of the culmination of rejection are revealed in chapters 11 to 13:

Matt. 11:20,26	'They repented not'. 'Even so Father'.
Matt. 12:6,41,42	'A greater than the temple, than Jonah and than Solomon' rejected (Priest, Prophet and King).
Matt. 13	The MYSTERY of the kingdom of heaven.

In these three chapters the gap and its antidote is anticipated. The miracles which the Saviour wrought, had as their primary purpose the repentance of Israel, and so to lead to the setting up of the kingdom (Matt. 11:20-24). Christ stood in their midst as Prophet, Priest and King, but they knew Him not.

In Matthew 12 we meet the first favourable use of the word 'Gentile'. In Matthew 10:5 the disciples were told 'go not into the way of the Gentiles' but upon it becoming manifest in Matthew 11, that Israel were not going to repent, a change is indicated.

> 'That it might be fulfilled which was spoken by Esaias the prophet, saying ... He shall shew judgment to the Gentiles ... And in His name shall the Gentiles trust' (Matt. 12:17-21).

The next chapter, Matthew 13, supplies the third key-word namely 'mystery'. Summing up these momentous chapters we have:

(1) No repentance of Israel, in spite of evidence of miracles.
(2) The inclusion of the Gentiles for the first time, consequent upon Israel's failure.
(3) The kingdom of heaven passes into its 'mystery' stage, and the parable form of speech is introduced.

The introduction of the Parable, contrary to popular interpretation, was NOT in order that the common people should be enabled to understand the message of the Gospel, but to veil the new aspect of truth from the eyes of those who were non-repentant. As this point of view is so contrary to that which is considered 'orthodox' let us consider what the Lord actually said in answer to His disciples' question, 'Why speakest Thou unto them in parables?' (Matt. 13:10). The very fact that the disciples were moved to ask such a question suggests that the parable form of speech was new to the Saviour's method hitherto. His answer is unambiguous and conclusive:

> 'He answered and said unto them, Because it is given unto you to know THE MYSTERIES of the kingdom of heaven, but to them it is not given' (Matt. 13:11).

The second part of the Lord's answer indicates that a great dispensational change was imminent:

> 'Therefore speak I to them in parables: because they seeing see not; and hearing they hear not, neither do they understand. And in them is fulfilled the prophecy of Esaias ... But blessed are your eyes, for they see: and your ears, for they hear' (Matt. 13:13-16).

The people of Israel had reached the point when the blindness prophesied by Isaiah had begun to take effect. It is a matter of importance to note the peculiar word used by the Lord here, that is translated 'fulfilled'. Up to Matthew 13:14 the accepted formula 'that it might be fulfilled' or 'then was fulfilled' translates the verb *pleroo*, and this on seven occasions (Matt. 1:22; 2:15,17,23; 4:14; 8:17 and

12:17). Once only in the whole record of the Saviour's utterances, is there a departure from this rule, and that is made at Matthew 13:14, where the intensive form *anapleroo* is employed. There is an element of completion about this word, as 1 Thessalonians 2:16 will show.

Even though the long-suffering of God waited throughout the whole period covered by the Acts of the Apostles, and there was granted a stay of execution consequent upon the Saviour's prayer and the witness of Pentecost, it is not without significance, that when the apostle in his turn quotes Isaiah 6:9,10 in a similar context, namely, upon the rejection of Israel, the favourable mention of the Gentile, and the bringing in of the dispensation of the Mystery, he *does not say*, 'in them is fulfilled' but instead says, 'well spake the Holy Ghost by Esaias the prophet unto our fathers' (Acts 28:25). What was *de jure* in Matthew 12 is *de facto* in Acts 28.

At the failure of Israel, the apostle Paul became the Prisoner of the Lord, and as such received the dispensation of the grace of God for the Gentiles, the dispensation of the Mystery (Eph. 3:1-9 R.V.), and while the church of this new dispensation is usually referred to by its title, 'the Church which is His Body' or 'the One Body', there is an extension of this title that is of vast importance. The full passage reads:

> 'And hath put all things under His feet, and gave Him to be the Head over all things to the Church, which is His body, THE FULNESS of Him that FILLETH ALL in all' (Eph. 1:22,23).

When the dispensation of the Mystery comes to an end, the successive dispensations that have suffered a rupture will be resumed, and the signs of the times thicken around us, that tell us plainly that the *lo-ammi* ('not My people') condition is nearing its close. Already believing Jews who accept Jesus as their Messiah are gathering and witnessing in complete independence of Gentile Christianity, and the claim of Israel for national recognition, made at Pentecost 1948, while not to be confused with the day when they shall be restored by the Lord Himself, is certainly an indication that the great epoch is upon us. The Church of the Mystery fills the last gap in the outworking of the ages, and in this dispensation of the Mystery, the conception of 'Fulness' receives its fullest exposition. The following are the references in the Prison Epistles that must be given attention before our study of this subject can be considered at all complete.

Pleroma in the Prison Epistles

'The dispensation of the fulness of times' (Eph. 1:10).

'The fulness of Him that filleth all in all' (Eph. 1:23).

'That ye might be filled unto all the fulness of God' (Eph. 3:19).

'The measure of the stature of the fulness of Christ' (Eph. 4:13).

'It pleased the Father that in Him should all fulness dwell' (Col. 1:19).

'For in Him dwelleth all the fulness of the Godhead bodily' (Col. 2:9).

These references fall into two groups:

(1) The one reference that speaks of the fulness of times.

(2) The five references that speak of the Church and the Lord.

In this study we will deal with the first reference, Ephesians 1:10 :

> 'That in the dispensation of the fulness of times He might gather together in one all things in Christ, both which are in heaven, and which are on earth; even in Him'.

It is evident that the passages flow out of something stated earlier. In verse 9 we read of 'the mystery of His will' which He hath purposed in Himself, and this leads to the opening word of verse 10, *eis* 'unto'. This preposition *eis* variously translated 'into', 'unto', 'in', 'to', 'for', 'towards', 'until', 'throughout', 'concerning', 'that', 'with' and 'on' in this one epistle to the Ephesians, has one underlying meaning however varied the translation; it indicates a goal 'unto' which something tends. We could freely translate *eis* here in Ephesians 1:10 by the words 'with a view to'. The secret of His will and its revelation at this time is with a view to a dispensation.

What is in view is 'a dispensation of the fulness of times'. When the Son of God came into the world it was 'when the fulness of the TIME was come' (Gal. 4:4), here in Ephesians we look forward to a dispensation of the fulness of TIMES. What is the difference between these two expressions 'time' and 'times'?

'Time' is from the same root as 'tide', and Aristotle observes 'our conception of time originates in that of motion'. Time is the measure of movement. To say that a motor-car was travelling at sixty miles, says nothing, the complete statement must be 'sixty miles per hour', or day as the case may be. 'Season' on the other hand derives from the Latin *sationem*, 'a sowing', and looks not so much at the time but at the fitness and suitableness of the period under review.

'How many things by season *season'd* are'
(Shakespeare).

We therefore should revise Ephesians 1:10 and read:

'A dispensation of the fulness of the seasons'.

Gap after gap has been succeeded by fulness after fulness, as we have already seen in the outworking of the age purpose, and at last we have arrived at the fulness of these seasons, the many sowings are past, the harvest is in view. The outstanding characteristic of the dispensation of the fulness of the seasons is that therein:

'He might gather together in one all things in Christ, both which are in heaven and which are on earth; even in Him'.

Where universality is intended, 'things under the earth' are added, as in Philippians 2:10. Here the all things headed up in Christ is limited to the redeemed.

Strictly speaking there is no Greek word for 'gather together', and no Greek word for 'in' or 'one', this is a free rendering of the one word *anakephalaioomai*. Had the apostle meant to say 'gather together' he had the word *sunago* ready to his hand.

The Greek word *kephale* means the 'head' and this both in the literal sense (Matt. 14:11) and in the spiritual (Eph. 4:15): *Kephalaion* means the 'sum' either a sum of money (Acts 22:28), or a summary or summing up (Heb. 8:1). It must be remembered that the ancients placed the sum of a column of figures at the head, and not at the foot as we do now. *Kephalis* (Heb. 10:7) may refer to the brief 'contents' that was written on the outside of a scroll, rather than the complete 'volume'. The word used by Paul in Ephesians 1:10 therefore means something more than 'to gather together in one', it means 'to head up' or 'to sum up' in Himself all that compose 'the all things' before the great day of glory dawns. In Ephesians 1:22,23 this glorious 'summing up' is foreshadowed and anticipated in the present position of Christ, and His relation with the Church of the present calling.

And hath put all things under His feet (this is quoted again in 1 Cor. 15:27 and Heb. 2:8 with age-purpose associations), and gave Him to be Head (*kephale*) over all things (*panta*, all things without exception, whereas in Ephesians 1:10 *ta panta* refers to the redeemed) to the Church which is His Body, the fulness of Him, that filleth all in all (*ta panta*, not the wider term).

(12) 'All the Fulness of God'

The Church of the One Body is the great outstanding anticipation of the goal of the ages. It is associated with Him, under Whose feet are *all things*, it is associated with a dispensation of the fulness of the seasons, when *all things* are to be summed up in Him, and it is itself called:

> 'The fulness of Him that filleth all in all' (Eph. 1:23).

How are we to understand this statement? It falls into line with the last occurrence of *pleroma* in Colossians, and as for that, the last, in the New Testament:

'For in Him dwelleth all the fulness of the Godhead bodily' (Col. 2:9).

The first occurrence of *pleroma* in Ephesians, stands by itself (Eph. 1:10); the remainder form a group that expand the theme, thus:

A 'The Church, which is His Body, the fulness of Him that filleth all in all' (Eph. 1:22,23). Head. Body. Filleth all.

B 'The whole family in heaven and earth ... that Christ may dwell in your hearts by faith ... filled unto all the fulness of God' (Eph. 3:14-19). Whole family. Heaven and Earth. Dwell.

C 'He ascended up far above all heavens, that He might fill all things ... Unto a perfect man, unto the measure of the stature of the fulness of the Christ' (Eph. 4:8-13). Fill all things.

B 'For in Him were all things created ... all things were created by Him and for Him .... He is the Head of the body the church ... for it pleased the Father that in Him should all fulness dwell ... to reconcile all things ... in earth or things in heaven' (Col. 1:16-20). All things. Dwell. Heaven and Earth.

A 'For in Him dwelleth all the fulness of the Godhead bodily, and ye are filled to the full in Him, Which is the Head of all principality and power' (Col. 2:9,10). Head. Principality. Filled.

Here is a very complete conspectus of this mighty theme, point answering point with such precision, that no approach to one corresponding member can be undertaken without due consideration of the other. This, the reader will perceive is fraught with immediate consequences. It forces a comparison between Ephesians 1:22,23 and Colossians 2:9,10.

The passage in Colossians 2:9 has been taken as one of the proof texts of the Deity of Christ. The doctrine of the Deity of Christ constitutes one of the four tenets of the Trust of the Berean Forward Movement, yet we believe it to be a mistake to use Colossians 2:9 as a proof of that wondrous doctrine. The Church of the One Body is 'the fulness of Him that filleth all in all', but such a revelation does not justify the thought that the Church is 'Divine'. The prayer of Ephesians 3 is that the believer may be 'filled with all the fulness of God' and if to be filled with all the fulness of the Godhead bodily teaches the Deity of

Christ in Colossians 2:9, what does Ephesians 3:19 teach of the believer? Identical language, *pan to pleroma* 'all the fulness', is found in Ephesians 3:19, Colossians 1:19 and 2:9, and these passages cannot be separated and interpreted independently of each other.

The 'fulness' of Christ dwells 'bodily' in the Church, even as the 'fulness' of the Godhead dwells 'bodily' in Him. There are, moreover, many contextual links that bind these references together as one whole. In Ephesians 1:21-23, the stress is upon the Headship of Christ as the Risen and Ascended One, with all things under His feet, the Church which is His Body, being the fulness of Him, Who in turn filleth all in all. In Colossians 1:15-20 the two creations are brought together, with Christ as 'Firstborn' in each (Col. 1:15,18), with Christ as pre-eminent in each (Col. 1:17,18). Things in heaven and earth were His creation (Col. 1:16) and they are to be the objects of reconciliation (Col. 1:20).

When we come to Colossians 2:4-23, we have left the positive revelation of truth, and have entered into the sphere of conflict with error. The complete structure of this passage has been set out on page 84 of Volume 23 of *The Berean Expositor*, but for our present purpose we will give the opening and closing members of this great correspondence:

A **a** 4-8. Plausible speech. Philosophy (*sophos*).
  b 8. Traditions of men.
    c 8. Rudiments of the world.
      CORRECTIVE. 8,9. Not after Christ. Fulness *pleroma*.
      10. Ye are filled full in Him *pleroo*.

* * *

A *c* 20-22. Rudiments of the world.
  b 22. Teaching of men.
a 23. Wordy show of wisdom (*sophos*).
      CORRECTIVE. 23. Not in any honour.
      23. Filling of the flesh *plesmone*.

Whatever is intended by Colossians 2:9, 'all the fulness of the Godhead bodily', is closely and intentionally carried forward into verse 10, for the word translated 'complete' is *pepleromenoi*, even as conversely, the title of the Church as 'the fulness' is carried upward to Christ, as the One Who is filling (*pleroumenou*) the all things in all. Colossians 2:4-23 combats the invasion of a vain and deceitful philosophy, supported by tradition and the rudiments of the world, but 'not after Christ', and later in the same argument, not only intruding philosophies and traditions, but even Divinely appointed 'new moons and Sabbath days' are alike set aside as 'shadows of things to come' because 'the body (substance here) is of Christ'.

The whole fulness toward which every age and dispensation has pointed since the overthrow of the world, is at last seen to be Christ Himself. All types and shadows that once filled the gap caused by sin, are now seen to be but transient, or of value only as they point the way to Him, and then disappear. He is Head, He is Pre-eminent, He is Creator and Redeemer, He is the Firstborn of all creation, and Firstborn from the dead. He is the beginning of the Creation of God (Rev. 3:14, Col. 1:18), the Alpha and Omega, the First and the Last, in deed and in fact 'Christ is all, and in all' (Col. 3:11) in the Church of the One Body, as He will yet be in the whole redeemed Universe.

No more glorious position for the redeemed is conceivable than that revealed in Ephesians 1:23. To be one of a kingdom of priests on the earth is a dignity so great, that Old Testament prophets have piled imagery upon imagery in setting it forth. Yet when we come to the Bride of the Lamb, and the description of the heavenly Jerusalem, we realize how much more glorious is that calling to the highest calling on earth. What shall be said then of that company of the redeemed, blessed neither on earth nor in the New Jerusalem, blessed neither as a kingdom nor as Bride, but blessed 'with Christ' where He now sits 'far above all', blessed not only as the members of

His Body which is dignity indeed, but actually destined to be 'the fulness of Him' in Whom dwells all the fulness of the Godhead bodily. Consequently we can the better hope to appreciate the climax prayer of Ephesians 3:14-21 and the three steps which the prayer takes upward to the goal of the ages.

The three stages in the progress of this prayer are indicated by the Greek word *hina*, 'a conjunction of mental direction and intention', translated three times in Ephesians 3:14-21 'that' and which could be translated 'in order that'.

The first step reaches out toward the spiritual condition that makes it possible for Christ 'to dwell in your hearts by faith'. The second stage is directed to comprehending what is breadth, length, depth and height, and the third, the climax of the prayer leads on by way of the knowledge of the love which 'passeth knowledge' to being 'filled with all the fulness of God'. The dwelling of Christ in the heart by faith, is a personal experimental anticipation of the fulness of God yet to be known in heaven and on earth.

The four-fold comprehension, breadth, length, depth, and height encompass all time and space, even as in order that He might fill all things, Christ descended to the lower parts, that is to say the earth, and ascended up far above all heavens, 'that he might fill all things'. Unfathomable love is seen to be the all-sufficient *cause* for this glorious *effect*, and the prayer of the apostle for the Church of the One Body is that it may be filled with all the fulness of God. This preposition 'with' is the translation of the Greek preposition *eis*, which, though it occurs over 1,400 times in the New Testament, is nowhere else translated 'with', and the R.V. corrects the translation and reads 'unto'. The Septuagint uses the simple verb *pleroo* without a preposition for the idea 'to fill with' or 'to be filled with' (Gen. 6:11; Num. 14:21), which rule is followed in Philippians 1:11.

We cannot say 'to be filled with, unto all the fulness of God' however, for this does not make sense. The believer is to be filled *up to* all the fulness of God, which implies the attainment of a goal, and the reaching of standard. This can be illustrated by a reference to the passage in Ephesians 4 which contains the last occurrence of *pleroma* in the epistle:

> 'Till we all come in the unity of the faith (namely that unity which is comprehended by the "one faith" of the unity of the Spirit), and of the knowledge (better "acknowledgment" *epignosis*) of the Son of God, unto a perfect man, unto the measure of the stature (or "full age" *helikia*, John 9:21; Heb. 11:11) of the fulness of the Christ' (Eph. 4:13).

Just as the fulness of Ephesians 1:23 flows from the exaltation of Christ 'far above all', so does it here (Eph. 4:10-13). What was the goal of the ministry of Ephesians 4 is the goal of prayer in Ephesians 3, just as in Colossians Paul's 'teaching' and Epaphras' 'praying' had the presenting and the standing 'perfect' of every man.

The purpose of the original creation of heaven and earth, the subsequent 'fillings' of the creation of the six days, the planting of Paradise, the provision of the Ark, the promise to Abraham, and the promotion of the Gentile upon the failure of Israel, and the perfect man of the present dispensation — Purpose, Planting, Provision, Promise, Promotion and Perfection — are all successive 'fillings' foreshadowing 'all the fulness of God' that could be contained alone in the Lord Himself.

We sincerely hope that enough has been brought to light to quicken the interest of the earnest student, supply him with much food for thought, theme for ministry, and above all to lead him to the place of praise, so fitly expressed in the doxology of the prayer concerning the pleroma.

> 'Now unto Him that is able to do exceeding abundantly above all that we ask or think, according to the power that worketh in us, unto Him be glory in the Church by Christ Jesus throughout all ages, world without end (literally "unto all the generations of the ages of the ages")'.
>
> (A description of *the pleroma* when at last it is complete) (Eph. 3:20,21).

Such a lengthy article as this upon one subject may appear out of place in this analysis, but it had to be considered at some length or not considered at all. In many ways it contains in germ all that we have endeavoured to teach these many years, and if taken together with the article on the SEED[4], will provide much to help in the due appreciation of Dispensational Truth and the Purpose of the Ages.

(13) ALL THE FULNESS OF THE GODHEAD BODILY-WISE

Three Greek words are translated 'Godhead' in the New Testament, namely: (1) *to theion* that which is Divine, the thing pertaining to *theos*; (2) *theiotes*, Divinity, the characteristic property of *theos*, that which is discernible from the works of creation, thereby making idolatry 'without excuse' (Rom. 1:20); (3) *theotes*, Deity, the being in Whom *theiotes* of the highest order resides (Col. 2:9).

The above is partly quoted from Dr. Bullinger's Lexicon, and it agrees with the definitions given by Trench, Cremer, Lightfoot and most commentators.

Some who believe the doctrine of the Deity of Christ, naturally turn to Colossians 2:9 as to a proof text, but this may not be the right attitude of heart and mind when dealing with the Sacred Scriptures. We do no honour to the Lord, if we misuse a portion of Scripture, even to 'prove' or to enforce the glorious doctrine of His Deity. *Truth needs no bolster*. One of the reasons that caused us to hesitate about this use of Colossians 2:9 is that when we apply the principle given in 1 Corinthians 2:13 namely, that we speak not in the words of man's wisdom, 'but which the Holy Ghost teacheth', and that we then go on to compare spiritual things with spiritual, we come up against a doctrinal difficulty. If the words 'all the fulness' of the Godhead prove the Deity of Christ, what do they prove in Ephesians 3:19? There, the prayer of the apostle is for the believer, that Christ may dwell, *katoikeo*, in their hearts by faith, and as a consequence, that they may be 'filled with (*eis* unto, with a view to) all the fulness of God'. If 'all the fulness of *theotes*' proves the Deity of Christ, should not 'all the fulness of *theos*' prove the Deity of the Church? To express the thought is to refute it. Such cannot be the meaning. In Colossians 1:19 we meet the expression 'all the fulness', but there it is not followed, either by 'God' or 'Godhead', yet this first reference must have a definite bearing upon the second reference found in Colossians 2:9.

> 'For it pleased the Father that in Him should all the fulness dwell' (*pan to pleroma katoikesai*) (Col. 1:19).

We cannot expect to understand the reference in Colossians 2:9 if we ignore the earlier reference in Colossians 1:19. They go together and constitute a united testimony. The first passage opens with Redemption 'through the blood' (Col. 1:14) and closes with 'peace through the blood of His cross' (Col. 1:20). He Who created 'all things, that are in heaven and that are in earth' (Col. 1:16) reconciled 'all things, whether they be things in earth, or things in heaven' (Col. 1:20). We move from Creation to Reconciliation *via* the headship of the Church which is His Body and the blessed fact that He Who was in the beginning 'the firstborn of every creature' is revealed as being Himself 'the beginning, the firstborn from the dead'. While the triumph of His resurrection is the feature that is stressed here, 'the blood of His cross' reminds us of His deep humiliation, and we believe we shall never understand the reference to 'fulness' in Colossians 2:9 if we do not know the corresponding 'emptying' of Philippians 2. In order to illustrate this approach we use the figure of Jacob's ladder, being fully justified so to do by the reference made to it by the Lord Himself.

In Genesis 28 we have the record of Jacob's dream, wherein he saw a ladder set up on earth, and the top of it reached to heaven, 'and behold the angels of God ascending and descending on it' (Gen. 28:12). In John 1, Nathanael is referred to by the Lord as 'an Israelite indeed, in whom is no guile' (1:47). The word translated 'guile' is *dolos* and is used in the LXX of Genesis 27:35, where Isaac tells Esau, 'thy brother came with subtilty (*dolos* guile), and hath taken away thy blessing'. One cannot avoid seeing an oblique reference in John 1:47 to Jacob, an Israelite who was most certainly not without 'guile'. However, that is by the way, our interest is more directly concerned with verse 51:

> 'Hereafter ye shall see heaven open, and the ANGELS of God ASCENDING and DESCENDING upon the Son of Man' (John 1:51).

Now observe, 'fulness' is associated with Christ in the fact that in order that He might FILL ALL THINGS, He that *descended* is the same also that *ascended* far above all heavens (Eph. 4:10).

Returning to John 1, we observe the following sequence of thought:

> 'In the beginning was the Word ... the Word was God'.
>
> 'All things were made by Him'.
>
> 'The Word was made flesh and dwelt (tabernacled, *skenoo*, not the permanent "dwelling" *katoikeo* of Col. 2:9) among us'.
>
> 'Of His FULNESS have all we received'.
>
> 'The angels of God ascending and descending upon the Son of Man'.

So in Colossians 1:15-20, He Who was the 'Image of the Invisible God' (compare John 1:1 and 18), Who created all things (see 1:3) Who became also the Firstborn from the dead, Who is before all things (even as John the Baptist acknowledged, John 1:30), in Him, in that capacity, not only as Creator but as the Firstborn from the dead (thereby assuming the death of the cross), in that capacity and in no other way, was it pleasing to the Father that 'in Him should all the fulness dwell'. It is for this reason, we find the word *somatikos* 'bodily' in Colossians 2:9. This word has been translated by several commentators 'bodily-wise', as though the fulness could not dwell in Him in any other way.

Earlier we spoke about the fact that if Colossians speaks of the Saviour's 'Fulness', Philippians speaks of His voluntary self-emptying. Philippians 2:6-11 has been given a fairly full exposition in the book entitled *The Prize of the High Calling* and the reader would be advised to consult chapter 5 of that volume. Here, we can deal with one item only, the meaning of the words, 'He made Himself of no reputation' (Phil. 2:7). First of all we give the structure of verses 6-11.

Philippians 2:6-11[*]

Example of Christ

K	2:6.			EQUALITY WITH GOD ORIGINALLY (*huparchon*).
	L 2:7,8. *Sevenfold Humiliation*	**r**	7.	He emptied Himself.
		s	7.	A bond servant.
		t	7.	Likeness as a man.
		u	8.	Fashioned as a man.
		r	8.	He humbled Himself.
		s	8.	Obedient unto death.
		t	8.	The death of the cross.
K	2:9. EXALTATION			THE NAME (inherited, see Heb. 1:4).
	L 2:9-11. *Sevenfold Exaltation*	**v**	9.	The Name above every name.
		w	10.	Every knee shall bow.
		x	10.	Things in heaven.
		y	10.	Things in earth.
		x	10.	Things under earth.
		w	11.	Every tongue confess.
		v	11.	Jesus Christ is Lord.

Here it will be observed 'things in heaven, and things in earth' occur as in Colossians 1:16.

'*He made Himself of no reputation*'. The Authorized Version has used the word 'reputation' twice in Philippians, the second occurrence being at 2:29, 'hold such in reputation'. The Revised Version has wisely omitted the word 'reputation' in both passages, reading in

---

* This structure is part of a complete outline extracted from *The Testimony of the Lord's Prisoner* by the same author.

2:7, 'but emptied Himself', and in 2:29, 'hold such in honour', for two different Greek words are used.

The change, however, while it makes some aspects of the truth clearer, introduces other problems for, to a modern mind, there is something strange about the idea of anyone 'emptying himself'. In modern usage 'empty' places foremost in the mind the idea of a 'jug without water', 'a room without furniture' and 'empty vessels' (2 Kings 4:3); these come naturally to mind. In order to avoid too crude an application of the figure of 'emptying a vessel' when speaking of the Saviour's humiliation, most of us slip into paraphrase and say, 'He divested Himself of His dignity and insignia of Deity', but this is confessedly an attempt to avoid a problem. The verb *kenoo* is cognate with *kenos* 'vain' and means 'empty'. That the word has a wider application than that of emptying a vessel, such expressions as 'seven empty ears' (Gen. 41:27), 'the sword of Saul returned not empty' (2 Sam. 1:22) will show.

Where *kenos* is translated 'empty' in the Authorized Version of the New Testament it refers in the parable to the treatment of the servant by the wicked husbandmen, who sent him 'empty away' (Mark 12:3; Luke 20:10,11), and to 'the rich' who were 'sent empty away' (Luke 1:53); in most cases, however, *kenos* is translated 'vain', as for example, in Philippians itself 'run in vain' and 'labour in vain', where it is evident that 'empty' would have no meaning (Phil. 2:16).

The verb *kenoo* translated 'to make of no reputation', occurs five times in the Greek New Testament and the four occurrences other than that of Philippians 2:7, render the word 'make void', 'make none effect' and 'be in vain' (Rom. 4:14; 1 Cor. 1:17; 9:15; 2 Cor. 9:3). In Philippians 2:3 we find the word *kenodoxia* 'vain glory'. We remember with adoring wonder that in the Psalm of the Cross, we read, 'I am poured out like water' (Psa. 22:14). He did indeed 'empty Himself'. The word translated 'offer' in Philippians 2:17 is found in the LXX of Genesis 35:14, where Jacob revisited the scene of the 'ladder', which he re-named 'Bethel', and this time 'he poured out a drink offering thereon'. Paul, following in His Master's footsteps faintly adumbrates that awful condescension which for our sakes left behind the glory of heaven, for the deep, deep humiliation of 'the death of the cross'. The Saviour 'emptied' Himself. The apostle was willing to be made 'a drink offering' (Phil. 2:7,17).

Above the ladder, in our illustration given elsewhere (see RECKONING AND REALITY[7]), is intimated 'the glory that He had' before the world was. This must not be confused with the glory that was 'given' Him, as the Man Christ Jesus, the One Mediator. We may, in resurrection 'behold' the one, but 'the glory which Thou gavest Me' the Saviour said, 'I have given them, that they may be one, EVEN AS we are one' (John 17:22). We do not pretend to understand this profound revelation, we would add not one syllable of our own lest we spoil and corrupt such unearthly beauty; but we can bow our heads and our hearts in adoring wonder, as we perceive that *this is* implied in the word 'fulness', for the Church of the One Body is revealed to be:

> 'The fulness of Him that filleth all in all' (Eph. 1:23).

Here the Church is 'one' with the Lord. On the left hand of the ladder, we see the wondrous descent, seven steps down to the death of the cross. Here at the foot, on the earth He is seen as Emmanuel 'God *with us*'. Here, it was fulfilled 'He was numbered *with* the transgressors'. And by virtue of that most wondrous 'reckoning', He became our Surety. The word translated 'surety' in the Old Testament is the Hebrew word *arab*, which in the form *arrabon* is brought over into New Testament Greek, occurring in Ephesians 1:14 as 'earnest'. This word corresponds with 'pledge' in Genesis 38:17,18, 'wilt thou give me a *pledge* till thou send it?' The root idea appears to be that of *mixing* or *mingling*:

'A mixed multitude' (*margin*: a great mixture) (Exod. 12:38).
'The holy seed have *mingled* themselves' (Ezra 9:2).
'A stranger doth not *intermeddle* with his joy' (Prov. 14:10).
'In the *warp*, or woof' (Lev. 13:48).

Arising out of the idea of this mixing and interweaving comes that of surety, who is so intimately associated with the obligations laid upon the one for whom he acts that he can be treated in his stead. So we get:

'Thy servant became surety for the lad' (Gen. 44:32).
'He that is surety for a stranger shall smart for it' (Prov. 11:15).
'We have mortgaged our lands' (Neh. 5:3).
'Give pledges to my lord the king' (2 Kings 18:23).

In Ezekiel 27:9,27 we find the word translated 'occupy' in the sense of exchange or bartering. In a way, we understand the expression, 'occupy, till I come', and still speak of a man's trade as his 'occupation'.

Such is the underlying meaning of the word 'surety', one who identifies himself with another in order to bring about deliverance from obligations. This is clearly seen in Proverbs 22:26,27: 'Be not thou one of them that strike hands, or of them that are sureties for debts. If thou hast nothing to pay, why should he take away thy bed from under thee?' It is evident from this passage that the surety was held liable for the debts of the one whose cause he had espoused, even to the loss of his bed, and this meant practically his all, as may be seen by consulting Exodus 22:26,27. 'If thou at all take thy neighbour's raiment to pledge, thou shalt deliver it unto him by that the sun goeth down; for that is his covering only, it is his raiment for his skin: wherein shall he sleep?' Judah, who became surety for his brother Benjamin gives us a picture of Christ's Suretyship, saying to Joseph:

'How shall I go up (ascend) to my father, and the lad be not WITH ME?' (Gen. 44:34).

If poor erring Judah could enter like this into the meaning of Suretyship, how much more must our Saviour have done so. At the foot of the ladder, the transfer is made, and the first of the seven steps up to the glory of the right hand of God is made. Elsewhere in this analysis, these seven steps 'with Christ' have been treated of (see RECKONING AND REALITY[7]). We but draw attention to them here. The self-emptying on the one hand is compensated by all the fulness on the other, but that fulness would never have been attained had the Saviour not become man, a man of flesh and blood, all the fulness dwells in Him 'bodily-wise'. The church is the fulness of Him that filleth all in all. The goal and standard of that church is the measure of the stature of the fulness of Christ. The personal experimental climax of the faith is that each member shall be filled with (or unto) all the fulness of God. It is difficult, with these features so clearly set forth in Ephesians, to think that the same word 'fulness' when dealt with in Colossians, a confessedly parallel epistle, should suddenly swing over to the doctrine of the deity of Christ.

It may be that our attempt to explain Colossians 2:9 is so defective that the gleam of truth we saw at the commencement of this article has already become dimmed by our very effort to explain it. Shall we then, writer and reader, pause — put aside our lexicons, our concordances, our interpretations and follow in the footsteps of Asaph, who tells us that not until he went into the Sanctuary of God, did he understand.

In conclusion, the following structure of the word 'Pleroma' in the New Testament may stimulate a fuller examination of the subject than we have been able to include in this *Analysis*.

PLEROMA

A John 1:16.			All things made by Him. GOD INVISIBLE. THE WORD. Only Begotten.	
B Gal. 4:4.			Weak and beggarly elements (9). Observance of days, moons, times, years. (10).	
Israel and the Gentile	C	**a**	Rom. 11:12	Provoke to jealousy (11,14).
		b	Rom. 11:25	Fulness of Gentiles.
		c	Rom. 13:10	Law fulfilled.
		b	Rom. 15:29	Fulness of Gospel.
		a	1 Cor. 10:26	Provoke to jealousy (22).
Christ and the Church	*C*	**a**	Eph. 1:10	Fulness of seasons. Head up.
		b	Eph. 1:23	Fulness of Him.
		b	Eph 3.19	Fulness of God.
		a	Eph. 4:13	Fulness of Christ. Till we come.
A Col. 1:19.			All things created by Him. GOD INVISIBLE. THE IMAGE. Firstborn.	
B Col. 2:9.			Philosophy and vain deceit. Elements. Observance of Meat, Drink, Feast, New Moon, Sabbath (8,16).	

PREDESTINATION. It is not easy for the mind to dwell upon this term, without it being influenced by the word 'destiny'. Destiny calls up the idea of fate, inexorable and unalterable, and so, we have this statement in the *Westminster Confession*:

> 'That the number of the predestinated to life, and of those foreordained to death, is so certain and definite, that it cannot be either increased or diminished'.

It is difficult to see how any one holding such a doctrine, could ever preach the gospel of salvation, could ever contemplate the 'plucking' of even 'one brand from the burning' or why anyone should bother to preach at all. The overshadowing of the word 'destiny' is plainly marked in this *Confession*, and many of the advocates of Calvinism are Necessitarians. In a letter to Archbishop Cranmer, the reformer, Melancthon complained:

> 'At the commencement of our Reformation, the Stoical disputations among our people concerning FATE were too horrible'.

The word 'destination' may convey in some contexts, the most fixed and unalterable of fates, while in another it may be the attaining of a journey's end. To meet one's 'Waterloo' may mean meeting one's *fate*; to be met at 'Waterloo', or 'Waterloo Station was his destination' can have no such element of 'destiny' about it. We must, therefore, avoid importing any ideas into the doctrine of predestination that derive from the composition of the English word. The Greek word translated 'predestinate' is a compound of *pro* 'before' and *horizo* 'to set bounds'. In the New Testament *horizo is* translated 'determinate', 'ordain', 'limit', 'declared'. This word gives the English 'horizon' which has no element of fate in its meaning, but means simply the 'boundary' where sea and sky appear to meet.

Predestination occurs twice in Ephesians, once it is 'unto adoption' and once to an 'inheritance' (1:5,11). This second occurrence falls into line with the usage of the LXX. *Horizo* in the LXX is found in the proximity of the words *kleros* and *kleronomia*, words that mean 'the obtaining of an inheritance by lot'.

> 'This shall be your west border' *horion* (Num. 34:6).
>
> 'Jordan shall be their boundary, *horion*, on the east: this is the inheritance (*kleronomia*) of the children of Benjamin' (Joshua 18:20 LXX).
>
> 'See, that I have given to you (lit. "cast upon you") these nations that are left to you by lots (*klerois*) to your tribes ... and the boundaries (or he shall be bound *horizo*) shall be at the great sea westward' (Josh. 23:4 LXX).

In the context of most of the references to *horizo* will be found words that mean an inheritance obtained by lot. Seeing that the apostle has linked 'predestination' *prohorizo* with 'obtaining an inheritance' (*kleroo*), this Old Testament usage must be recognized.

Predestination, or 'marking off beforehand' is what every one does when he makes a will. Here, in the Will of the Father, we are permitted to see that 'adoption' and 'inheritance' are secured. That a human 'will' is a permissible analogy, Galatians 3:15 and 4:1,2 will make clear, and no legatee under a human will has ever been heard to raise an objection on the lines of 'fatalism'. Those who were chosen in Christ before the overthrow of Genesis 1:2, were also 'marked off before hand' and as the R.V. reads were 'foreordained unto adoption'.

The same goal, 'adoption', is associated with predestination in Romans 8. First let us see the structure.

Romans 8:1-39

A 1-4. No condemnation. God sent His own SON (*huios*).
  B 5-15. Led by Spirit of God. SONS now (*huios*).
    C 15-17. Spirit itself bears witness. SONSHIP (*huiothesia*).
      D 17-21. Suffering and glory. Manifestation of SONS (*huios*).
    C 22-28. Spirit Itself intercedes. SONSHIP (*huiothesia*).
  B 29,30. Conformed to the image of His SON then (*huios*).
A 31-39. Who condemns? He spared not His Own SON (*huios*).

Just as the chapter opens with a statement concerning the believer's immunity from condemnation, so it closes with the same fact, and upon the same ground, namely, the gift of God's Son:

> 'There is therefore now no CONDEMNATION to them which are in Christ Jesus ... God sending His Own Son ... CONDEMNED sin in the flesh' (Rom. 8:1-3).
>
> 'He that spared not His own Son ... who is he that CONDEMNETH? It is Christ that died, yea rather, that is risen again, Who is even at the right hand of God, Who also maketh intercession for us' (Rom. 8:32-34).

This, then, is the beginning and end of the matter, even as it is the beginning and end of the structure — 'His own Son'. The next fact that emerges is that all who are thus blessed are 'sons of God' too. The member marked B 5-15 is full of references to the Spirit, the spirit of resurrection anticipating now in this life and in these mortal bodies, that glorious consummation when we shall in actual fact be 'conformed to the image of His Son' in resurrection glory. And so the two corresponding members read:

B 5-15 Led by the Spirit of God. SONS now (*huios*).
B 29,30 Conformed to the image of His SON then (*huios*).

Added to this leading by the Spirit of God is His 'witness' and His 'intercession'.

> 'The Spirit Itself beareth witness with our spirit, that we are the children of God' (Rom. 8:16).
>
> 'The Spirit Itself maketh intercession ... for the saints according to the will of God' (Rom. 8:26,27).

This 'witness' and 'intercession' are closely associated with the fact that these sons of God are not yet in glory, but here in the midst of a groaning creation. They are strengthened to suffer because of the glory that is to come; they are 'saved by hope'; and while they often know not what to pray for, they do know that all things work together for good. It is in this realm that the witness and intercession of the Spirit have their place. In the structure it will be seen that the word SON gives place to SONSHIP, which is the word translated 'adoption' in the A.V.:

C 15-17 Spirit Itself bears witness. SONSHIP (*huiothesia*).
C 22-28 Spirit Itself intercedes. SONSHIP (*huiothesia*).

This brings us to the centre of the structure:

D 17-21 Suffering and Glory. Manifestation of SONS (*huios*).

Until the reign of sin and death actually ceases, until creation itself emerges into the liberty of the glory of the children of God, the day of complete emancipation for the believer must be future. For the present, it is enough that we have passed from Adam to Christ, that there is *now* no condemnation, that during this pilgrimage we have the witness and the intercession of the Spirit, and that with all our ignorance of what to pray for, we know that all things work together for good to them that love God.

We commend this outline to the prayerful interest of the reader, believing that, as it is based upon the occurrence of words used by the Holy Spirit and not upon headings of our own devising, it does 'divide aright' this precious portion of truth. It shows us the seven great sections into which the subject matter falls, and provides us with well-defined bounds for our subsequent studies.

Turning to the section that speaks of predestination we read:

> 'For whom He did foreknow, He also did predestinate to be conformed to the image of His Son, that He might be the Firstborn among many brethren. Moreover, whom He did predestinate, them He also called: and whom He called, them He also justified: and whom He justified, them He also glorified' (Rom. 8:29,30).

The analysis of the passage is simple, and is as follows:

A PREDESTINATION — Conformity. Steps leading to.
    B PURPOSE — Christ. Firstborn among many brethren.
A PREDESTINATION — Glory. Steps leading to.

But before we can appreciate its magnificence we shall have to arrive, with some certainty, at the meaning of several of the words used.

Foreknowledge. How are we to understand this word? The word *proginosko*, to foreknow, occurs five times in the New Testament, and the noun, *prognosis*, twice, making seven references in all. The passages are as follows:

> 'Him, being delivered by the determinate counsel and *foreknowledge* of God, ye have taken, and by wicked hands have crucified and slain' (Acts 2:23).
>
> 'My manner of life from my youth, which was at the first among mine own nation at Jerusalem, know all the Jews; which *knew* me from the beginning' (Acts 26:4,5).
>
> 'For whom He did *foreknow*, He also did predestinate' (Rom. 8:29).
>
> 'God hath not cast away His people which He *foreknew*' (Rom. 11:2).
>
> 'Elect according to the *foreknowledge* of God the Father' (1 Pet. 1:2).
>
> 'Who verily was *foreordained* before the foundation of the world' (1 Pet. 1:20).
>
> 'Ye, therefore, beloved, seeing *ye know* these things *before*' (2 Pet. 3:17).

It will be observed that the usage subdivides this list into three groups. (1) *God.* It is used of God in connection with Christ and His sacrifice for sin. (2) *God.* It is used of God in connection with His people who are called the elect, or the chosen. (3) *Man.* It is used of man in the sense of knowing beforehand, or of having previous information. The grouping of these occurrences may be made more evident if set out as follows:

A Reference to Christ and His sacrifice (Acts 2:23).
  B Reference to man and his previous knowledge of facts (Acts 26:4,5).
    C Reference to the elect people of God (Rom. 8:29; 11:2; 1 Pet. 1:2).
A Reference to Christ and His sacrifice (1 Pet. 1:20).
  B Reference to man and his foreknowledge as a result of Scriptural testimony (2 Pet. 3:17).

To Know Beforehand

Commentators are divided in their treatment of the meaning of the 'foreknowledge' of God. The Calvinist sees in the word a synonym for predestination. Others an indication of love and favour. Apart from theological necessity, the word means to know beforehand, without responsibility, as to the event. Dr. Liddon says of the earlier suggestions, 'the New Testament use of the word does not sanction this (not even Rom. 11:2; 1 Pet. 1:20), or any other meaning than *to know beforehand*'. To us, creatures of time and space, such knowledge borders upon the impossible. Indeed, some, like Jonathan Edwards, have boldly said, 'it is impossible for a thing to be certainly known, to any intellect, without evidence', and have come to the conclusion that the foreknowledge of God compels Him, the Most High, to decree, foreordain, and unalterably fix every act and word that He has foreknown. It is extraordinary that any should thus presume to say what is or is not possible to the Lord; nor can such avoid the logical conclusion of their argument, that God must be, if they are right, the author of sin, a conclusion diametrically opposed by the Word of God, and odious to the conscience of His children.

Time is the measure of motion, and in our limited state, the idea of a timeless state expressed by the title I AM, is beyond our comprehension. A very crude illustration, however, may be of service in arriving at some understanding of the matter. Suppose the reader to be standing at a small table upon which there rest books, paper, ink, and pens. As he stands, he comprehends the whole table and contents as one; there is neither a first nor a last. The articles could as well be enumerated from the left hand as from the right. Now, further, suppose that an ant has crawled up one of the table legs, and that he visits each article in turn. To the ant there will be a definite sequence because the element of time is introduced and, resultingly, there will be a first and a last and moreover there will be a limit to its vision. So also, if a spider crawl up the opposite leg, its enumeration and experience would be reversed. But God, as it were, sees all at a glance; He knows the end from the beginning. With us, the future is hid from our eyes because of our human limitations.

We shall be wise, therefore, to leave the word foreknowledge to mean just what it says and no more. The infinite knowledge of God makes it impossible that He shall not know who will preach and who will teach; where they will go, and when they will go; who shall hear, who reject, who accept, and who be left without a word of the gospel. The one great demand upon all who hear the gospel is that they believe the testimony of God concerning His Son. Whoever so believes passes into all the blessings purchased by the blood of Christ. Whoever does not believe makes God a liar (1 John 5:10). If there were any idea of preordination in this, refusal to believe would be as much a part of God's predeterminate decrees as is election to glory, and it would not be possible to make God a liar by so refusing His testimony. Further, in the passage before us, foreknowledge is differentiated from predestination, for we read, 'whom He did foreknow He also did predestinate'. If we alter the word 'foreknow' to any word bearing the sense of predetermining or predestining, the sentence ceases to have meaning, as, for example, if we read, 'whom He did foreordain He also did predestinate'.

We, therefore, understand the passages before us to declare that God, Who is not under the limitation of time and space as we are, and needs no external evidence to attain unto knowledge, knows all things, past, present and future; knows them perfectly and completely, and can therefore act with absolute certainty where, to us, all would appear in a contingent light.

No Fatalism

Those who were foreknown of God were also predestined to conformity to the image of His Son. Here is another term that demands care in application.

The word 'predestinate' as we have already observed is a translation of the Greek *prohorizo*. The word *horos*, from which *horizo* is formed, does not occur in the New Testament, but it has the well-established meaning of boundary or limit, as in the word horizon. This word, in turn, is from *horao*, to see, boundaries generally being marked to make them visible and conspicuous. Those whom God foreknew He also marked out beforehand for a glorious end — conformity to the image of His Son.

There are three related words which should be considered together, and each of these three commences with the prefix *pro*, in the original.

(1) Purpose (*prothesis*). Something set or placed before the mind, a proposition.
(2) Foreknowledge (*proginosko*). To know beforehand, and
(3) Predestinate (*prohorizo*). To mark off beforehand.

The whole testimony of the Scriptures is to the effect that God has a purpose before Him, according to which He works and, in accord with that purpose of peopling heaven and earth with the redeemed, He foreknew every one who would respond to the call of grace, and accordingly marked them off beforehand for the various spheres of glory that His purpose demanded. If we believe that God fixed unchangeably from all eternity, whosoever should in time believe, then however much we may hedge and cover the fact, there is but one logical conclusion, a conclusion that, in days gone by, has driven many to the edge of despair. That conclusion is, that He Who absolutely and unalterably fixed the number of those who should believe, just as surely fixed unalterably the number of those who should not believe, a conclusion so monstrous that it has only to be expressed to be rejected:

> 'How then shall they call on Him in Whom they have not believed? and how shall they believe in Him of Whom they have not heard?' (Rom. 10:14).

The Goal of Predestination

In the original the word 'conformed' in Romans 8:29 is *summorphos*, which is made up of sum, 'together with', and *morphe*, 'form'. The English word 'form' is from the Latin *forma*, which is but a translation and transposition of the letters of the Greek *morpha* or *morphe*. While the word *morphe* indicates visible shape, its usage, both in its simple form and as a compound, compels us to see in it a resemblance that is much deeper than mere outward conformity. We have, for example, in Romans 2:20, 'a form of knowledge', and in 2 Timothy 3:5 'a form of godliness' which was merely external and 'formal'. In Mark 16:12 and Philippians 2:6,7, we have the word used in the account of the appearance of the Lord to His disciples on the way to Emmaus, and in the exhortation based on that most wonderful condescension, when He laid aside the 'form' of God by taking upon Him the 'form' of a servant. In combination with the preposition *meta*, we have the familiar word *metamorphosis*, a word used in the study of insect development to indicate the change from pupa to perfect butterfly, a wonderful illustration comparable with the argument based on the sowing of seed used by the apostle in 1 Corinthians 15.

Again we find the word in Matthew 17:2 and Mark 9:2, where it is translated 'transfigured'. In Philippians 3:21, future resurrection glory is in view, the word, 'change' being *metaschematizo*, and the words 'fashioned like' being *summorphon.*

The primary meaning of 'form' is uppermost in most of these references. We note the change from that which is external to that which is within in Galatians 4:19 when the apostle says, 'my little children, of whom I travail in birth again until Christ be formed in you', and again in Romans 12:2, where we have the two words *suschematizo* and *metamorphoo* translated 'conformed' and 'transformed' respectively. The difference between the two words may be better appreciated if we remember that *morphe* deals more with organic form, and *schema* with external appearance.

> 'And be not conformed to this world (age): but be ye transformed by the renewing of your mind' (Rom. 12:2).

Here it is most evident that the transformation is internal and not merely outward and visible. Again, in 2 Corinthians 3:18, the words 'changed into the same image' must not be construed to refer only to a future resurrection likeness, but to a present spiritual anticipation. Lastly, the words occurring in Philippians 3:10, 'being made conformable unto His death', refer to the present spiritual transfiguration that anticipates 'conformity to the body of His glory' in that day (Phil. 3:21).

With this thought we return to Romans 8:29. Conformity to the image of His Son is to be both a present experience, and a future hope; the one, associated with the 'renewing of our mind' *now* (Rom. 12:2), the other, associated with the 'redemption of our body', *then* (Rom. 8:23). In Romans 8, sonship is here and now essentially associated with resurrection, the 'spirit' of sonship being expressed in Christ-likeness, while literal sonship itself ('adoption', 8:23) will be expressed in complete likeness to the glorified Lord, in body as well as in spirit. God's goal for His children should also be consciously their goal. To be like Christ, the Son, is to satisfy all that Scripture demands in holiness, righteousness, wisdom and acceptance. All growth in grace and all advance in knowledge must be submitted to this one standard — conformity to the image of His Son. We have borne the image of the earthly; we look forward to bearing the image of the heavenly in resurrection glory (1 Cor. 15:49), the teaching in this passage being associated with the two Adams. While in Romans 8:29 the subject of the two Adams is in the foreground (see Rom. 5:12 to 8:39 as a whole), a closer, family figure is used of the Lord, namely, 'that He might be the Firstborn among many brethren'. The following passage in Hebrews 2 vividly comments on this truth:

> 'It became Him, for Whom are all things, and by Whom are all things, in bringing many sons unto glory, to make the Captain of their salvation perfect through sufferings. For both He that sanctifieth and they who are sanctified are all of one: for which cause He is not ashamed to call them brethren ... Forasmuch then as the children are partakers of flesh and blood, He also Himself likewise took part of the same' (Heb. 2:10-14).

The reader will remember that the structure of Romans 8 as a whole throws into prominence the words 'son' and 'sonship'. Whether it be deliverance, life, peace, growth or victory, the spirit of sonship must never be forgotten. To attempt an entry into the position of Romans 8 in any other spirit is to court disaster. The Lord foreknew us, and He predestinated us to the glorious goal of conformity to 'the image of His Son'. May He see of the travail of His soul, and be satisfied in some measure *now*, even as He shall be fully satisfied when we shall stand in all the glory of His resurrection before God our Father.

PRESENTATION. Two Greek words are employed to speak of the believer's presentation to God, namely *histemi* 'to set, place, station' (Jude 24), and *paristemi* 'to set, place, or station alongside' (Eph. 5:27; Col. 1:22,28). Full and rich as the doxology of Jude is, it will be observed that the presentation there envisaged is not so near, so intimate as that of the Church of the Mystery, the one is to be set or stationed *before* the presence of the glory, the other adds the preposition *para* 'alongside' a signal mark of super-heavenly glory. This presentation is associated with such terms as 'without blemish', 'without spot or wrinkle or any such thing' and with being 'faultless'. These terms are borrowed from the character of the Old Testament sacrifice and priesthood and something of the picture that is introduced may be gathered by reading the preparation of Esther for her presentation to the king (Esther 2:1-4 and 8-20). Especially let us note Esther's modest restraint. She could have decked herself from a wardrobe as fantastic and voluptuous as any described in *The Arabian Nights*; instead, in blessed anticipation of the believer's ground of acceptance 'she required nothing but what Hegai the king's chamberlain, the keeper of the women appointed'.

The two presentations of Colossians 1:22 and 28, must be distinguished. One is the result of *the offering* of Christ, the other is the consequence of the apostle's *warning and teaching.* The structure of Colossians places two members in correspondence thus:

E	1:23 to 2:1	Preaching to present PERFECT.
E	4:12,13	Prayer to stand PERFECT.

In order that this new section shall be seen from the Word itself, and not merely from our disposition of the matter, we will quote the two passages from the A.V.:

> 'Warning every man, and teaching every man in all wisdom; that we may present every man perfect in Christ Jesus: Whereunto I also labour, striving according to His working, which worketh in me mightily. For I would that ye knew what great conflict I have for you, and for them at Laodicea, and for as many as have not seen my face in the flesh' (Col. 1:28 to 2:1).

> 'Epaphras, who is one of you, a servant of Christ, saluteth you, always labouring fervently for you in prayers, that ye may stand perfect and complete in all the will of God. For I bear him record, that he hath a great zeal for you, and them that are in Laodicea, and them in Hierapolis' (Col. 4:12,13).

The items that link these two passages together are the double reference to Laodicea, the use of *agonistic* terms, *agon* 'conflict' (Col. 2:1), *agonizomai* 'striving' (Col. 1:29) and 'labouring fervently' (Col. 4:12). These are subordinate, however, to the central theme:

> 'That we may present every man perfect in Christ Jesus' (1:28).
>
> 'That ye may stand perfect and complete in all the will of God' (4:12).

The correspondence will be the more readily perceived if set out as follows:

Paul (Col. 1:28 to 2:1)

A METHOD — Warning and teaching.
  B ACCOMPANIMENT — Striving (*agonizomai*).
    C OBJECT — Present perfect.
      D ANNOUNCEMENT — For I would that you should know.
        E ACCOMPANIMENT — What great conflict I have for you.
          F OBJECTS — For Laodicea and for as many as have not seen my face in the flesh.

Epaphras (Col. 4:12,13)

A METHOD — Prayers.
  B ACCOMPANIMENT — Labouring fervently (*agonizomai*).
    C OBJECT — Stand perfect.
      D ANNOUNCEMENT — For I bear him record.
        E ACCOMPANIMENT — That he hath great zeal for you.
          F OBJECTS — For Laodicea and for Hierapolis.

Let us follow the teaching of these passages step by step. First as to the methods adopted by these two servants of the Lord. The one employed 'warning and teaching' the other 'praying'. The apostle has recognized this double ministry elsewhere:

> 'I have planted, Apollos watered; but God gave the increase. So then neither is he that planteth any thing, neither he that watereth; but God that giveth the increase. Now he that planteth and he that watereth are one: and every man shall receive his own reward according to his own labour. God's fellow-workers are we, God's husbandry, God's building are ye' (1 Cor. 3:6-9).

The ministry of the apostle in this special labour for the Colossians is described as 'warning and teaching'. If the reader will refer to the structure of the epistle given in the article entitled COLOSSIANS[1], he will see that the central member commences with the word '*beware*'. The great difference between Ephesians and Colossians is in this central section (Col. 2:4-23) with its warning notes:

> 'And this I say, lest any man should beguile you'.
> 'Beware lest any man spoil you'.
> 'Let no man therefore judge you'.
> 'Let no man beguile you of your reward'.

Admonition or warning belongs to the training and discipline of children; it presupposes life and position in the family:

> 'Ye fathers, provoke not your children to wrath: but bring them up in the nurture and *admonition* of the Lord' (Eph. 6:4).

Admonition or warning belongs to growth, to walk, to the things that accompany salvation, to the prize or reward, not so much to salvation in its first phase:

> 'Know ye not that they which run in a race run all, but one receiveth the prize? So run, that ye may obtain ... All our fathers were under the cloud, and all passed through the sea; and were all baptized ... and did all eat ... and did all drink ... But with many of them God was not well pleased ... Now all these things happened unto them for ensamples: and they are written for our *admonition*' (or warning) (1 Cor. 9:24 to 10:11).

'Warning and teaching' are related as 'practice and doctrine' are related.

We must now turn our attention to the central theme. In this chapter there are two 'presentings', and they are intimately associated:

(1) 'In the body of His flesh through death, *to present* you holy and unblameable and unreproveable in His sight' (Col. 1:22).

(2) 'That *we may present* every man perfect in Christ Jesus' (Col. 1:28).

The reader is sufficiently taught, we trust, to realize that the work of Christ on our behalf is so complete, that to speak of adding to it or 'perfecting' it is nothing short of treason. The words used preclude all possible addition. What can be added to holiness? and what improvement can there be upon a condition which is both unblameable and unreproveable in God's sight? That which is *unreproveable there* is surely *unimproveable here*; and yet the fact remains that Paul does say, and in the near context, 'that I may present every man perfect', even though the ink that wrote verse 22 was scarcely dry.

He does also use the expression 'perfecting holiness' in 2 Corinthians 7:1.

The difficulty lies in the word 'perfect' and the meaning that it has attached to it in modern speech. The derivation of the English word, however, takes us nearer to the meaning of the Greek original. 'Perfect' has come into English through the old French *parfait*, which in its turn comes from the Latin *per* 'throughly' and *facere* 'to make'. Now the word 'fact' comes from the same verb *facere*, and if we can see in the word 'perfect' the idea of making that which is a 'fact' in Christ, a 'fact' also in our own experience, we shall be near the truth contained in the two presentings of Colossians 1, and perfecting of 2 Corinthians 7:1. There is, however, only one true method of arriving at the meaning of a word, and that is by a canvass of its usage together with its etymology. The word translated 'perfect' in Colossians 1:28 is *teleios*, and if we bring together the various words that are derived from the same root or stem, we shall be in a position to understand its essential meaning.

(1)	*Telos*	An end	'Then cometh the end' (1 Cor. 15:24).
(2)	*Teleo*	To end	'I have finished my course' (2 Tim. 4:7).
(3)	*Teleios*	What has reached its end	'Every man perfect' (Col. 1:28).
(4)	*Teleiotes*	Perfection	'Let us go on unto perfection' (Heb. 6:1).
(5)	*Teleioo*	To finish	'That I might finish my course' (Acts 20:24).
(6)	*Teleios*	Perfectly	'Hope to the end' (1 Pet. 1:13).
(7)	*Teleiotes*	Finisher	'Author and Finisher' (Heb. 12:2).

There are other words used in the New Testament derived from the same source, and also quite a number of compounds, but we have sufficient for our purpose in the list above. The etymology of the word suggests that 'perfect' has something to do with the 'end', with a 'finish'. The usage of the word leaves us without any doubt. It is found as an antithesis to 'begin' and 'beginning', and is employed in association with the running of a race with a prize in view. It is used of Christ Himself in connection with the 'finishing' of His work, although the idea of His 'being made perfect' as a result of His sufferings cannot be tolerated, if by the word 'perfect' we mean moral or spiritual improvement. Let us take a few occurrences of the word 'perfect' in order to establish its meaning by its usage.

> 'Having begun in the Spirit, are ye now *made perfect* by the flesh?' (Gal. 3:3).

Here the word is used in its natural meaning. Over against 'begun' the apostle places 'made perfect' where the mind thinks of the idea of 'ending' or 'finishing':

> 'Therefore leaving the word of *the beginning* of Christ (A.V. margin), let us go on *unto perfection*' (Heb. 6:1).

Here once more a literal rendering throws 'beginning' and 'perfecting' or 'ending' into prominence:

> 'That as he had begun, so he would also *finish*' (2 Cor. 8:6).

Here, the word translated 'to make perfect' in Galatians 3:3 is translated 'to finish' as also:

> 'I have fought a good fight, I have *finished* my course, I have kept the faith' (2 Tim. 4:7).

The figure that occurs with the use of this word in 1 Corinthians and Hebrews, also in Ephesians, is that of a full grown adult.

> 'Howbeit we speak wisdom among them that are *perfect* ... I ... could not speak unto you as unto spiritual, but as unto carnal, even as unto babes in Christ. I have fed you with milk, and not with meat' (1 Cor. 2:6; 3:1,2).

> 'For when for the time ye ought to be teachers, ye have need that one teach you again which be the first principles of the oracles of God, and are become such as have need of milk, and not of strong meat. For every one that useth milk is unskilful in the word of righteousness: for he is a babe. But strong meat belongeth to them that are of full age (*perfect*), even those who by reason of use have their senses exercised to discern both good and evil. Therefore leaving the word of the beginning of Christ, let us go on unto perfection' (Heb. 5:12 to 6:1).

> 'Till we all come ... unto a *perfect man* ... that we henceforth be no more *children*' (Eph. 4:13,14).

With the knowledge that we now have of the word under discussion, we can return to Colossians 1 and realize that there is no intrusion into the finished work of Christ by Paul's statement, but rather the idea that the believer, whose holiness is already an unalterable fact *in Christ*, should by teaching and admonition make that fact real *experimentally*, that he should take to the end, or to its logical conclusion, such a glorious position as is his by grace. When the same apostle speaks of yielding the body as a living sacrifice, he calls it a 'reasonable' or 'logical' service, in other words the exhortation of Romans 12 is but the logical sequel of the doctrine of Romans 6 or the perfecting of holiness of 2 Corinthians 7:1.

See article PERFECTION OR PERDITION (p. 176), for further notes on this aspect of truth.

PRINCIPALITIES. It is impossible to speak of the peculiar sphere of blessing that belongs to the dispensation of the Mystery, without referring to principalities and powers. The Greek word translated 'principality' is *arche*, a word rendered 'beginning' forty times, and recognizable in the English *arch*-bishop, *arch*-itecture, etc. In English, the word principality implies sovereign power.

'Yet let her be a principality
Sovereign to all creatures on the earth' (Shakespeare).

The term is applied to Wales, as giving the title 'Prince' to the heir apparent of the throne of England.

Arche occurs fifty-eight times. We omit the forty references which are translated 'beginning' and any that deal with time, like 'at the first', and give a concordance to the remaining occurrences.

Arche

Luke 12:11	Unto *magistrates*, and powers.
Luke 20:20	Unto the *power* and authority of the governor.
Rom. 8:38	Nor *principalities*, nor powers.
1 Cor. 15:24	Put down all *rule* and all authority.
Eph. 1:21	Far above all *principality*, and power.
Eph. 3:10	Now unto *principalities* and powers.
Eph. 6:12	Against *principalities*, against powers.
Col. 1:16	Dominions, or *principalities*, or powers.
Col. 1:18	Who is the *Beginning*.
Col. 2:10	The Head of all *principality* and power.
Col. 2:15	Having spoiled *principalities* and powers.
Titus 3:1	Subject to *principalities* and powers.
Jude 6	Angels which kept not their *first estate*.
Rev. 3:14	The *Beginning* of the creation of God.

The ordinary believer has had no personal acquaintance with heavenly principalities, but the use of the term in the New Testament enables us to proceed from the known to the unknown. The first reference in the list given above renders the word *arche* 'magistrate' and the second 'power', the power and authority of a governor. With this may be linked the reference in Titus 3:1. Principality, therefore, while it may include more, cannot include less than a magistrate. A magistrate is a public officer invested with authority to carry out executive government. The Sovereign is thus the chief magistrate in the kingdom, but by reason of the fact that the labours involved are delegated, this title is seldom, if ever, used of the king. In both references in Luke, the word *exousia* is added and is translated in Luke 12:11 'powers' and in Luke 20:20 by 'authority'. This is the word which in Ephesians and Colossians is coupled with principalities and translated 'powers'. It is rather a pity that *exousia* should be translated 'power', this term should be reserved for the translation of *dunamis*. *Exousia* is translated 'authority' twenty-nine times, 'jurisdiction' once, 'liberty' once and 'right' twice, and these terms more aptly render the meaning of *exousia* in English than power. Both Peter and Paul associated principalities with angels.

> 'Who is gone into heaven, and is on the right hand of God; angels and authorities (*exousion*) and powers (*dunameon*) being made subject unto Him' (1 Pet. 3:22).
>
> 'Neither death, nor life, nor angels, nor principalities, nor powers (*dunameis*)' (Rom. 8:38).

Principalities, therefore, are the chief rulers among angels. These principalities appear to be divided into two companies. First, we read that Christ is the Head of all principality. Then we read that the Church of the One Body finds in one section of these mighty spiritual beings, attentive spectators, learning through the lowly ministry of the Church the wonders of Divine wisdom (Eph. 3:10), but that another section constitute their foes against whom the whole armour of God has been provided (Eph. 6:12). (See, for a new translation of Ephesians 6:12, the article entitled SAINTS[4]). One company of these principalities seems to have exercised its authority to the prejudice of the Church and was 'spoiled' at the cross (Col. 2:15), and fallen angels are said to have left their 'first estate' or 'principality' (Jude 6). Further, Christ is Head of all principality and power because He is their Creator (Col. 1:16), and then by virtue of Redemption and Resurrection is invested with the title 'The Beginning', i.e. THE Principality *par excellence* (Col. 1:18). This Mediatorial office is held by the Saviour until all 'rule' (i.e. principality) has been subjected under His feet, and the goal of the ages has been reached.

Although Colossians 1:16-20 is prominent among the advocates of universal reconciliation, no created being is named there but spiritual rulers, the argument of the passage leading up to the Pre-eminence of His Principality (*arche* 'beginning'); verse 20 should read, 'reconcile all these things', as in Colossians 3:8.

THE PRIZE

The Greek word translated 'prize' is *brabeion*, and occurs in two passages.

1 Cor. 9:24	Run all, but one receiveth the prize.
Phil. 3:14	I press toward the mark for the prize. (According to a mark, I press toward the prize, literally).

The word prize is derived from *brabeus*, the judge at a public game who assigns the prize. *Brabeuo*, to preside at the games, occurs in Colossians 3:15 where it is translated 'rule' and *katabrabeuo* also found in Colossians 2:18, means 'to defraud or deprive of a prize, to so manage affairs that the umpire shall pronounce against the contestant'. In Colossians the thought is not so much that of being cheated of the reward, but of failing to attain unto the required standard. The atmosphere of 1 Corinthians 9:24 and of Philippians 3:14 is that of the arena, and the race course. In the article entitled the CROWN[1], we have shown that 'prize' and 'crown' are related, as genus and species.

Philippians 3:10-14 reveals a series of steps toward the goal in view.

First Step 'The Power of His Resurrection'

When the apostle cried, 'that I may know Him and the power of His resurrection' it is this aspect of resurrection that he has before him. He knew the historic fact, he knew its fundamental character for all doctrine, he knew all preaching and all faith was vain without it, but he also realized that there was a personal and experimental side to the fact of resurrection that had a peculiar bearing upon the great theme of the Philippian epistle. Let us follow the apostle in his quest.

(1) That I may know Him, and the power of His resurrection.
(2) The fellowship of His sufferings.
(3) Being made conformable unto His death.
(4) If by any means I might attain unto the resurrection of the dead.

It will be seen that this fourfold subdivision falls into an introversion.

A That I may know. Power. Resurrection. Something to attain.
  B Fellowship of His sufferings } Something to endure in the process.
  B Conformity to His death }
A If by any means I might attain. Resurrection. The Consequence.

It is evident that the prayer 'that I may *know* Him' speaks of a knowledge that is deeper than either that which is historical or even doctrinal. A person may be said 'to know' when a subject has simply come within the sphere of his perception, and where this aspect of knowledge is intended, the Greek word *oida* is used, a word that is derived from *eido* to see, or perceive by means of the senses. This knowledge, however, is not deep, it lies near the surface of things. To know as represented by the word *ginosko* implies insight, acquaintance and personal relationship. It is this word *ginosko* that the apostle uses in Philippians 3:10. Relation with the object is readily seen in such passages as 'Who knew no sin', 'I had not known sin'. The special use of the word 'know' in Matthew 1:25 and Luke 1:34 shows how intimate this knowledge is considered to be. In Philippians 3:10 the apostle was not seeking fuller *information* about the Person or the History of Christ; he was not concerned about the number of prophecies that were fulfilled by His advent, he desired a closer, more intimate acquaintance, a personal relationship even though it involved suffering and shame; he desired a fellowship and a conformity.

When the full meaning of knowledge is perceived, we can the better understand how it is that it stands at the very dividing of the ways in Genesis 3, and will be the great and glorious possession of the redeemed in the ages to come (Isa. 11:9). This intimate, personal knowledge of Christ, if taken in its widest scope, is so vast, that like the love of Christ 'it passeth knowledge'. Here in Philippians 3:10, the apostle's desire is focussed upon one aspect of His great work, 'the power of His resurrection'. Even so, we must remember that he has given evidence in other epistles that he was acquainted with this mighty power. He speaks of this in Ephesians 1:19; 3:7,20 and 6:10, in relation to believing, ministry, answer to prayer, and Christian warfare, but here, in Philippians, he has something more in view. He desires to attain unto the resurrection of the dead (a term that awaits examination) and he perceives that this is only possible by a descent with Christ, comparable in his limited degree, to the great humiliation and exaltation of Philippians 2:6-11. The great Sacrifice which the Saviour came to offer, and which underlies the whole plan of salvation, was completely accomplished when He died 'the just for the unjust'. For this purpose He had been born and to make this offering 'a body had been prepared Him'. In this great act the believer can have no share. It was done 'for' him.

Moreover, in making this offering He laid down His life voluntarily, 'no man taketh it from ME' He declared. To this, however, man's wickedness and enmity added the cross, the shame and the sufferings, and *in these added aspects* of His great sacrificial work, the believer may have some fellowship. Christ is said to have suffered 'being tempted'; to have learned obedience by the things which He 'suffered'; of being reproached, to have suffered 'without the gate' (Heb. 2:18; 5:8; 13:12). Peter speaks of Christ suffering for us, and thereby 'leaving us an example', associating this suffering with that endured by the believer who with a clear conscience takes unmerited evil patiently, and actually telling him that in these things he can 'follow His steps'. It will be found that this is the character which attaches to the sufferings of Christ in the New Testament In these sufferings the believer can be a 'partaker' (2 Cor. 1:5-7; 1 Pet. 4:13).

The reader will expect a reference to the apostle's statement that he filled up 'that which was behind of the afflictions of Christ in my flesh' (Col. 1:24). It should be noted that here the word is not *pathema*, but *thlipsis* often rendered 'tribulation' (Eph. 3:13; Rev. 7:14), and in many passages associated with future glory as a consequence. The apostle desired to have 'fellowship' with these sufferings of Christ, and because of this, he also desired a deeper acquaintance with the power of His resurrection; without such power, fellowship with Christ's sufferings would be suicidal.

Second Step 'The Out-resurrection'

Resurrection is not only a blessed hope, it is inescapable. The unjust as well as the just, they that have done good, and they that have done evil, those who form the Body of Christ, and those who stand before the Great White Throne, each and every one of the seed of the woman, Jew or Gentile, must be raised from the dead. The fact that the apostle could preface his reference to resurrection in Philippians 3:11 with an 'if' after having expressed his complete surrender to the grace of God in Christ, is of itself an indication that he is not speaking of the fundamental doctrine of resurrection.

'If by any means I might attain unto'. No ambiguity attaches to the original here, the R.V. makes but one alteration, the exchange of 'may' for 'might'. The simple way of 'putting the condition' is attained by using the particle *ei*, as in Philippians 1:22. In the passage before us *ei* is combined with the adverb *pos* 'how', and so means 'if somehow'. The word *eipos* occurs but four times in the

New Testament and in every case the contingency is very real, the possibility of *failure* is stressed. The passages are:

'If by any means they might attain to Phenice' (Acts 27:12).

'If by any means now at length I might have a prosperous journey' (Rom. 1:10).

'If by any means I may provoke to emulation' (Rom. 11:14).

'If by any means I might attain unto the resurrection' (Phil. 3:11).

The grafting of the Gentile, as a wild olive, *failed* to provoke Israel to emulation. The attempt to reach Phenice, *ended* in shipwreck. The original of Philippians 3:11 reads *eipos katanteso eis*, the original of Acts 27:12 reads *eipos dunainto katantesantes eis*. The differences are purely grammatical, *katanteso* being singular, and *katantesantes* being plural, and the added word *dunainto* being the addition of the word meaning 'be able'.

The experiences of the apostle recorded in Acts 27 and 28 must have left an indelible impression upon his mind, and as he penned the words, 'if by any means I might attain unto the resurrection', *he knew*, that there was the possibility of failing to arrive, just as surely as the venture to attain unto Phenice met with such disaster. In the verse following, he emphasizes the fact that he had not 'already attained' but that he 'followed after', still further adding 'brethren, I count not myself to have apprehended'. Now it is certain that Paul could have entertained no doubt concerning his standing in grace and his acceptance in the Beloved, his hope like an anchor was sure, and if he used words that express contingency and uncertainty, then it is morally certain that he was *not* speaking of *the hope* of the believer. In verse 14, he reveals that his uncertainty was related to a 'prize', and this attitude of mind he had already exhibited in relation to the same theme in 1 Corinthians 9:24 to 10:13. The 'resurrection', therefore, that was the object of the apostle's desires here in Philippians 3:11, for which he suffered and was willing to endure, must be something equivalent to 'the first resurrection' of Revelation 20:4-6, or the 'better resurrection' of Hebrews 11:35. The words 'first' and 'better' stand visible for all to read in the passages cited, but neither the A.V. nor the R.V. use any such qualifying prefix in Philippians 3:11. The A.V. reads:

> 'If by any means I might attain unto the resurrection of the dead'.

The R.V. reads:

> 'If by any means I may attain unto the resurrection from the dead',

but that is all the difference that there is between the two versions. The reader will by this time be desirous of consulting the original, and to this we accordingly turn. The Received Text reads *ten exanastasin ton nekron* 'the out-resurrection of or from the dead', the Critical Texts read *ten exanastasin ten ek nekron* 'the out-resurrection, that which is out from dead ones'. In order to appreciate the intention of the apostle here, it will be necessary to review the teaching of the New Testament on this great question of resurrection. Two sects divided the religious beliefs of Israel into conflicting camps, the Sadducees and the Pharisees. Of the Sadducees it is written that they say 'there is no resurrection' (Matt. 22:23). When the Saviour challenged the faith of Martha concerning the resurrection of her brother Lazarus, she replied in the language of the common creed of the day, 'I know that he shall rise again ... at the last day' (John 11:24). The simplest statement concerning the resurrection is that given by the apostle before Felix and the Sanhedrin, a belief which Israel and the believer could share 'and have hope towards God which they themselves also allow, that there shall be a resurrection of the dead, both of the just and unjust' (Acts 24:15). Here in the words *anastasin nekron* we have the most elementary form in which the resurrection of the dead can be expressed, a form used by the Pharisees, and by Paul, by the sister of Lazarus and by the common people, for the Apocrypha, written long before Christ, contains the words *anastasin eis zoen* 'a resurrection unto life'.

It is, therefore, somewhat disconcerting to read in Mark 9:10 of the disciples that they questioned one with another, 'what the rising from the dead should mean?' Are we to understand that the very disciples who had been selected to witness the Transfiguration on the mountain, were not so mature in their faith as an unconverted Pharisee? Did Martha outstrip the apostles in this article of faith? Once again, therefore, we must turn to the actual words as recorded in the original before attempting a conclusion. The words that troubled the disciples were those used by the Lord when He said, 'till the Son of Man were risen from the dead', *ek nekron anaste*, 'risen OUT FROM dead ones'. It is the presence of this word *ek* that caused the questioning. It was something additional to the common creed. It was this resurrection *ek nekron* that declared Christ to be the Son of God with power (Rom. 1:4). The first to rise out from the dead was Christ, as Paul testifies in Acts 26:23 :

> 'That Christ should suffer, and that He should be the first that should rise out from dead ones'.

We now take one further step forward and discover a reference that is nearer to the form found in Philippians 3, *tes anastaseos tes ek nekron* in Luke 20:35 :

> 'But they which shall be accounted worthy to obtain that world, and the resurrection that which is out from dead ones'.

Here it will be observed that not only have we words similar to those used in Philippians 3:11, but a similar context — 'accounted worthy to obtain'. Believers can be accounted worthy to obtain that age and the out-resurrection, they may be accounted worthy to escape the dreadful things that are coming on the earth and to stand before the Son of Man, they were counted worthy to suffer shame for His name; and the persecutions which they endured were a manifest token of the righteous judgment of God, that they may be counted worthy of the kingdom of God, for which they suffered (Luke 20:35; 21:36; Acts 5:41; 2 Thess. 1:5).

The word 'obtain' in Luke 20:35 is used by the apostle in 2 Timothy 2:10, 'that they may also obtain that salvation which is with eternal glory', where the context associates 'suffering' with 'reigning', and in Hebrews 11:35, 'that they might obtain a better resurrection' which is an obvious parallel with the 'out resurrection' of Philippians 3:11. While Paul was sure of the 'hope' of his calling, he could not be sure of attaining unto the 'prize' of this same calling, and associated with that prize is the special resurrection, the out-resurrection and the desire for conformity unto the death of Christ, which we have been considering.

In the verse following, the apostle makes it very clear that this uncertainty is legitimate, and one or two added words are employed in making this fact clear. 'Not as though I had already attained', ('not that I have already obtained' R.V.), 'either were already perfect' ('or am already made perfect' R.V.), 'but I follow after' ('but I press on' R.V.). 'If that I may apprehend that for which also I am apprehended of Christ Jesus' ('if so be that I may apprehend that for which also I was apprehended by Christ Jesus') (Phil. 3:12 R.V.). The A.V. repeating the word 'attain' in Philippians 3:12 gives a continuity to the apostle's argument, but as two very different words are employed *katantao* in verse 11, and *lambano* in verse 12, the R.V. is preferable. The change from 'attaining' to 'obtaining' moreover, reveals a change in the apostle's objective. He sought first to 'attain' to the out-resurrection, and then subsequently to 'obtain' the prize. This comes out clearly when we remember that *lambano* 'obtain' occurs in 1 Corinthians 9:24,25, 'one *receiveth* the prize', 'they do it to *obtain* a corruptible crown'.

It is, moreover, evident from the apostle's language, that one who 'obtained' the prize, could be considered as 'perfect'. Here the Greek word *teteleiomai* 'I have been perfected' awaits the triumphant *teteleka* 'I have finished' of 2 Timothy 4:7, where once again we have the race course, the conflict, and the crown. The reader will recognize that in both of these Greek words, there is the common root *tel* which means that the 'end' has been reached, the race run. *Telos* 'end' (Phil. 3:19) gives us *teleo* 'to reach an end, and finish' (2 Tim. 4:7); and so *teleioo* 'to make perfect' (Phil. 3:12), and *teleios* 'perfect' (Phil. 3:15). The apostle said, 'I follow after', and what he sought for was that he might 'lay hold of' that for which he had been 'laid hold of' by Christ. Meanwhile his 'confidence' in Philippians 1 and his 'diffidence' in Philippians 3 give us the two sides of truth that present a perfect whole.

The Third Step. The Prize Itself

The figure of a race, a conflict with a crown or prize at the end is used by the apostle in more places than one. If this 'prize' is something for which we have been apprehended by Christ, then if for no other reason, than to please Him, we should get to know what it is and how it may be obtained. While it is right for every believer to sing:

> 'Not for weight of glory, not for crown or palm,
> Enter we the army, raise the warrior's psalm
> But for love that claimeth, lives for whom He died',

it is also right for every believer to believe what God has said regarding 'the prize' that is attached to our 'High Calling', as it is right that we should understand the High Calling itself. When one has perceived the riches of grace that characterize the calling of the Mystery, there is a temptation which is very strong, to put out the hand to save the ark of God, and to deny the possibility of 'reward' in the Prison Epistles at all, lest by so doing the character of unmerited grace should be impaired. While sympathizing with this regard for grace, we must nevertheless resist it, for we have a higher regard for 'truth' of which grace is a part, and truth demands that we shall allow a rightful place in the dispensation of the Mystery to the undiluted meaning of 'crown', 'prize' and 'reward'.

Let us turn to the epistle to the Colossians, an epistle which stresses the fact of the believer's 'completeness' in

Christ, and observe what it says concerning this aspect of revealed truth.

First, in chapter 2 the apostle gives a warning against that attitude of mind that 'beguiles of the reward'.

'*Let no man beguile you of your reward*'. The word that demands attention here is *katabrabeuo. Kata* means 'against', and *brabeuo* means to be a judge or umpire, and so to assign the prize in a public game. *Brabeuo* occurs in Colossians 3:15 where the peace of God is said to 'act the umpire (rule) in your hearts', a precious thought. *Brabeion* is a prize. It is found in 1 Corinthians 9:24 and Philippians 3:14, 'the prize of the high calling of God in Christ Jesus'. We are, therefore, not without guidance as to the subject of this section. It has to do with the prize. Now Colossians, whilst running very parallel with Ephesians, has much in its central section that bears upon Philippians. Philippians is the epistle of the 'prize' and the 'perfecting', and if we look at Colossians 1 we shall find under the idea of being 'presented' the two aspects of truth set forth by Ephesians and Philippians. We shall distinguish between that which can never be lost, and that which may be lost, and return to Colossians 2 with clearer views:

The first presentation.

> 'In the body of His flesh through death, to present you holy and unblameable and unreproveable in His sight' (Col. 1:22).

The second presentation.

> 'Warning every man, and teaching every man in all wisdom; that we may present every man perfect in Christ Jesus' (Col. 1:28).

The first presentation rests solely upon the finished work of Christ; the second involves the idea which is found in the word 'perfect', of pressing on to the end. In the first no effort of our own could ever present us 'holy'; in the second we stand in need of 'warning'.

Satan does not waste his energies in attempting to deprive us of our acceptance in the Beloved. 'Your life is hid with Christ in God'. Scripture nowhere says: 'Hold that fast which thou hast, that no man take away thy *life*' but it does say: 'Hold that fast which thou hast, that no man take thy *crown*' (Rev. 3:11). Satan was permitted to touch everything belonging to Job *except his life*.

The same is true of all the redeemed. There is a prize to be won, a crown to be gained, but no man is crowned, except he strive lawfully. If, therefore, Satan can turn the saint away from the fulness of Christ, and get him occupied with other means and ways, be they ordinances, days, feasts, meats, drinks, false humility, neglect of the body, unscriptural mediators, or any other thing save 'holding the Head', then the prize is lost, the saint dishonoured, and above all the Saviour robbed, for what is a crown to us, but an added crown to Him?

> 'Servants, obey in all things your masters according to the flesh; not with eyeservice, as menpleasers; but in singleness of heart, fearing God: and whatsoever ye do, do it heartily, as to the Lord, and not unto men; knowing that of the Lord ye shall receive the reward of the inheritance: for ye serve the Lord Christ. But he that doeth wrong shall receive for the wrong which he hath done: and there is no respect of persons' (Col. 3:22-25).

'*The reward of the inheritance*'. In this phrase is the key to the apostle's object in writing the epistle. The Colossian believers, being members of the Body of Christ, were already potentially 'seated together in heavenly places in Christ'; already 'accepted in the Beloved'; already sure of their presentation, 'holy and unblameable and unreproveable' in the sight of God. Already the apostle had said, 'giving thanks unto the Father, which *hath made* us meet to be partakers of the inheritance of the saints in light' (Col. 1:12).

Words cannot make clearer the assured position of the believer nor the completeness of this acceptance. Nevertheless, before the chapter is finished we have found Paul 'warning' and 'teaching' that he may 'present every man perfect in Christ Jesus', and also at the close of the epistle we find Epaphras praying for the selfsame thing

(Col. 4:12). As it is evident that neither Paul nor Epaphras have any doubt that what has already been written of the saints as to standing in Colossians 1:12,13 and 22 remains unalterably true; it becomes necessary to distinguish between the common 'inheritance of the saints in light', for which all believers have been made meet, and 'the reward' attaching to that inheritance, which was associated with individual faithfulness. That is the 'prize attached to the high calling' which, as in Philippians 3, is associated with 'perfecting' (Col. 1:28; 4:12).

We must distinguish between that 'holy, and unblameable, and unreproveable' position which is ours because of the offering of 'the body of His flesh through death', and the possibility of being *blamed and reproved* for the things done in service. If we 'try the things that differ', we shall see that 'hope' is on a basis of pure unalloyed grace, which excludes all possibility of either gain or loss, running or serving; and that the 'prize' is on a basis of reward, given only to those who strive lawfully. Knowing these distinctions we shall be saved a multitude of vexations, and moreover not be found false witnesses of God, for without doubt, He teaches us that membership of the One Body and participation in its one hope is entirely outside the range of attainment on our part. And with equal certainty He assures us that the *prize* of the high calling, the *reward* of the inheritance, and the *crown* of righteousness, fall within the category of attainment. True, nothing but grace will avail, but it is grace *used.* The reason for the apostle's assurance that our life is hid with Christ in God, is that we might know that *life* is not in question. He does not say in Colossians 2:18, let no man beguile you of your *life*, or *membership*, or *position*: these are never in question. But he does echo the words of another dispensation and say, 'take heed, that no man take your *crown*'.

The word translated 'wrong' in Colossians 3:25 is translated 'hurt' in Revelation, where it speaks of being 'hurt of the second death'. Reward or forfeiture belong to both contexts. (See MILLENNIAL STUDIES[9]).

In 1 Corinthians 9:24-27 the apostle enlarges upon this figure of the race and the crown, supplementing his own inspired figures by the 'ensamples' provided by Israel in the wilderness (1 Cor. 10:1-13). Grace is emphasized in the epistles of Paul written before Acts 28 as an examination of Galatians and Romans will demonstrate. No single chapter repudiates the flesh and its efforts more strongly than does 1 Corinthians, chapter 1, yet the apostle sees no incongruity in stressing in the same epistle with equal emphasis the running of a race, the fact that only one receives the prize, and the necessity for discipline and temperance on the part of all who enter the lists, with the final warning, that he himself could possibly become 'disqualified' (*adokimos* 1 Cor. 9:27, not 'castaway'), even as with many of Israel even though redeemed out of Egypt the Lord was not 'well pleased' (*eudokeo* 1 Cor. 10:5).

In the last epistle Paul wrote, he speaks not only of the association of 'crown' and 'running the race' in connection with himself, but applies the same principles to 'all that love His appearing' (2 Tim. 4:8); at the same time he distinguishes very clearly between the unalterable position of those who 'died with' Christ, as compared with the condition attached to 'reigning with him' (2 Tim. 2:11-13). Life with Christ is one thing, reigning with Him is another.

We trust the passages which have been brought before our notice make it clear that the doctrine of Prize, Crown and Reward is by no means absent from the epistles of the Mystery. We can, therefore, return to the passage in Philippians 3, which speaks of the 'prize of the high calling of God in Christ Jesus', assured that we are examining a passage of Scripture that applies with undiminished force to ourselves.

> 'Brethren, I count not myself to have apprehended: but this one thing I do, forgetting those things which are behind, and reaching forth to those things which are before, I press toward the mark for the prize of the high calling of God in Christ Jesus' (Phil. 3:13,14).

'Forgetting ... I press'. What things did the apostle wish to 'forget'? What things if remembered would hinder his running and spoil his chances for the Prize? It cannot refer to the fact that Paul was once a Pharisee and an enemy of the Gospel, for this is remembered with deep appreciation of grace in 1 Timothy 1:11-16, and urged upon the remembrance of Timothy himself in 2 Timothy 1:3; 3:10-14. In Hebrews 12, in connection with 'running the race that is set before us' the apostle urged his readers to 'lay aside every weight', which turns us back to Hebrews 6 where he says, 'leaving the word of the beginning of Christ, let us go on unto perfection'. The Hebrews were hindering their ability to run the race that was set before them, and to go on unto perfection, by clinging to the doctrines and practices of a dispensation that had passed.

So, even although the Philippians were called to salvation and the preaching recorded in Acts 16, and referred to in Philippians 4:15, they must nevertheless beware of bringing over from the Pentecostal dispensation which had now fallen into abeyance, doctrines and practices which were once right and proper, but now obsolete and hindrances. They must 'forget the things which are behind'. For the apostle himself, the things that were 'behind' would embrace all that he had counted loss for Christ's sake, and for each one of us, there will be a similar and personal assessment that we alone can make. From the prison where the apostle was held on the Palatine Hill at Rome (Phil. 1:13) he would hear the shouting and the cheering of the multitudes as they encouraged their favourite charioteers in the *circus maximus*. Paul, though a prisoner, was also a charioteer, he too had a 'mark', he too 'stretched himself forward' as the racer did in the tests.

Clement of Rome, who is probably the same person as is mentioned in Philippians 4:3, associates the 'prize' *brabeion*, with Paul's Apostolic career. 'St. Paul (he says) gained the *brabeion* of endurance, having worn chains seven times for Christ (probably an allusion to the seven rounds of the racecourse before the final run up of the mark)'. From this Greek word for 'prize' *brabeion*, some think the English 'bravo' is ultimately derived. Coming to the prize itself. Are we to understand the apostle to teach:

(1) The prize, that is to say, the high calling of God?
(2) The prize, that is to say, the upward call?
(3) The prize which is attached to the high calling of God?

If the apostle is allowed to speak for himself, then the prize *brabeion* is equivalent with a crown *stephanos*, both words being used in 1 Corinthians 9:24-27 and both words being used in connection with a race or a conflict. *Katabrabeuo* is 'to beguile of reward', A.V., 'rob you of your prize' R.V. (Col. 2:18), and *ho brabeus* was the judge who assigned the prizes at the games, an umpire or an arbitrator. It is exceedingly difficult to find support from any passage of Paul's epistles, to suppose that the prize *was itself* the high calling. Just as 'the reward OF the inheritance' in Colossians 3:24, means the reward attached to an inheritance already assured by grace (Col. 1:12), so the prize OF the high calling of God, means the prize which is attached to the high calling already received and entered by grace.

There is, however, an objection to be considered here. The word translated 'high' is *ano*, an adverb, and as adverbs qualify *verbs*, 'calling' must be a verb, and if so, the passage means 'the prize of the summons on high' and refers, say some, to a special exemption from death granted to those who attain unto the out-resurrection. While it is true that *ano* is an adverb, it is not true that in Greek adverbs qualify verbs only, as can be demonstrated by the use of this very word in Paul's writings. 'Jerusalem which is *above*' (Gal. 4:26), uses *ano* to qualify *the noun* Jerusalem; 'seek those things which are *above*' uses the phrase *ta-ano* 'the above things', so Philippians 3:14 employs *ano* to qualify the noun 'calling'. *Klesis* is not a verb and cannot be translated other than 'a calling or vocation'. It is used eleven times in the New Testament and ten of the occurrences are found in Paul's epistles.

Ephesians 1:18; 4:1,4 and 2 Timothy 1:9 will indicate the way the word is used by the apostle.

It was Sir Robert Anderson who said, that those who translated Philippians 3:14 'the upward call', meaning a future 'summons on high', rarely complete the quotation. Paul *does not say* 'the prize of the high calling of God', what he says is 'the prize of the high calling of God which is IN CHRIST JESUS'. The out-resurrection segregates the believer who has obtained the prize, but is not itself the prize for which the apostle was running. When at the last he could say 'finished', he then speaks not in generic terms of a 'prize' but in specific terms 'a crown', which he also associates with 'reigning together' in the second chapter of the same epistle (2 Tim. 2:12 and 4:8).

The Fourth Step

'THE MARK' set before those who would be 'perfect'
(Phil. 3:17-21)

The majority of commentators see no difficulty in the accepted translation of Philippians 3:15, 'let us therefore, as many as be perfect', or if they had any problem, the difficulty is left unexpressed. Most take the word 'perfect' here to mean 'mature' as contrasted with 'babes' and immature, and in other contexts this is quite true (Heb. 5:14). If, however, we look back to Philippians 3:12, where the apostle says of himself that he was not already 'perfect' or 'mature', we shall have a difficulty in accepting the usual rendering of verse 15. If Paul was not then 'perfect' who among the Philippians or his readers down the ages could hope to be? Further, it reflects upon the intelligence of the apostle to make him say in verse 12 that he was not 'mature' yet at verse 15 to continue his argument with the word 'therefore' and assume that nevertheless both he and others were at the same time 'mature' or 'perfect'.

It is an axiom that requires no demonstration to prove that a thing cannot both be, and not be, at one and the same time. Conybeare and Howson sense the difficulty saying 'the translation in the A.V. of *teteleiomai* (verse 12) and *teleioi* by the same word, makes Paul seem to contradict himself' and their way out of the difficulty is to translate verse 15 by 'ripe in understanding'. This, however, only conceals the difficulty from the English reader. Macknight is the only Commentator we have consulted who senses the difficulty. He translates Philippians 3:15, 'As many, therefore, as WISH TO BE perfect'. *Hosoi oun teleioi* contains no verb. The 'be' is supplied in the A.V. to make sense. If we must supply a verb, why not keep the unity of the apostle's argument? Why make him contradict himself within the space of three verses? Why accuse him of using a term in two different meanings without the slightest warning to the reader? 'As many as would be', or who 'wish to be perfect', makes all clear and straightforward. All who would emulate the apostle's desire and eagerness, must emulate his 'mind'; they must be 'thus minded' and we have only to go back to the opening of the great argument in chapter 2, to realize that the apostle is turning back to the 'mind that was in Christ Jesus'. The Received Text reads at verse 16:

> 'Nevertheless, whereto we have already attained, let us walk by the same rule, let us mind the same thing'.

The use in the A.V. of the word 'attain' in Philippians 3:11,12 and 16 to represent *three different Greek words*, has robbed the English reader of the means to appreciate the transition of thought in the apostle's argument. We have already observed that in verse 12, the word should be 'obtain', we now draw attention to the original of verse 16, where *phthano* is the word translated 'attain'. Dr. Bullinger's *Concordance and Lexicon* here says, '*phthano*, to come or go before another, to be beforehand with, to overtake, outstrip; to come first'. It is this word that is found in 1 Thessalonians 4:15 and translated 'prevent' which is from the Latin *provenio* 'to come before'. The recognition of this Greek word 'to outstrip', while it brings us closer to the apostle's language, makes the suggested translation offered by Lewin untenable, 'but whereunto we have outstript, walk in the same'. While it is of the very nature of a race that competitors should endeavour to outstrip others, the race set before the believer would appear to the worldling as though the prize was awarded to the last man in rather than the first.

The Great Example of chapter 2, appeared at all points to be giving away advantages. His humble follower Paul, pursued the *prize* while at the same time counting all things *loss*. Whoever won a race, and 'esteemed the affairs of others, of far more importance than his own' (Phil. 2:3)? In this competition there is no thought of elbowing the weak brother out of the way, but rather of losing place and pace while we pause to help him on to his feet. The apostle exhorted the runner to 'lay aside every weight' yet at the same time revealed that the law of Christ called upon every entrant 'to bear one another's burdens'. This somewhat paradoxical state could obtain only in the realm of grace. The hymn expresses something of this quality when it says:

'Through weakness and defeat,
He won the mead and crown;
Trod all His foes beneath His feet
By being trodden down'.

Some MSS. omit the words 'by the same rule, let us mind the same thing'. Others omit the word 'rule'; yet others omit 'let us mind the same thing'. Griesbach simply cancels the whole passage, and many critics take it for granted that the reference to the 'rule' has crept in from Galatians 6:16, which is a gratuitous piece of criticism. The 'rule' *kanon* refers to 'the white line by which the course in the stadium was marked out, including the whole space between the starting-place and the goal, and that those who ran out of that space did not contend lawfully. The runners, in endeavouring to pass one another, were in danger of going out of that space' (Hammon quoting Julius Pollux, A.D. 180-238). Aquila uses the word *kanon* in his Greek version of Job 38:5. The apostle taught the Ephesians that the spirit of wisdom and revelation was given 'in the acknowledgment' of Christ, so here in Philippians the apostle says, 'I follow along the mark' *kata skopon dioko*, 'and as many as would be perfect' and obtain the prize, they too will 'think this'. There are other things, such as the observance of one day above another, or the eating or not eating of certain foods, in which there will be considerable differences of opinion, but provided that all press on in the right spirit, God will reveal these things to such. We are to be 'strivers together' for the faith, but not strivers with one another (Phil. 1:27; 2:3).

The apostle has, by his exhortation, thrown the believer back upon the example both of the Lord and of himself, he now proceeds to enforce the need for observing this example both positively, 'be followers together of me' and negatively, 'and mark them which walk so as ye have us for an ensample' (Phil. 3:17). The words of verses 18 and 19 are a parenthesis, the whole passage being constructed as follows:

Examples

A	17.	*Positive*	Be followers together of me ... us for an ensample.
B	17.	*Negative*	Mark them which walk.
B	18,19.	*Negative*	Their end — destruction.
A	20,21.	*Positive*	Our citizenship is in heaven ... we shall be changed.

Five things are enumerated by the apostle when speaking of those whose example was to be avoided.

(1) They were enemies of the cross of Christ (see Heb. 6:6; 10:29) .
(2) Their end was destruction (or 'Perdition' as Heb. 10:39).
(3) Their god was their belly (as Esau, Heb. 12:16).
(4) Their glory was in their shame.
(5) They minded earthly things.

It is impossible to believe that a church of so high a spiritual standard as that of the Philippians could need a solemn warning not to follow a worldly crowd, yet at first sight such a list as that given above does not seem of possible application to a believer.

Let us examine them a little more closely, and start with the last named 'who mind earthly things'. It will be conceded after a moment's thought, that the unsaved man of the world has no option, *he can mind nothing else.*

Philippians 3:15-19 is a section complete in itself, and the word *phroneo* 'mind' occurs in it as follows:

A 3:15. As many as would be perfect (one thing, *to hen* verse 13) be thus minded.

B 3:15. Otherwise (*heteros*) minded.

A 3:16. Whereto ... outstripped others ... mind the same thing (*to auto*).

B 3:19. Who mind earthly things (*ta epigeia*).

It will be seen that those who mind earthly things are in correspondence with those who think differently from the apostle in his single-eyed effort to attain the prize. 'Earthly things' therefore need not mean things positively sinful, but things that come in between the runner and his goal; 'every weight' as Hebrews 12 suggests. 'Earthly things' are in the original *ta epigeia* (Phil. 3:19). 'Things on the earth' are *ta epi tes ges* (Col. 3:2). 'Earthly things' are spoken of in John 3:12, James 3:15, 1 Corinthians 15:40, 2 Corinthians 5:1 and in Philippians 2:10 and 3:19. In each case, 'earthly things' are set over against 'heavenly', 'from above' and 'celestial'. Those who may have been persuaded that the 'earth' not 'heaven' is the sphere of blessing for all the redeemed should heed this warning. 'Our citizenship is (*huparchei*) in *heaven*'.

Those, therefore, who mind earthly things, are those who do not act in accordance with their heavenly citizenship (Phil. 3:20) and whose example and teaching will 'beguile' them of their reward. This must be shunned by all who seek the prize of the high calling.

The example of Abraham, as set out in Hebrews 11:8-16, who desired a better country, 'that is, an heavenly', can be added to that of the apostle here. If the last of the list of five things to avoid can describe those who are believers, let us return to the head of the list and ponder again the dreadful words, 'the enemies of the cross of Christ'. James declares that friendship with the world makes one 'the enemy of God' (Jas. 4:4), but will it be denied that such friendship is possible to a child of God? One may become an enemy in the eyes of another by telling him unpalatable truth (Gal. 4:16), and enmity can be exhibited and maintained by a middle wall of partition (Eph. 2:15). A believer can, therefore, by adopting some attitude make himself an enemy of the truth for which the cross of Christ stands.

To many, the cross of Christ is seen only in an evangelical light, the central testimony to *unsaved* sinners. To those who see no further than this aspect of the cross, those referred to in Philippians 3:18 cannot possibly be believers. To those who have examined the place which the cross occupies in Paul's testimony and have seen its essential message to the believer who is already saved, the warnings of these verses will present no problem. We have demonstrated the many ways in which the epistle to the Hebrews runs parallel with that to the Philippians, and the only reference to the cross in that epistle is found in Hebrews 12:2, in direct connection with 'running the race which is set before us'. This is the last reference to the cross in the New Testament, the earliest references (Matt. 10:38; 16:24) which relate to the cross, speak also of discipleship and future reward. Paul uses the doctrine of the cross to counter the fleshly wisdom of the Corinthian believers (1 Cor. 1:17,18; 2:2), he teaches the Galatian believers that by the cross the world and its boasting are repudiated (Gal. 5:11; 6:12,14), and that the emancipation of the believer, together with the complete reconciliation of the One Body, are accomplished by the cross of Christ (Eph. 2:16; Col. 1:20; 2:14).

Those who are 'otherwise minded' and whose associations with the world and the flesh run in opposition to the 'one thing' that characterized the apostle's testimony, would be, though believers, 'enemies' of all that the cross of Christ stood for, and so become examples for the Philippians to shun.

PROMISE. The Greek words *epaggelia* and *epaggelma* are translated 'promise' and *epaggellomai, exomologeomai* and *homologeo* are translated by the verb 'to promise'. While there are a number of promises mentioned in the New Testament two features are characteristic of them all.

(1) They are 'great and precious' (2 Pet. 1:4).
(2) They are all 'yea and amen' in Christ (2 Cor. 1:20).

The promises of the New Testament are distributed under a number of headings of which the following is a fair presentation.

(1) The promise of the Holy Spirit, which took place at Pentecost.

'The promise of My Father' or 'the Father', (Luke 24:49; Acts 1:4).

'The promise of the Holy Ghost' (Acts 2:33 cf. 38,39).

'The promise of the spirit' (Gal. 3:14).

(2) The promise of the Coming of the Messiah.

(1) His First Advent (Acts 13:23,32).
(2) His Second Advent (2 Pet. 3:4,9).

(3) The promise made to Abraham.
Romans 4:13,14,16,20, summed up in verse 16 as follows:

> 'Therefore it is of faith, that it might be by grace; to the end the promise might be sure to all the seed; not to that only which is of the law, but to that also which is of the faith of Abraham; who is the father of us all'.

Galatians 3:16,17,18 and 21. In this presentation, the subject is divided under two headings:

(a) 'Now to Abraham and his seed were the promises made. He saith not, And to seeds, as of many; but as of one, And to thy seed, which is Christ'.

(b) 'And this I say, that the covenant that was confirmed before of God in Christ, the law, which was four hundred and thirty years after, cannot disannul, that it should make the promise of none effect'.

(4) The promises to Israel.
Romans 9:4 and 8, show that these are Israel's prerogative and Ephesians 2 shows just as clearly that no promises were made to the Gentiles who were 'aliens from the commonwealth of Israel and strangers from the covenants of promise'. In Romans 15:8 the apostle makes another very important statement concerning the place of Israel in the mind and purpose of God, and which throws a vivid light upon the earthly ministry of the Saviour. 'Now I say that Jesus Christ was a minister of the circumcision for the truth of God, to confirm the promises made unto the fathers'. These promises include the hope of resurrection, as Acts 26:6-8 testifies.

(5) The promises upon which the New Covenant are based are said to be 'better promises', even as Christ is set forth as the Mediator of a 'better covenant' (Heb. 8:6).

(6) The goal of the ages, which includes a new heaven and a new earth is based upon 'His promise' (2 Pet. 3:13).

(7) The word promise in the Prison Epistles is never found in the plural. There is but one promise, and that a promise that was made before the age times.

The believer is sealed with that Holy Spirit of promise (Eph. 1:13) which is not to be confused with the promise OF the Spirit as in Acts 1:4.

The unique calling and constitution of the Church of the Mystery as revealed in Ephesians 3:6, is according to 'His promise in Christ by the gospel' whereof Paul was made a minister. In 2 Timothy 1:1 we have 'the promise of life', closely associated with the testimony of our Lord and of Paul His prisoner, and with the purpose and grace which was given us in Christ Jesus before age times, and with the abolishing of death and with the bringing to light of 'life and immortality'.

PROPHECY. Peter tells us that prophecy is like a light that shineth in a dark place, until the day dawn (2 Pet. 1:19). Strictly speaking the Mystery cannot be the *subject* of prophecy, as it was hid in God and not revealed until it was entrusted to Paul the Prisoner. While the Mystery cannot be the subject of prophecy, it has a prophetic view of its own which is gathered up in 1 Timothy 4 and in 2 Timothy 3 and 4, where 'the light shines in the darkness' that will obtain just before the day of the Lord's appearing. The subject matter of these prophetic portions of the epistles of the Mystery have been examined in the article entitled LAST DAYS AND LATTER TIMES[2].

While there were prophets as well as apostles in the beginning of this dispensation, the gift of prophecy as exercised by the church of Corinth was not continued. Like the apostle, the prophet was a 'foundation' ministry (Eph. 2:20), and has no successor. The continuing ministry being that of the evangelist, pastor and teacher. These we find in the epistles to Timothy and Titus, the bishop being equivalent to the pastor (see Acts 20:28; 1 Pet. 2:25). The great prophetic book of the New Testament is the book of the Revelation, called 'This

Prophecy' (Rev. 22:19), and this is given full attention in the article entitled REVELATION[4].

Note. Parts 8 and 9 of *An Alphabetical Analysis* are devoted entirely to Prophecy and allied subjects.

PURPOSE. We have considered the meaning and place of the word Dispensation, and have likewise given considerable space to the references in Scripture to the Ages, and both Ages and Dispensations are vehicles of Purpose.

The Bible a Book of Purpose

Having considered the fact that there are many and great differences in the various dispensations, it will be well to observe that all these different lines of truth are united, inasmuch as God is working out a mighty purpose, affecting heaven and earth, and that these changes of dispensational dealings instead of indicating experiment or caprice, are so many links in a wondrous chain. (See PLEROMA, p. 197). None but a superficial reader of the Bible will assume that the Scriptures are given to explain everything, or to answer all the inquiries of the human mind. There are some things which God kept secret for thousands of years, never revealed until He committed them to the apostle Paul (see Eph. 3). There are some things concerning which we are told hardly anything. Take for example the Bible record of Satan. His first introduction into the page of Scripture is as a *fallen* being (Gen. 3). No explanation is offered, no reason is given. We start the record of the purpose of God as pertains to man with a revealed yet unexplained fact. As it is with Satan's beginning, so with the last we hear of him. In Revelation 20 he is put into the lake of fire there to be tormented unto the ages of the ages. What happens to him at the end of that period Scripture does not say.

The nearer Scripture approaches that section of God's purpose that is connected with Israel, the plainer and more definite it becomes. Israel's history fills the bulk of the Bible. The Nations have a comparatively small space, while the Church occupies a small portion of the New Testament. Things in heaven, the spiritual powers, are concerned with the great purpose unfolded in the Word, yet we know very little of what their place in that purpose will be.

There are many references in the Scriptures to the fact of a purpose, and it may be well for us to establish this before we proceed to inquire into details. Romans 8:28; 9:11; Ephesians 1:11 and 2 Timothy 1:9 are sufficient to show that the salvation of men is part of a purpose. The word *prothesis* means 'a placing before', and indicates a well-considered plan. That this plan or purpose is unalterable Ephesians 1:9 and Jeremiah 51:29 will be sufficient to prove. The words in 2 Timothy 1:9, 'before the world began', are not strictly true as a translation. The original reads *pro chronon aionion* and should be rendered 'before age-times'. Another occurrence of this same expression is found in Titus 1:2, where a somewhat parallel doctrine is discovered. Before the age-times, then, the purpose of God was formed, and in harmony with this is the teaching that the members of the One Body were 'chosen in Him *before* the foundation of the world'. Not only is it important to see that the purpose or plan of God was made before the age times, but that the very ages themselves are a necessary part and platform for the unfolding and ripening of that purpose. Ephesians 3:11 (A.V.) speaks of an 'eternal purpose'. Now while the thought in these words is very majestic, the teaching of the passage is not strictly rendered by them. The word 'eternal' is an adjective, whereas in Ephesians 3:11 it is not the adjective *aionios* that is used, but *aion*, 'age'. The true rendering of the passage, therefore, should be, 'according to a purpose of the ages'.

The Bible is occupied with that purpose. The Bible spans the ages. What was *before* the ages, and what lies *beyond*, is not strictly within the scope of the Book. Men labour to explain and emphasize *eternity*. Philosophy may burden the mind with the effort to grasp 'that which has neither beginning nor end, that which has neither centre nor circumference', but the Bible does not. Scripture commences with, 'In the beginning God'. From that basis, the Scriptures unfold the purpose of the ages.

Having surveyed the Scriptures with regard to the *fact* of the purpose, we next consider some passages which relate to its *fulfilment*. Here at once we learn that the accomplishment of God's purpose does not rest with the creature, but with God Himself. Ephesians 1:11 is emphatic on this:

> 'Being predestinated according to the purpose of Him Who worketh all things after the counsel of His own will'.

Isaiah 46:9-11 also shows that the Old Testament equally with the New demonstrates this fact:

> 'I am God, and there is none like Me, declaring the end from the beginning, and from ancient times the things that are not yet done, saying, My counsel shall stand, and I will do all My pleasure ... yea, I have spoken it, I will also bring it to pass; I have purposed it, I will *also do* it'.

We will not multiply passages; the Bible is insistent on this grand fact that God Who purposes is the God also Who fulfils. This was the secret of Abraham's faith, for it is recorded in Romans 4:17-21:

> 'Before Him Whom he believed, even God, Who quickeneth the dead, and calleth those things which be not as though they were ... being fully persuaded that, what He had promised, He was able also to perform'.

Nothing is so strengthening to faith, even in the small details of life, as this glorious fact that God is the fulfiller of His own will.

The next truth we would bring to notice is that the great centre of the purpose of the Ages is the Lord Jesus Christ. Going back into the past we find that creation is the work of the Son of God. John in chapter 1 of his Gospel speaks of Christ as the Word, Who was God (verse 1), Who became flesh, the only begotten of the Father (verse 14), and says:

> 'All things were made by Him; and without Him was not any thing made that was made' (John 1:3).

Hebrews 1:10 says of Him:

> 'And Thou, Lord, in the beginning hast laid the foundation of the earth; and the heavens are the works of Thine hands'.

Colossians 1:16 speaks further of the creation, not only of visible but of invisible and mighty beings in the heavens, yet all the creatures of the Son of God. The first man Adam is 'a figure of Him that was to come' (Rom. 5:14), and is placed in contrast with 'the last Adam', Who is a life-giving Spirit, 'the Second Man' Who is the Lord from heaven (1 Cor. 15:45-47). The promise of the seed of the woman (Gen. 3) finds its fulfilment in the Person and Work of the Son of God. All typical events and institutions, such as the Ark built by Noah, and the Passover Lamb, the Tabernacle, the Offerings, the Priesthood, all find their anti-type and fulfilment in Christ.

Every prominent figure of the Old Testament prefigures either Christ or Antichrist. We have only to think of men like Joseph, David, Moses, Pharaoh and Joshua to see how fully this can be demonstrated. However stupendous may have been such interferences with the course of nature as the Flood, the redemption from Egypt, the giving of the Law from Sinai, or however important such events as the fresh start after the Flood, the entry into Canaan, the setting up of David's throne, yet all these events but lead on to one point called by God 'the fulness of the time', marked by the most wonderful event made known to men:

> 'When the fulness of the time was come, God sent forth His Son, made of a woman, made under the law, to redeem them that were under the law' (Gal. 4:4,5). (See PLEROMA, p. 197).

So the purpose unfolds, ever revealing more and more the central place that the Son of God holds in its development, until we read of its fruition and full accomplishment when the Son, having brought the purpose of the ages to a glorious consummation, hands over to the Father a perfected kingdom, that 'God' (not specifically the Father or the Son) may be all in all (1 Cor. 15:24-28).

Not only have we the fact, the fulfilment, and the glorious centre of this purpose, but we further learn that all creatures are in some way agents in the mighty plan. So far as mankind is concerned it is divided into three classes, two of them racial and one spiritual. First, we have the two national divisions of Jew and Gentile. Israel's agency in the great purpose may be summed up in three particulars: (1) a chosen people, (2) a city (Jerusalem), and (3) a king (David typically, but Christ really). The Church, the spiritual agency, made up of an election from Jew and Gentile, constitutes the third agency. These three divisions run their appointed ways without fusing, but are drawn near together by two great outstanding events, namely, the First and Second Coming of Christ.

Satan works along lines that closely resemble the working of God in some particulars, and his activities constitute a great opposing feature, overruled and made to contribute finally to the outworking of the purpose of the God of all grace.

The one great purpose of God is displayed under varying forms again and again:

First we have a perfect creation (Gen. 1:1). Then a fall, darkness and chaos. Then a renewal (Gen. 1,2).	Cosmic.

If we leave the cosmic platform and limit ourselves to the human plane, the purpose is again displayed in Genesis 3:

First a perfect creation. Man. Then a fall, death and expulsion. But a restoration promised and typified.	Racial.

Leaving the wider circle of the human race we notice the story of the nations:

First the nations divided by God (Gen. 10) Then their rebellion (Gen. 11) Then their only hope of restoration (Gen. 12)	National.

This is as far as Genesis takes us. Exodus now expands the theme, but confines itself to the fortunes of the one nation Israel. The same order is observed.

First the fruitful and mighty people (Exod. 1:1-7).
Then the bondage.
Followed by the deliverance and exodus.

Up to the book of Exodus, the purpose of God can be demonstrated by concentric circles, cosmic, racial and national. With the redemption of Israel, the elective character of the purpose takes shape, which, as the New Testament shows, issues in an election, from among Jews and Gentiles, first as heirs of the promise to Abraham, and joint heirs with him of the heavenly calling, and then of a church whose calling and constitution was unknown until revealed to the apostle Paul, the steward of this great Mystery. One suggestive feature is the way in which the Greek word *prothesis* is translated. The word occurs twelve times. In Acts, Romans, Ephesians and 2 Timothy it is translated 'purpose', but in Matthew 12:4, Mark 2:26, Luke 6:4 and Hebrews 9:2 it is combined with the word 'bread' to give the word 'shewbread'. This typical feature suggests that in the purpose of God the redeemed are ever before His face, even though in themselves they may wander as did Israel, from the path of righteousness, even though the ten tribes seemed to be 'lost', there were never less than twelve loaves on the table of shewbread. Ecclesiastes reminds us that there is a time for every purpose under the heaven (Eccles. 3:1,17; 8:6), and Jeremiah declares that every purpose of the Lord shall be performed (Jer. 51:29) and in Isaiah the Lord says, 'as I have purposed, so shall it stand' (Isa. 14:24). The fact that the word 'according to' is associated with the purpose of God (Rom. 8:28; 9:11, Eph. 1:11 and 2 Tim. 1:9) shows that the calling and the election of both Israel and the Church is in harmony with this Divine purpose of the Ages.

One of the most illuminating words employed in the Scriptures in connection with the Purpose of the Ages is the word PLEROMA and we draw the reader's attention to the articles and chart bearing that name.

ISBN for complete set of 10 volumes: 0 85156 200 0

ISBN for this volume: 0 85156 203 5

SUBJECT INDEX TO ALL 10 PARTS OF THIS ALPHABETICAL ANALYSIS

Main articles are printed in **bold** type capitals thus: **ADOPTION**. Subsidiary articles are printed in small capitals thus: ASCENSION.

Each article has been given its Part number in bold, followed by the page number. The Part number and the page number are separated by a colon. Thus:

SEATED.................... **4**:218,

indicates that an article on the subject 'Seated' may be found on page 218, in Part 4 of this 10 Part Analysis.